Codependent No More

Codependent No More

HOW TO STOP
CONTROLLING OTHERS
AND START CARING
FOR YOURSELF

Melody Beattie

*Spiegel
and Grau*

S&G

Spiegel & Grau, New York
www.spiegelandgrau.com

Cover design adapted by Strick & Williams
Interior design by Meighan Cavanaugh

Library of Congress Cataloging-in-Publication Data Available upon Request

ISBN 978-1-954118-21-8 (paperback)
ISBN 978-1-954118-22-5 (eBook)

Printed in the United States of America

First Spiegel & Grau Edition

10 9 8 7 6 5 4 3 2 1

*This book is dedicated to me—and to
all the people who have learned from me
and allowed me to learn from them.*

It is not easy to find happiness in ourselves, and it is not possible to find it elsewhere.

—AGNES REPPLIER

Contents

Preface to the Revised Edition

On Valentine's Day, 1986—on assignment from the publisher—
Terry Spahn, a neighbor who worked at Hazelden, drove to my
home in Stillwater, Minnesota, to wrest from my hands the daisy
wheel–printed pages that would become *Codependent No More*.

I'd written it on a floppy disc on a Kaypro—one of the first
home computers released into the world. I was enamored with this
new writing technology that allowed me to edit endlessly and (unlike word processors) distract myself on breaks by playing *Pong*.
That's also why Terry needed to show up and physically take possession of the manuscript. After clutching it close and dancing for
a moment while Terry tried to take it from my arms, I let go and
released the book into the world.

Codependent No More has worn well since that day in Stillwater,
Minnesota. It established proof of concept. I still feel good about
the rhythm and essential truth of the book.

Yet over the past two decades, and especially with the techno-
logical advances that have had such a widespread impact on our

lives, I've found myself wincing at the sometimes archaic, dated language and references; the cautious way I told *my* story; the waffling I sometimes did (in my life and the book) about whether it was okay, really okay, to love ourselves, and if so, how much and exactly what that means.

We were in the grip of a different consciousness when I researched and wrote the book in the 1980s, but we were beginning to question ideas we'd taken for granted. Women were moving from being chattel with few rights to full personhood. And people were hungry for information to help them make sense of life in a rapidly changing world. Bookstores didn't yet have self-help sections, but people were becoming curious about their inner lives. Though the essential truths of the book remain solid, some of the trappings felt so dated that they obscured the helpful information. The book needed an update.

"Do you think younger readers will even know who Bob Newhart is?" I asked my new editor, referring to a chapter's epigraph.

"No," she said, "but they'll know how to Google him."

· · ·

There have also been many changes in my life since *Codependent No More* was first published that have shaped me and my beliefs: relocating to California; the death of my ex (my children's father) and the death of my father—two of my three original qualifiers for codependency; and caring for my mother at the end of her life (my original love-hate relationship).

The most profound loss, though, was the death of my son Shane the day after his twelfth birthday. It plummeted me undeniably into the world of grief, crippling me with trauma.

Through this dreadful crucible, I would gain an understanding of the ways trauma, anxiety, and PTSD intersect with codependency. Of course I had no appreciation for these lessons when I was learning them. *Trauma* wasn't even in our vernacular, save for soldiers returning from war, until 9/11, when we experienced it collectively. The recovery community had begun to recognize that the chaos and fear instilled in us from growing up in an alcoholic family or living through sexual assault or physical abuse was like being at war. Personally, I realized that I needed to address the residual trauma in me, to find my own healing and peace.

That's what ultimately inspired the writing of the new chapter, "Soothe Yourself," in this book. I'm grateful to have written it.

• • •

While working on the revision, I also decided to come out about my codependency story. Because the people I was most codependent on were still alive back in 1986, I disguised them and myself. I felt I didn't have the right to tell their stories. I'm now including those stories here. I'm not doing it to speak ill of the deceased, but I'm no longer codependently covering for them either. We can lovingly and compassionately tell the truth about our experiences—without demeaning others or ourselves.

Another goal in the revision was to de-pathologize the writing—to separate people from their afflictions, labels, struggles, and illnesses. Many spectrums exist on which many of us land . . . somewhere. Although much of the writing focuses on codependency triggered by someone's substance abuse, you'll also find stories and anecdotes that don't involve substance abuse. The recovery behaviors discussed in this book can apply to a wide range of code-pendency triggers.

In this revised edition I've also included an inclusive resources guide that's mindful of the many areas where people may need extra or urgent help. Kudos to Lauren Barragan, who expertly assembled this section.

. . .

The longer this lifetime goes, the more convinced I am that our primary responsibility in life is to find a way to make peace with ourselves, our past, and our present—no matter what we face and no matter how often we need to do that. It's also our job to mindfully practice self-love. Every day. For all our lives. It's not a narcissistic or obnoxiously selfish attitude toward life and our relationships. Self-love is a humbler, quieter thing. You'll get used to it. I like it; you may too.

On Valentine's Day, 2022, I turned in the newly revised and updated *Codependent No More*. It's my legacy and long overdue gift to *us* as we move from the chaotic close of the past age and enter the Age of Aquarius.

May God bless this new edition.

Introduction

My first encounter with codependents occurred in the early sixties. This was before people, tormented by other people's behavior, were called codependents, and before people addicted to alcohol and other drugs were labeled chemically dependent. Although I didn't know what codependents were, I usually knew who they were. As someone who struggled with alcoholism and addiction, I stormed through life, helping create other codependents.

Codependents were a necessary nuisance. They were hostile, controlling, manipulative, indirect, guilt producing, difficult to communicate with, generally disagreeable, sometimes downright hateful, and a hindrance to my compulsion to get high. They hollered at me, hid my pills, made nasty faces at me, poured my alcohol down the sink, tried to keep me from getting more drugs, wanted to know why I was doing this to them, and asked what was wrong with me. But they were always there, ready to rescue me from self-created disasters. The codependents in my life didn't understand me, and the misunderstanding was mutual. I didn't understand me, and I didn't understand them.

My first professional encounter with codependents occurred years later, in 1976. At that time in Minnesota, addicts and alcoholics had become *chemically dependent*, their families and friends had become *significant others*, and I had become a *recovering addict* and *alcoholic*. By then, I also worked as a counselor in the chemical dependency field, that vast network of institutions, programs, and agencies that helps chemically dependent people get well. Because I'm a woman and most of the significant others at that time were women, and because I had the least seniority and none of my co-workers wanted to do it, my employer at the Minneapolis treatment center told me to organize support groups for wives of addicts in the program.

I wasn't prepared for this task. I still found codependents hostile, controlling, manipulative, indirect, guilt producing, difficult to communicate with, and more.

In my group, I saw people who felt responsible for the entire world, but they refused to take responsibility for leading and living their own lives.

I saw people who constantly gave to others but didn't know how to receive. I saw people give until they were angry, exhausted, and emptied of everything. I saw some give until they gave up. I even saw one woman give and suffer so much that she died of "old age" and natural causes at age thirty-three. She was the mother of five children and the wife of an alcoholic who'd been sent to prison for the third time.

I worked with women who were experts at taking care of everyone around them, yet these women doubted their ability to care for themselves.

I saw mere shells of people, racing mindlessly from one activity to another. I saw people pleasers, martyrs, stoics, tyrants, withering vines, clinging vines, and, borrowing from H. Sackler's line in his play *The Great White Hope*, "pinched up faces giving off the miseries."

Most codependents were obsessed with other people. With great precision and detail, they could recite long lists of the other person's deeds and misdeeds: what they thought, felt, did, and said; and what they didn't think, feel, do, and say. The codependents knew what the other person should and shouldn't do. And they wondered extensively why they did or didn't do it.

Yet these codependents who had such great insight into others couldn't see themselves. They didn't know what they were feeling. They weren't sure what they thought. And they didn't know what, if anything, they could do to solve their problems—if, indeed, they had any problems other than the other person.

It was a formidable group, these codependents. They were aching, complaining, and trying to control everyone and everything but themselves. And, except for a few quiet pioneers in family therapy, many counselors (including me) didn't know how to help them. The chemical dependency field was flourishing, but help focused on the addicted person. Literature and training on family therapy were scarce. What did codependents need? What did they want? Weren't they just an extension of the alcoholic, a visitor to the treatment center? Why couldn't they cooperate, instead of always making problems? The alcoholic had an excuse for being so crazy—he was drunk. These significant others had no excuse. They were this way sober.

Soon, I subscribed to two popular beliefs: These crazy codependents (significant others) are sicker than the alcoholics. And, no wonder the alcoholic drinks; who wouldn't with a crazy spouse like that?

By then, I had been sober for a while. I was beginning to understand myself, but I didn't understand codependency. I tried, but couldn't—until years later, when I became so caught up in the chaos of *my alcoholic* that I stopped living my own life. I stopped thinking. I stopped feeling positive emotions, and I was left with rage, bitterness, hatred, fear, depression, helplessness, despair, and guilt. At times, I wanted to stop living. I had no energy. I spent most of my time worrying about people and trying to figure out how to control them. I couldn't say no (to anything but fun activities) if my life depended on it, which it did. My relationships with friends and family members were in shambles. I felt terribly victimized. I lost myself and didn't know how it had happened. I didn't know what had happened. I thought I was going crazy. And, I thought, shaking a finger at my alcoholic, it's *his* fault.

Sadly, aside from myself, nobody knew how bad I felt. My problems were my secret. Unlike the alcoholic, I wasn't going around making big messes and expecting someone to clean up after me. In fact, next to the alcoholic, I looked good. I was so responsible, so dependable. Sometimes I wasn't sure I had a problem. I knew I felt miserable, but I didn't understand why my life wasn't working.

After floundering in despair for a while, I began to understand. Like many people who judge others harshly, I realized I had just taken a very long and painful walk in the shoes of those I had judged. I now understood those crazy codependents. I had become one.

Gradually, I began to climb out of my black abyss. Along the way, I developed a passionate interest in the subject of codependency. As a counselor and a writer, my curiosity was provoked. I also had a personal stake in the subject. What happens to people like me? How does it happen? Why? Most important, what do codependents need to do to feel better? And to stay that way?

I talked to counselors, therapists, and codependents. I read the few available books on the subject and related topics. I reread the basics—the therapy books that have stood the test of time—looking for ideas that applied. I went to meetings of Al-Anon, a self-help group based on the Twelve Steps of Alcoholics Anonymous but geared toward the person who has been affected by another person's drinking.

Eventually, I found what I was seeking. I began to see, understand, and change. My life started working again. Soon, I was conducting another group for codependents at another Minneapolis treatment center. But this time, I had a vague notion of what I was doing.

I still found codependents hostile, controlling, manipulative, and indirect. I still saw all the peculiar twists of personality I previously saw. But, I saw deeper.

I saw people who were hostile; they had felt so much hurt that hostility was their only defense against being crushed again. They were that angry because anyone who had tolerated what they had would be that angry.

They were controlling because everything around and inside them was out of control. Always, the dam of their lives and the lives of those around them threatened to burst and spew harmful consequences on everyone. And nobody but them seemed to notice or care.

I saw people who manipulated because manipulation appeared to be the only way to get anything done. I worked with people who were indirect because the systems they lived in seemed incapable of tolerating honesty.

I worked with people who thought they were going crazy because they had believed so many lies they didn't know what reality was.

I saw people who had gotten so absorbed in other people's problems they didn't have time to identify or solve their own. These were people who had cared so deeply, and often destructively, about other people that they had forgotten how to care about themselves. The codependents felt responsible for so much because the people around them felt responsible for so little; they were just taking up the slack.

· · ·

I saw hurting, confused people who needed comfort, understanding, and information. I saw victims of alcoholism who didn't drink but were nonetheless victimized by alcohol. I saw victims struggling desperately to gain some kind of power over their perpetrators. They learned from me, and I learned from them.

Soon, I began to subscribe to some new beliefs about codependency. Codependents aren't crazier or sicker than alcoholics, but they hurt as much or more. They haven't cornered the market on agony, but they have gone through their pain without the anesthetizing effects of alcohol or other drugs, or the other high states achieved by people with compulsive disorders. And the pain that comes from loving someone who's in trouble can be profound.

"The chemically dependent partner numbs the feelings and the nonabuser is doubled over in pain—relieved only by anger and occasional fantasies," wrote Janet Geringer Woititz in an article from the book *CoDependency, An Emerging Issue.*[1]

Codependents are that way sober because they went through what they did sober.

No wonder codependents are so crazy. Who wouldn't be, after living with the people they've lived with?

It's been difficult for codependents to get the information and practical help they need and deserve. It's tough enough to convince people who struggle with compulsive disorders to seek help. It's more difficult to convince people who struggle with codependency—those who by comparison look, but don't feel, normal—that they have problems.

Codependents suffered in the backdrop of the afflicted person. If they recovered, they did that in the background too. For many years, counselors (like me) didn't know what to do to help them. Sometimes codependents were blamed; sometimes they were ignored; sometimes they were expected to magically shape up (an archaic attitude that has not worked with alcoholism and doesn't help with codependency either). Rarely were codependents treated as individuals who needed help to get better. Rarely were they given a personalized recovery program for their problems and their pain. Yet, by its nature, alcoholism and other compulsive disorders turn everyone affected by the illness into victims—people who need help even if they are not drinking, using other drugs, gambling, overeating, or overdoing a compulsion.

That's why I wrote this book. It grew out of my research, my personal and professional experiences, and my passion for the subject. It is a personal and, in some places, prejudiced opinion.

I'm not an expert, and this isn't a technical book for experts. Whether the person you've let yourself be affected by struggles with substance abuse, gambling, eating disorders, or sex addiction;

whether they are a rebellious teenager, a neurotic parent, another codependent, or any combination of the above, this book is for you, the codependent.

This book is not about how you can help the other person, although if you get better, their chance of recovery improves too.[2] This book is about your most important and probably most neglected responsibility: taking care of yourself. It's about what you can do to start feeling better.

I've compiled some of the best, most helpful information on codependency. I've also included quotes and stories to show how real people dealt with real codependency problems. Although I've changed names and certain details to protect privacy, all the stories are true and are not composites.

. . .

A friend, Scott Egleston, who is a professional in the mental health field, told me a therapy fable. He heard it from someone, who heard it from someone else. It goes:

Once upon a time, a woman moved to a cave in the mountains to study with a guru. She wanted, she said, to learn everything there was to know. The guru supplied her with stacks of books and left her alone so she could study. Every morning, the guru returned to the cave to monitor the woman's progress. In his hand, he carried a heavy wooden cane. Each morning, he asked her the same question: "Have you learned everything there is to know yet?" Each morning, her answer was the same. "No," she said, "I haven't." The guru would then strike her over the head with his cane.

This scenario repeated itself for months. One day the guru entered the cave, asked the same question, heard the same answer, and raised his cane to hit her in the same way, but the woman grabbed the cane from the guru, stopping his assault in midair.

Relieved to end the daily batterings but fearing reprisal, the woman looked up at the guru. To her surprise, the guru smiled. "Congratulations," he said, "you have graduated. You now know everything you need to know."

"How's that?" the woman asked.

"You have learned that you will never learn everything there is to know," he replied. "And you have learned how to stop the pain."

That's what this book is about: stopping the pain and gaining control of your life.

Many people have learned to do it. You can too.

PART I

What's Codependency,
and Who's Got It?

1

My Story

The sun was shining, and it was a beautiful day when I met him.

Then, everything went crazy.

—MELODY, MARRIED TO AN ALCOHOLIC

When we met, I was two years clean and sober from alcohol and drugs. I worked as a legal secretary at a prestigious Minneapolis law firm on the top floor of the then newly built IDS Center, while taking courses at the University of Minnesota to become a chemical dependency counselor. Our introduction had been arranged by my Alcoholics Anonymous (AA) sponsor. I was ecstatic.

David was everything I could have hoped for and more: six feet four, good-looking, smart, well-read, and funny. He was part of the founding family of a major therapeutic community/rehabilitation center in Minneapolis (not the rehab I'd attended) and served as a director there. He was in the newspapers frequently, associating with judges and bigwigs. He worked in diversion, helping people get out of prison and into treatment for crimes related to substance abuse, both pre- and post-sentencing. This work was as exciting as it was novel. As a society, we were just beginning to discover—and get honest about—the depth, width, and impact of substance abuse. Everybody loved David, from the people he helped to the judges to his friends and family.

Soon, I did too. By then, I'd made my amends—emotional and financial; I'd worked my recovery program hard. The process was everything to me. David had achieved five more years of sobriety than I had, though he didn't attend AA. He said that through the therapeutic community in which he worked, he'd found another way to stay clean and sober. Because he worked in recovery and was so respected and loved, I took him at face value.

Our relationship progressed quickly. He moved into my small, one-bedroom apartment in South Minneapolis. Because we both worked—David often through evenings, weekends, and holidays—our time together was limited and precious. I was busy studying, working at the law firm, and attending AA.

Six months after we met, we got married in Sioux Falls, South Dakota. I'd been excited about the ceremony, but it felt . . . off. Instead of staying in South Dakota for a honeymoon, David changed plans at the last minute and wanted to return to Minneapolis immediately so he could stand in for his brother, Jim, in a theater production. (He and Jim both worked in theater, boxing, and rehabilitation.) I asked if he'd like me to attend; he said no. When he came back to the apartment after the show—our first night home as a married couple—David told me his father had suffered a stroke and died that evening. He needed to go to the hospital, be with his brothers, and make arrangements.

I asked if he wanted me to come with him; he said no. At six thirty the next morning, he walked into the apartment and said that he had decided to play cards with his friends to distract himself from his loss. I'd been up all night crying and waiting for word. David paced back and forth, his large frame filling the apartment and towering over me from my spot on the sofa, while I tried to repress how distraught I felt.

"I took a big chance when I married you," he said, scowling. "You're only two years sober. You're iffy when it comes to sobriety. You're new at it. Don't let me down. Don't prove I made a mistake."

His words hit their target. The truth was, I knew nothing about marriage, even less about love. My mom had been married eight times; no marriage lasted longer than two years. She was an aggressive, demanding, controlling woman—in pain—who'd been raised on a farm with seven brothers, two of whom would later be sent to prison on charges of child molestation. I was the youngest of her four children by ten years. Mom had placed the father of my three elder siblings in the hospital when they were young and then divorced him. She married my father years later when she found herself pregnant with me. Her favorite thing to say to me? "I should have aborted you when I could."

Hurt people hurt people, even sometimes their kids.

All the kids in my family ran from home as soon as they could, including me. Mom was a screamer. She walked into a room screeching and yelling and walked out of it the same way. Judgmental, accusatory, blaming, and without mercy, she beat my siblings. I still remember hiding behind a chair when I was very young, watching her pin my thirteen-year-old brother to the wall. She held his hair with one hand and beat him across the face with a heavy wooden paddle. Back and forth. One blow after another. Because I had heart problems, I escaped beatings, unless she asked Stepdad of the Year to punish me. Then he did as he pleased. *You'll be gone from this house before I am*, I'd think as I waited for him to leave my room.

I started medicating with alcohol at age eleven; my brother and I slowly consumed all the booze under the sink that Mom kept for the men she entertained. (Mom didn't drink; she barely took an aspirin when her head hurt.) I marked off the days until I turned eighteen on a large calendar that I kept under my mattress.

At the private academy where I attended high school, I excelled—learning to type 150 words per minute, take shorthand, and speak other languages. I also fell in love with writing when I worked on the school paper—the youngest student ever on staff. But I had zero social life. Since a stranger had abducted me at age four from the street where I lived and molested me, I wasn't allowed one. It was my mom's way of protecting me.

My dad had left when I was two. He was a skilled and extremely creative musician who worked as a fireman. He was also an alcoholic. I can't remember the exact mumbled, drunken, and devastating words he said the night he walked out for good, but they marked me with profound subliminal guilt and shame, making me feel that it was my fault I didn't have a dad who loved me.

It shouldn't have surprised me that I was clueless about how to be married, how to participate in a good marriage, or even what being in a good marriage looked like. I wasn't allowed to date or have friends until I turned eighteen and left home. Soon after, I stumbled into my first real relationship. My boyfriend was ten years older than I and dealt pot and pills. (He later got sober and started Narcotics Anonymous in Minneapolis.) Two years later I ran off with a hard-narcotics dealer, a rich kid from the suburbs who still lived in a posh home with his posh parents. Then I discovered I was pregnant.

I wanted to have the baby, then place him for adoption. My boyfriend said he'd found a family, but then I learned that all he knew about these people was that they were willing to pay him $20,000 for the baby. I put a stop to that; no way would I let him sell our baby. After John was born, the boyfriend and I lived together in an apartment for a few months. We got a marriage license, which I ripped into pieces less than twenty-four hours later. I wasn't 100 percent sane, but despite my actions and addiction, I had the mental presence to know that this marriage would never work.

But if we didn't marry, John would be labeled "illegitimate" for the rest of his life. I taped the marriage license back together, and we got married a week later.

By then, I was working as a legal secretary to help with our financial situation. The firm I worked at represented a new clinic within the Mount Sinai Hospital complex that opened sometime around 1970. Methadone is an opiate substitute that helps addicts avoid using drugs. One day I walked into my boss's office, closing the door behind me. "I'm an addict," I told him. "On coffee breaks, I shoot Dilaudid. Can you please help my husband and me get on the methadone program? Please," I asked. "Their waiting list is long, and we can't wait."

After a moment, he agreed to help. The next day, we got on the methadone program. But I lost my job. The firm couldn't afford to have a drug addict on their payroll.

My first marriage dissolved only one month after that. My husband took our baby and returned to his parents. I knew deep in my soul that I couldn't raise the child; I also knew that I couldn't allow my mom to have him. As much as one could find peace in such circumstances, I knew allowing his paternal grandparents to raise him was the right thing to do, but after I made that decision, I was lost. For the next year or so, I dove into as much darkness and oblivion as I could find, resulting in a court sentence to treatment and an admonition that even so much as a parking ticket thereafter would result in jail time.

Now, five years later, I was attempting to sort my marriage to David. Maybe everything that was happening to us was normal. Maybe this overwhelming mess of feelings in my gut was normal too. My sponsor was of the opinion that David and I were a match made in heaven. I wasn't so sure. I wanted it to work; I needed it to work. My hope was that our marriage would not only be good for us but could also inspire others.

My soul and self-esteem couldn't handle another divorce. I'd discussed my marriage with one other woman my age who had been married for twelve years to another cofounder of the rehab program where David worked. She and her husband seemed so in love; their marriage clicked. One day I asked her, "How do you stay married and not get divorced?"

"Just . . . Do. Not. Ever. Get. Divorced," she said. "No matter what."

Seems simple enough, I thought.

• • •

One month after David and I married, I became pregnant with our daughter, Nichole. Being pregnant with her inspired me to go for my dream of working as a chemical dependency counselor. I wanted to help others the way my counselor had profoundly helped me transform my life. I started taking job interviews at any chemical dependency treatment center in Minneapolis that was hiring.

In the mid-1970s, there were not many treatment center openings for women outside of office work. After I'd taken every interview available and come up empty-handed, then surrendered to my despair, David came home from work and said his rehab had decided to hire me. "It's an office job; it involves working with the board of directors," he explained. "But something else might open up later, down the line."

I took it.

David and I moved into a larger apartment in Edina; I worked until Nichole was born.

David seemed jubilant about the baby, though he worked all the time. And he traveled a lot for business.

Three weeks after Nichole was born, I was at home with her and David when the toilet wouldn't stop running. I went into the bathroom and jiggled the handle a few times. It didn't help. Finally, I removed the lid of the toilet tank.

Like a scene from a bad movie, a bottle of vodka was wedged in the tank. This was too on the nose, too *Days of Wine and Roses*.

David drinking? I could barely take it in; this hadn't even occurred to me. Not ever. Not for a second.

When I confronted David later, I threatened to leave. But where would I go with a three-week-old baby? David promised that the vodka had been a one-off; it wouldn't happen again. His older brother dropped by, encouraging—begging—me to give David another chance.

It struck me as odd that out of the three of us, I was the only one who thought David's drinking was a problem. I knew that it wouldn't be smart for my own sobriety to stay with a substance abuser.

But I stayed.

Around that time, our little family moved to a home on Pleasant Avenue in South Minneapolis. My mother had loaned us the money for a down payment; the place was a dilapidated mess. It had been used as a rental property, and it clearly hadn't received any TLC for many years. I quickly learned that David's familiarity with screwdrivers extended only to the drink, not the tool. I learned how to repair and paint walls; I sanded and refinished the floors; I patched a huge hole in the bathroom wall that went clear through to the outside; I made the kitchen pretty and welcoming. I turned the house into a warm, comfortable home.

I was also promoted at work. Federal funding required that the rehab facility where I worked fund groups for the family members and loved ones of substance abusers.

"We want you to organize and run that group," David said. "For the families."

Horrifying visions of working with women like my mother filled my head. While AA had opened its doors and heart to us, most of the younger people in the program didn't participate in Al-Anon, which was started in 1951 for family members affected by someone else's drinking. I mostly thought of it as a program for elderly Catholic women.

"I don't know what to do with . . . *them*," I said.

"Neither do we," David said. "That's why you get the job."

I wasn't excited. I wanted to work with the substance abusers, the people with the real problem. Not the "significant others" who weren't significant—not to themselves or anyone else.

Nevertheless, I bucked up and accepted the challenge. My goal was to facilitate the most helpful, effective group I could. It took not more than a minute for me to realize that I belonged in this group too. We were mirrors, the people in this group and me. As I watched and listened, I began hearing *myself.* Though I dug deeply into the literature and my education at the university on how to deal with families of substance abusers, I found little that was tangibly helpful in terms of therapeutic technique. However, when I started looking inside and around myself and following my curiosity, I began to find answers—though slowly at first.

Forty years in the future, I would discover a universal synchronicity. While our culture was still raising its consciousness about the prevalence of substance abuse and starting to spread information about how to heal from it, American astronomer Charles Kowal identified the minor asteroid Chiron, which was finally big and bright enough to see. Chiron became known as the "wounded healer" planet, referring to the Greek god Chiron's ability to heal everyone but himself. In 1951, Carl Jung had been the first to apply the term "wounded healer" to the way in which a healer's own soul disease and pain can train them to help others heal.[1]

If that's true, I was well trained.

To quote Rumi, "The wound is the place where the Light enters you."

David's drinking "relapses" became more severe and frequent, causing more damage to him, our family, and, ultimately, his career.

I became more incensed, frightened, curious, trapped, despondent, uncertain, overwhelmed, suspicious, controlling, rigid, miserable, and unhappy. There was no peace between his relapses; only unexpressed anger and fear about when it would happen again. Our finances were constantly in chaos; I became an expert at fending off the gas company workers showing up at our door to shut off utilities. David didn't believe in paying bills; I was compulsive about it. I saw over time that we shared very few values except one: we both loved our daughter. I also knew he was having affairs, though I could never prove it. (After we divorced, I learned that he had never ended his relationship with the lover he'd had before we married. She lived a mile from us.) How can you confront someone when they so effectively and wholeheartedly deny your claims and you have no proof? The gaslighting was enough to make me go crazy.

I had to let go.

I didn't want all this angst; I didn't want a broken family.

I didn't want to be codependent.

I hated being codependent.

Two years and two months after Nichole was born, our son Shane was born. David barely showed up at the hospital, even though I had one of those lovely rooms where both parents could sleep with the baby. Nichole was with her grandmother; I'm certain David was with his lover. Little by slowly, the lies and betrayals—and the disease of alcoholism—disabused me of any feelings of love I had for David.

I divorced him when the time was right, when I felt empowered to do that. I waited until the last possible moment; the kids loved their daddy so much. By the time we moved out of Pleasant

Avenue, I found dozens of empty vodka bottles hidden in the basement.

David was my karma. He was my qualifier, the person who qualified me for codependency (and Al-Anon), and my trigger (and he triggered a lot). He was also my motivation, the driving force behind me learning about codependency and wanting to share my healing with others. He wasn't a bad guy, though his behaviors hurt the family and me a lot. Many of our mutual acquaintances knew of his affairs—and his drinking. It was embarrassing and humiliating. I've since learned to let his behavior reflect on him and not take it on myself.

He had a compulsion to drink and screw around; he'd lost control.

I had a compulsion to control him; I'd lost control too.

* * *

I was about to learn three fundamental ideas.

First, I wasn't crazy; I was codependent. Alcoholism and other compulsive disorders are truly family illnesses. The way the illness affects other family members is called *codependency*.

Second, once family members have been affected, codependency takes on a life of its own. It's similar to catching pneumonia or picking up any destructive habit. Once you've got it, it's yours.

And third, if we want to get rid of it, *we* have to do something to make it go away. It doesn't matter whose fault it is. Our codependency becomes *our* problem—and our challenge. Solving our problem is our responsibility.

If we're codependent, we need to find our own recovery or healing process—our own path to well-being. To begin that recovery, it helps to understand codependency and certain attitudes, feelings, and behaviors that often accompany it. It's also important to change some of these attitudes and behaviors and understand what to expect as these changes occur.

This book will search for those understandings and encourage those changes.

There's more to my story. I found a new beginning. I got better. I started living my own life. You can too.

••• ACTIVITY •••

1. At the end of the following chapters, you'll find prompts to record your responses to what you've read. You might find it helpful to get a notebook and write down thoughts and feelings you have as you read this book.

2

Other Stories

When I say I'm codependent, I don't mean I'm a little
bit codependent. I mean I'm really codependent. I don't
marry men who stop for a few beers after work.
   I marry men who won't work.

—ELLEN, AN AL-ANON MEMBER

Maybe you identified with my story in the last chapter.
It's an example of codependency, but it's not the only
type of codependency. There are as many variations of
my story as there are people to tell them.
   Here are a few.

· · ·

Jason, a handsome and personable man in his early forties, has
called himself "a success in business but a failure in relationships
with women." During high school and college, Jason dated many
women. He was popular and considered a good catch. However,
after graduation, Jason stunned his family and friends when he

married Lisa. Lisa treated Jason worse than any other woman he had dated. She was cool and hostile toward Jason and his friends, shared few interests with him, and didn't seem to care much for or about him. Thirteen years later, the marriage ended in divorce when Jason discovered that some things he had suspected for years were true: Lisa had been dating other men since they were married, and she was (and had been for some time) abusing alcohol and other drugs.

Jason was devastated. But, after mourning for about two months, he fell wildly in love with another woman, who was a start-in-the-morning-and-drink-'til-she-passed-out alcoholic. After spending several months worrying about her, trying to help her, trying to figure out what he was doing that caused her to drink, trying to control her drinking, and ultimately getting angry with her because she wouldn't stop drinking, Jason terminated the relationship. Soon he met another woman, fell in love with her, and moved into her apartment. Within months, Jason suspected she, too, was chemically dependent.

Jason began spending much of his time worrying about his girlfriend. He checked up on her, rummaged through her purse looking for pills or other evidence, and questioned her about her activities. Sometimes, he simply denied she had a problem. During those times, he kept busy, tried to enjoy his time with her (although he said he felt uneasy), and told himself, *It's just me. Something's wrong with me.*

During one of the many crises in his most recent relationship, when Jason was temporarily jolted out of denial, he went to a chemical dependency counselor for advice.

"I know I should end the relationship," Jason said, "but I'm just not ready to let her go. We can talk about anything and everything together. We're such good friends. And I love her. Why? Why does this always happen to me?"

He confided, "Give me a room full of women, and I'll fall in love with the one with the most problems—the one who will treat me the worst. They're more of a challenge. If a woman treats me too well, it turns me off."

Jason considered himself a social drinker who had never had problems as a result of his drinking. He told the counselor he'd never used drugs. His older brother had abused alcohol since he was a teenager. For many years Jason adamantly denied that either of his deceased parents had been alcoholics, but as time passed, he reluctantly admitted that his dad, a restaurant/bar owner, may have "drank too much."

The counselor suggested the alcoholism and excessive drinking in Jason's immediate family may still be affecting him and his relationships.

"How could their problems be affecting me?" Jason asked. "Dad has been dead for years, and I rarely see my brother."

After a few counseling sessions, Jason began to identify his codependent behaviors, but he wasn't sure exactly what that meant or what to do about it. When he became less angry about the immediate problem in his relationship, he discontinued counseling. Jason decided his girlfriend's problems with drugs weren't that bad. He became convinced his problems with women were his fault. He was attracted to women who were trouble. Maybe one day he'd get tired of the drama and change his pattern.

• • •

Patricia was in her midthirties and had been married for eleven years when she sought help from a private therapist. She had three children, the youngest of whom had cerebral palsy. Patricia had given up her career to devote herself to raising her kids. She told her therapist she loved her children and didn't regret her decision to stay home but hated her daily routine.

Before her marriage, Patricia had many friends and interests; she worked as a nurse and liked to be active—going on hikes, working out, even training for marathons. However, in the years following the birth of her children, particularly her child with disabilities, she had lost her enthusiasm for life. She had few friends, had gained over eighty pounds, didn't know what she was feeling, and if she did, felt guilty for feeling that way. She had tried to stay active by doing volunteer work at her kids' school, but her efforts usually resulted in feelings of ineffectiveness and resentment. She thought about returning to work, but she didn't because, as she told her therapist, "All I know is nursing, and I'm sick of taking care of people."

She also shared, "My family and friends think I'm a tower of strength. Good ole dependable Patty. Always there. Always in control. Always ready to help. The truth is, I'm falling apart, very quietly but very certainly. I've been depressed for years. I can't shake it. I cry at the drop of a hat. I don't have any energy. I scream at the kids all the time. I don't have any interest in sex, at least not with my husband. I feel guilty all the time about everything. I even feel guilty about coming to see you," she told the therapist. "Therapy is a ridiculous waste of time and money. I should be able to solve my own problems. I should be able to just snap out of this. But I had to do something.

"Lately, I've been thinking about suicide," Patricia confessed. "Of course, I'd never actually kill myself. Too many people need me. Too many people depend on me. But I'm worried. And scared."

Patricia told the therapist that before their marriage, her husband had a problem with alcohol. After they got married, he drank less, had held the same job, and was well-liked at work. But when the therapist pressed her, Patricia revealed that her husband did not attend AA meetings or any other support group. Instead, he would be sober for months and then fall off the wagon and go on weekend drinking binges. When he drank, he lost his mind. When he wasn't drinking, he was angry and hostile.

"I don't know what happened to him. He's not the man I married. What's even more frightening is I don't know what's happening to me or who I am," Patricia said. "It's difficult to explain exactly what the problem is. I don't understand it myself. There's no major problem I can point to and say, 'That's what's wrong.' But it feels like I've lost myself. At times, I wonder if I'm losing it. What's wrong with me?"

"Maybe your husband is an alcoholic, and your problems are caused by the family disease of alcoholism," the therapist suggested.

"How can that be?" Patricia asked. "Most of the time my husband doesn't drink."

The therapist dug into Patricia's background. Patricia talked with fondness about her parents and her two adult brothers. She came from a good family that was close and successful. The therapist dug deeper. Patricia mentioned that her father had attended AA since she was a teenager.

"Dad sobered up when I was in high school," she said. "I really love him, and I'm proud of him. But his drinking years were a pretty crazy time for our family."

Patricia was not only married to someone who was probably an alcoholic but was also what's called "an adult child of an alcoholic." The entire family had been affected by the family disease of alcoholism. Her dad had stopped drinking; her mother went to Al-Anon. But Patricia, too, had been affected. Was she expected to magically overcome the ways she had been affected just because the drinking stopped?

Instead of suggesting ongoing therapy, Patricia's therapist referred her to a self-esteem course and an assertiveness-training class. The therapist also recommended Patricia attend Al-Anon meetings or Adult Children of Alcoholics (ACOA) meetings, which are self-help groups based on the Twelve Steps of Alcoholics Anonymous.

Patricia followed the therapist's advice. She didn't find an overnight cure, but as the months passed, she found herself making decisions with greater ease, expressing her feelings, saying what she thought, paying attention to her needs, and feeling less guilty. She became more tolerant of herself and her daily routine. Gradually, her depression lifted. She cried less and laughed more. Her energy and enthusiasm for life returned. Incidentally, with no prodding from Patricia, her husband joined AA. He became less hostile, and their marriage began to improve. The point here is that Patricia gained control of her life. Her life started working.

Now, if you ask Patricia what her problem is or was, she will answer: "I'm codependent."

• • •

Clients who seek help from mental health and chemical dependency agencies are not the only people who suffer from codependency. Randell was a chemical dependency counselor and a recovering alcoholic with several years of sobriety when he found himself struggling with codependency. Randell was also an adult child of an alcoholic; his father and three brothers were alcoholics. He was an intelligent, sensitive man who enjoyed his work, but his problem was his leisure time. He spent most of it worrying about—obsessed with—other people and their problems. Sometimes he tried to untangle messes that alcoholics created; other times he felt angry with them for creating the messes he felt obligated to clean up. Sometimes he felt upset because people, not necessarily alcoholics, behaved in particular ways. He ranted and felt guilty, sorry, and used by people. Rarely, however, did he feel close to them. Rarely did he have fun.

For many years, Randell believed his duty was to worry about people and get involved in their problems. He called his behavior kindness, concern, love, and, sometimes, righteous indignation. Now, after getting help for his problem, he calls it codependency.

• • •

Sometimes, codependent behavior becomes inextricably entangled with being a good wife, mother, father, friend, child, or worker. Sometimes it's entangled with religion. Now in her forties, Marlyss is an attractive woman—when she takes care of herself. Most of the time, however, she's busy taking care of her five children and her husband, who is a recovering alcoholic. She's devoted her life to making them happy, but she hasn't succeeded. Usually, she feels angry and unappreciated for her efforts, and her family feels angry at her. She has sex with her husband whenever he wants, regardless of how she feels. She spends too much of the family's budget on whatever toys and clothing the children want. She chauffeurs, reads to, cooks for, cleans for, cuddles, and coddles those around her, but nobody gives to her. Most of the time, they don't even say thank you. Marlyss resents her constant giving to the people in her life. She resents how her family and their needs control her life. She chose teaching as her profession, and she often resents that.

"But I feel guilty when I say no. I feel guilty when I don't live up to my standards of what a wife and mother should be. I feel guilty when I don't live up to other people's expectations of me. I feel guilty all the time," she said. "In fact, I schedule my day, my priorities, according to guilt."

Does endlessly taking care of other people, resenting it, and expecting nothing in return mean Marlyss is a good wife and mother? Or could it mean she's codependent?

• • •

Substance abuse is not the only family problem that can create codependency. Alissa, the mother of two teenagers, worked part-time at a mental health organization when she sought out a new family counselor because her oldest child, a sixteen-year-old boy, was constantly causing problems. He ran away, stayed out past his curfew, skipped school, smoked weed, and generally did whatever he wanted, whenever he wanted.

"This child," Alissa told the counselor, "is driving me crazy."

She meant it. She was worried sick. Some days she was so depressed and troubled she couldn't get out of bed. Alissa had tried everything she could think of to help this child. She'd placed him in treatment three times, sent him to teenage boot camp, and dragged the whole family from counselor to counselor. Alissa had tried other techniques too: She had threatened, cried, hollered, and begged. She had gotten tough and called the police on him. She had tried gentleness and forgiveness. She'd even tried acting like he hadn't done the inappropriate things. She had locked him out. And she had traveled halfway across the state to bring him home after he ran away. Although her efforts hadn't helped her son, Alissa was obsessed with finding and doing the one thing that would "make him see the errors of his ways" and help him change.

"Why is he doing this to me?" she asked the counselor. "He's running and ruining my life!"

The counselor agreed that the problem with Alissa's son was painful, upsetting, and required action. But the problem also didn't have to run and ruin Alissa's life.

"You haven't been able to control your son, but you can gain control of yourself," the counselor said. "You can deal with your own codependency."

. . .

Sheryl, a successful fashion model, also labels herself codependent. Shortly after marrying the man of her dreams, she found herself in a nightmare. Her husband, she learned, had a sex addiction. In his case, that meant he was addicted to pornography. He was also compulsively drawn into affairs with other women and, as Sheryl put it, "God only knows what and who else." She learned about his addiction one week after their wedding, when she discovered him in bed with another woman.

Sheryl's first response was panic. Then she got angry. Then she felt concern—for her husband and his problem. Her friends advised her to leave him, but she decided to stay in the marriage. He needed help. He needed her. Maybe he would change. Wasn't she enough?

Her husband joined Sex Addicts Anonymous (SAA), a Twelve Step self-help group similar to Alcoholics Anonymous. Sheryl refused to join COSA (similar to Al-Anon) for family members of sex addicts. She didn't want to go public with her problems; she didn't even want to discuss them privately.

Over several months, Sheryl found herself accepting fewer work assignments, turning down evenings out with friends, and sticking closer to home. She compulsively checked her husband's cell phone. She wanted to be home when he left the house and there when he returned. She wanted to see what he looked like, how he acted, and how he talked. She wanted to know exactly what he was doing and with whom he was doing it. She often called his SAA sponsor to complain, to report, and to inquire about her husband's progress. She refused, she said, to be tricked and deceived again.

Gradually, she alienated herself from friends and activities. She was too anxious to work, too ashamed to talk to her friends. Soon enough, she caught her husband cheating on her again; her friends were frustrated with her for staying with him.

"I couldn't stand the sight of him. I felt nothing but contempt for him. Yet I couldn't bring myself to leave," Sheryl reported later. "I couldn't make myself do much of anything except worry and obsess over him."

She said, "My turning point was the night I chased him with a butcher knife. It was an absolute low point. I was running through the house screaming at him when I suddenly became aware, for the first time, of *me*. I had gone completely mad. I was crazy—out of control—and he just stood there, calmly looking at me. I knew then I had to get help—for me."

Sheryl joined COSA shortly after that incident and began to label her loss of control as codependency. She is now separated from her husband and seeking a divorce. She is also feeling better about herself.

• • •

Although the preceding examples have been dramatic, codependency doesn't necessarily have to be so intense. And it doesn't always involve experiences with deeply troubled people. Kristen is married, has two young children, and knows of no alcoholism or compulsive disorders in her immediate or extended family. Yet she calls herself codependent. Her problem, she says, is that other people's moods control her emotions; she, in turn, tries to control their feelings. "I'm a people pleaser," she said.

"If my husband is happy, and I feel responsible for that, then I'm happy. If he's upset, I often feel responsible for that too. Then I become anxious, uncomfortable, and upset until he feels better. I try to *make* him feel better. I feel guilty if I can't. And he gets angry with me for trying. And it's not only with him that I behave codependently," she said. "It's with everyone: my parents, my children, guests in my home. Somehow, I just seem to lose myself in other people. I get enmeshed in them."

"I'd like to do something about it—this thing called codependency—before it gets any worse. I'm not terribly unhappy, but I'd like to learn how to relax and start enjoying myself and other people."

A colleague of mine summarized the condition this way: "Some people are *really* codependent, and some of us are a *little bit* codependent."

. . .

I chose the preceding examples because they represent a variety of experiences. They also illuminate a point that needs to be made: no single example illustrates codependency or the typical codependent experience. Codependency is complex. People are complex. Each person is unique, and each person's situation is different. Some people have extremely painful and debilitating experiences with codependency. Others don't and may be only mildly affected. Sometimes codependency is a person's response to another person's substance abuse; sometimes it isn't. Each person who struggles with codependency has a unique experience born of their circumstances, history, and personality.

Yet a common thread runs through all stories of codependency. It involves our responses and reactions to people around us. It involves our relationships with other people, whether they are substance abusers, gamblers, sex addicts, overeaters, or so-called normal people. Codependency involves the effects these people have on us and how we, in turn, try to affect them.

As Al-Anon members say, "Identify, don't compare."

··· ACTIVITY ···

1. Did you identify with any people in this chapter? What resonated with you and why?

2. Are you involved in any relationships right now that feel out of control to you?

3

Codependency

Relationships are like a dance, with visible energy racing back and forth between the partners. Some relationships are the slow, dark dance of death.[1]

—COLETTE DOWLING, *The Cinderella Complex*

Up to this point, I have been using the words *codependent*
and *codependency* as lucid terms. However, the definitions
of these words remain vague.

The definition of *chemical dependency* is being dependent (psychologically and/or physically) on alcohol or other drugs. *Overeating* and *gambling* are also words that bring specific actions to mind.
But what is codependency?

The obvious definition is: being a partner in dependency. This
definition is close to the truth but still unclear. It brings no specific
actions to mind. *Codependency* is treatment-center jargon, professional slang that's probably unintelligible to people outside that
profession and even gibberish to some inside the trade.

Jargon may mean different things to different people. Or, even if people can sense what a term means, they may not be able to define it clearly because it's never been clearly defined.

Those are some of the problems I've encountered with researching and attempting to define *codependency* and *codependent*. Many people haven't heard the terms or can't define them. Those who can define them each offer a different definition or rely on more jargon. To complicate matters, for many years I couldn't find the words in any dictionaries. My computer would tag them as misspelled, trying to convince me they weren't real words.

Yet *codependency* does have a particular and important definition to me and millions of other people. Let's get rid of the jargon and look at that meaning.

WHAT'S CODEPENDENCY?

In an article from the book *Co-Dependency, An Emerging Issue*, Robert Subby writes that codependency is "an emotional, psychological, and behavioral condition that develops as a result of an individual's prolonged exposure to, and practice of, a set of oppressive rules—rules which prevent the open expression of feeling as well as the direct discussion of personal and interpersonal problems."[2]

Earnie Larsen, another codependency specialist and a pioneer in the field, defines codependency as "those self-defeating, learned behaviors or character defects that result in a diminished capacity to initiate or to participate in loving relationships."[3]

Some less-professional definitions are as follows:

One woman said, "Codependency means that I'm a caretaker."

Another responded, "Being codependent means I'm married to an alcoholic. It also means I need to go to Al-Anon."

"Codependency," replied another, "means I'm up to my elbows in alcoholics."

"It means I'm always looking for someone to glom onto."

"Codependency? It means I know any man I'm attracted to, fall in love with, or marry will be chemically dependent or have some other equally serious problem."

"Codependency," explained one person, "is knowing all your relationships will either go on and on the same way (painfully) or end the same way (disastrously). Or both."

There are almost as many definitions of codependency as there are experiences that represent it. In desperation (or perhaps enlightenment), some therapists proclaim: "Codependency is *anything*, and *everyone* is codependent."

So who's got the inside story? Which definition is accurate? A brief history of codependency will help answer this question.

A BRIEF HISTORY

The word *codependency* appeared on the treatment scene in the late 1970s. I don't know who discovered it. Although several people may claim to have done so, the word emerged more or less simultaneously in several different treatment centers in Minnesota, according to information from the office of Sondra Smalley, a licensed psychologist and a leader in the codependency field. Maybe Minnesota, the heartland of chemical dependency treatment and Twelve Step programs for compulsive disorders, discovered it.

Robert Subby and John Friel, in an article from the book *Co-Dependency, An Emerging Issue,* write: "Originally, it was used to describe the person or persons whose lives were affected as a result of their being involved with someone who was chemically dependent. The codependent spouse or child or lover of someone who was chemically dependent was seen as having developed a pattern of coping with life that was not healthy, as a reaction to someone else's drug or alcohol abuse."[4]

It was a new name for an old game. Professionals had long suspected something peculiar happened to those who were closely involved with chemically dependent people. Some research had been done on the subject, indicating a physical, mental, emotional, and spiritual condition similar to alcoholism seemed to appear in many who did not struggle with alcoholism or chemical dependence but were close with someone who did. Words (more jargon that would later become synonymous with *codependent*) surfaced to describe this phenomenon: *co-alcoholic, nonalcoholic, para-alcoholic.*

Codependents certainly felt the effects of codependency long before the word was coined. In the 1940s, after the birth of Alcoholics Anonymous, a group of people—primarily wives of alcoholics—formed self-help support groups to deal with the ways their spouses' alcoholism affected them.[5] They didn't know they would later be called codependents. They did know they had been directly affected by their mates' alcoholism. And they were envious that alcoholics had a Twelve Step program to help them through recovery. The wives also wanted a program. So they used the Twelve Steps, revised the AA Twelve Traditions, changed its name to Al-Anon, and it worked! Millions of people have since benefited from Al-Anon.[6]

The basic thought, both then and in the late '70s when the word *codependency* emerged, was that codependents (co-alcoholics or para-alcoholics) were people whose lives had become unmanageable due to living in committed relationships with alcoholics.[7]

However, the definition for codependency has expanded since then. Professionals began to better understand the effects of a person's chemical dependency on the family and the effects of the family on the person struggling with chemical dependency. They also began to identify other problems, such as overeating and undereating, gambling, and certain sexual behaviors. These compulsive disorders paralleled the compulsive disorder—or *illness*—of alcoholism. Many people in close relationships with these compulsive people developed patterns of reacting and coping that resembled the coping patterns of people in relationships with alcoholics.

Something peculiar had happened to these families too. As professionals began to understand codependency better, more groups of people appeared to have it: adult children of alcoholics; people in relationships with emotionally or mentally disturbed persons; people whose partners had chronic illnesses; parents of children with behavior problems; people in relationships with irresponsible partners; professionals—nurses, social workers, and others in "helping" occupations. Even recovering alcoholics and addicts noticed they were codependent and perhaps had been long before becoming chemically dependent.[8] Codependents started cropping up everywhere.

When a codependent discontinued their relationship with a troubled person, the codependent frequently sought another troubled person and repeated the codependent behaviors with that new person. These behaviors, or coping mechanisms, seemed to prevail throughout the codependent's life—if they didn't change these behaviors.

Was it safe to assume codependency was triggered through relationships with people who have serious illnesses, behavior problems, or destructive compulsive disorders? Alcoholism in the family helped create codependency, but many other circumstances seemed to produce it too.

One common denominator was having a relationship, personally or professionally, with troubled, needy, or dependent people. But a second, more common denominator seemed to be the unwritten, silent rules that usually develop in the immediate family and set the pace for relationships.[9] These rules prohibit discussion about problems; open expression of feelings; direct, honest communication; realistic expectations (e.g., we are all human, vulnerable, and imperfect); selfishness; trust in other people and one's self; playing and having fun; and rocking the delicately balanced family canoe through growth or change—however healthy and beneficial that movement might be. These rules are common to alcoholic family systems but can emerge in other families too.

Now, I return to an earlier question: Which definition of codependency is accurate? They all are. Some describe the cause, some the effects, some the overall condition, some the symptoms, some the patterns, and some the pain. Codependency either meant, or has come to mean, all the definitions listed earlier.

I'm not trying to confuse you. Codependency has a fuzzy definition because it is a gray, fuzzy condition. It is complex, theoretical, and difficult to define in one or two sentences.

Why all this fuss about a definition? Because I'm going to attempt the difficult: I am going to try to define *codependent* in one sentence. And I want you to see the broader picture before I show you the narrower one. I hope this approach might help you identify codependency in yourself if that identification is appropriate. *Defining the problem is important because it helps determine the solution.* Here, the solution is vital. It means feeling better. It means recovery.

So, here is my definition of a codependent:

> A codependent person is one who has let another person's behavior affect them and who is obsessed with controlling that other person's behavior.

The other person might be a child, an adult, a lover, a spouse, a brother, a sister, a grandparent, a parent, a client, or a best friend. They could be an alcoholic, an addict, a person with mental or physical disabilities, a person who occasionally has sad feelings, or anyone else.

But the heart of the definition and recovery lies not in the other person—no matter how much we believe it does. It lies in ourselves, in the ways we have let other people's behaviors affect us and in the ways we try to affect them: the controlling, the obsessive "helping," caretaking, low self-worth bordering on self-hatred, self-repression, an abundance of anger and guilt, a peculiar dependency on peculiar people, an attraction to and tolerance for the bizarre, other-centeredness that results in abandonment of self, communication problems, intimacy problems, and an ongoing whirlwind trip through the five-stage grief process.[10]

Is codependency an illness? Some professionals say it isn't a disease; it's a normal reaction to abnormal people.[11]

Other professionals say codependency is a disease; it's a chronic, progressive illness. They suggest codependents want and need sick people around them to be happy in an unhealthy way. They say, for instance, the wife of an alcoholic needed to marry an alcoholic and chose him because she unconsciously thought he was an alcoholic. Furthermore, she needed him drinking and creating need and chaos in her life to feel fulfilled.

This latter judgment may be overly harsh. I'm convinced codependents need less harshness in their lives. Other people have been hard enough on us. We have been hard enough on ourselves. Friends, we have suffered enough. We have been victimized by diseases and people. Each of us must decide what part we played in our own victimization.

I don't know if codependency is or isn't an illness. I'm not an expert; I'm a writer with a passionate personal and professional interest in codependency. But to tell you what I believe, let me complete the brief history of codependency that I started earlier in this chapter.

Although the first Al-Anon groups appeared in the 1940s, I am certain we could go back to the beginning of time and human relationships and find glimmers of codependent behavior. People have always had problems, and others have always cared for their troubled friends and relatives. People have likely been caught up with the problems of others since relationships began.

Codependency probably trailed humans as they struggled through the remaining BCE years, right up to "these generally wretched times of the twentieth century," as Morley Safer of *60 Minutes* has been quoted as saying—and beyond. Ever since people first existed, they have been doing all the things we label "codependent." They have worried themselves sick about other people. They have tried to help in ways that didn't help. They have said yes when they meant no. They have tried to make other people see things their way. They have bent over backward to avoid hurting people's feelings, and, in so doing, have hurt themselves. They have been afraid to trust their feelings. They have believed lies and then felt betrayed. They have wanted to get even and punish others. They have felt so angry they wanted to kill. They have struggled for their rights while other people said they didn't have any. They have worn sackcloth because they didn't believe they deserved silk.

Codependents have undoubtedly done good deeds too. By nature, they are benevolent—concerned about and responsive to the needs of the world. As Thomas Wright wrote in *Co-Dependency, An Emerging Issue*:

> I suspect codependents have historically attacked social injustice and fought for the rights of the underdog. Codependents want to help. I suspect they have helped. But they probably died thinking they didn't do enough and were feeling guilty.
>
> It is natural to want to protect and help the people we care about. It is also natural to be affected by and react to the problems of people around us. As a problem becomes more serious and remains unresolved, we become more affected and react more intensely to it.

The word *react* is important here. However you approach codependency, however you define it, and from whatever frame of reference you choose to diagnose and treat it, codependency is primarily a reactionary process. Codependents are reactionaries. They overreact. They underreact. But rarely do they act. They react to the problems, pains, lives, and behaviors of others. They react to their own problems, pains, and behaviors. Many codependent reactions are reactions to the stress and trauma of living or growing up with alcoholism and other problems. It's normal to react to stress. But it's heroic and lifesaving to learn how *not* to react and to act in healthier ways. Most of us, however, need help to learn to do that.

Perhaps one reason some professionals call codependency a disease is because many who struggle with it are reacting to an illness such as alcoholism.

Another reason codependency is called a disease is because it is progressive. As the people around us become sicker, we may begin to react more intensely. What began as a little concern may trigger isolation, depression, emotional or physical illness, or suicidal ideations. One thing leads to another, and things get worse. Codependency may not be an illness, but it can make you sick. And it can help the people around you stay sick.

Another reason codependency is called a disease is because codependent behaviors—like many self-destructive behaviors—become habitual. We repeat habits without thinking. Habits take on a life of their own.[12] Whatever problem the other person has, codependency involves a habitual system of thinking, feeling, and behaving toward ourselves and others that can cause us pain. Codependent behaviors or habits are self-destructive. We frequently react to people who are destroying themselves; we react by learning to destroy ourselves. These habits can lead us into, or keep us in, destructive relationships—relationships that don't work. These behaviors can sabotage relationships that may otherwise have worked.

These behaviors can prevent you from finding peace and happiness with the most important person in your life—yourself. These behaviors belong to none other than ourselves. These are our problems. In the next chapter, we will examine these behaviors.

··· ACTIVITY ···

1. Which definition of codependency resonated with you?

2. Do you know anybody who has significantly affected your life, somebody whom you worry about and wish you could change? Who? Write several paragraphs about that person and your relationship. Afterward, read what you wrote. What feelings did you express? What feelings did you fail to express?

4

Codependent Characteristics

God, grant me the serenity
To accept the things I cannot change,
Courage to change the things I can,
And wisdom to know the difference.

—REINHOLD NIEBUHR, THE SERENITY PRAYER

A lthough two codependents might disagree on the definition of codependency, if they discuss the issues with each other, each will probably sense what the other person means. They will share ideas about things they have in common—things they do, think, feel, and say—that are characteristic of codependency. It is on these points—symptoms, problems, coping mechanisms, or reactions—that most definitions and recovery programs overlap and agree. These points dictate recovery. They are the things we need to recognize, accept, live with, deal with, struggle through, and frequently change.

Before I list the things people with codependency issues tend to do, however, I will make an important point: having these problems does not mean we're bad, defective, or inferior. Some of us learned these behaviors as children. Other people learned them later in life. We may have learned some of these things from our interpretation of religion. Some women, in particular, may have been taught that these behaviors were desirable feminine attributes. Wherever we learned to do these things, most of us learned our lessons well.

Most of us started doing these things out of necessity to protect ourselves and meet our needs. We performed, felt, and thought these things to survive—emotionally, mentally, and sometimes physically. We struggled to understand and cope with our complex world. It's not always easy to live with other people. It's particularly difficult to live with people who are sick, disturbed, or troubled. It's horrible to live with someone gripped by compulsive, out-of-control behaviors. Many of us have been trying to cope with outrageous circumstances, and these efforts have been both admirable and heroic. We've done the best we could.

However, these self-protective devices may have outgrown their usefulness. Sometimes, the things we do to protect ourselves turn on us and hurt us. They become self-destructive. Many codependents are barely surviving, and most aren't getting their needs met. As counselor Scott Egleston observes, codependency is a way of getting needs met that doesn't get needs met. We've been doing the wrong things for the right reasons.[1]

Can we change? Can we learn healthier behaviors? I don't know if mental, spiritual, and emotional health can be taught, but we can be inspired and encouraged. We can learn to do things differently. We can change. I think most people want to be healthy and live the best lives they can. But many of us don't know it's okay to do things differently. Many of us don't even understand that what we've been doing hasn't been working. Most of us have been so busy responding to other people's problems that we haven't had time to identify, much less take care of, our own problems.

Many professionals say the first step toward change is awareness. The second step is acceptance.[2] With that in mind, let's examine the characteristics of codependency. These characteristics have been compiled from my research and from my personal and professional experience.

CARETAKING

Codependents may:

- think and feel responsible for other people—for other people's feelings, thoughts, actions, choices, wants, needs, well-being, lack of well-being, and ultimate destiny

- feel anxiety, pity, and guilt when other people have a problem

- feel compelled—almost forced—to help another person solve their problem, such as offering unwanted advice, giving a rapid-fire series of suggestions, or fixing feelings

- feel angry when our help isn't effective

- anticipate other people's needs

- wonder why others don't do the same for us

- find ourselves saying yes when we mean no, doing things we don't really want to do, doing more than our fair share of the work, and doing things other people can and should do for themselves

- not know what we want and need or, if we do, tell ourselves what we want and need isn't important

- try to please others instead of ourselves

- find it easier to feel and express anger about injustices done to others than injustices done to us

- feel safest when giving

- feel insecure and guilty when somebody gives to us

- feel sad because we spend our whole lives giving to other people and nobody gives to us

- find ourselves attracted to needy people

- find needy people attracted to us

- feel bored, empty, and worthless if we don't have a crisis in our lives, a problem to solve, or someone to help

- abandon our routines to respond to or do something for somebody else

- overcommit ourselves

- feel harried and pressured

- believe deep inside that other people are somehow responsible for our unhappiness

- blame others for whatever predicament we are in

- say other people make us feel the way we do

- believe other people are making us crazy

- feel angry, victimized, unappreciated, and used

- find other people become impatient or angry with us for all the preceding characteristics

LOW SELF-WORTH

Codependents tend to:

- come from troubled, repressed, or dysfunctional families

- deny our families were troubled, repressed, or dysfunctional

- blame ourselves for everything

- pick on ourselves for everything, including the way we think, feel, look, act, and behave

- get angry, defensive, self-righteous, and indignant when others blame and criticize us—something we regularly do to ourselves

- reject compliments or praise

- get depressed from a lack of compliments and praise

- feel different from the rest of the world

- think we're not quite good enough

- feel guilty about spending money on ourselves or doing unnecessary or fun things

- fear rejection

- take things personally

- have been victims of sexual, physical, or emotional abuse, neglect, abandonment, or alcoholism

- feel like victims
- tell ourselves we can't do anything right
- fear making mistakes
- wonder why we have a tough time making decisions
- expect perfection from ourselves and others
- wonder why we can't get anything done to our satisfaction
- have a lot of "shoulds"
- feel a lot of guilt
- feel ashamed of who we are
- think our lives aren't worth living
- try to help other people live their lives instead
- get artificial feelings of self-worth from helping others
- overly identify with the failures and problems of the people we love
- wish good things would happen to us
- believe good things will never happen to us
- believe we don't deserve good things and happiness
- wish other people would like and love us
- believe other people couldn't possibly like and love us
- try to prove we're good enough for other people
- settle for being needed

REPRESSION

Many codependents:

- push our thoughts and feelings out of our awareness because of fear and guilt
- become afraid to let ourselves be who we are
- appear rigid and controlled

OBSESSION

Codependents tend to:

- feel terribly anxious about problems and people
- worry about the silliest things
- think and talk a lot about other people
- lose sleep over problems or other people's behaviors
- worry
- never find answers
- check on people
- try to catch people in acts of misbehavior
- feel unable to quit talking, thinking, and worrying about other people and their problems
- abandon our routines because we're so upset about somebody or something
- focus all our energy on other people

- wonder why we never have any energy
- wonder why we can't get things done

CONTROLLING

Many codependents:

- have lived through events and with people that were out of control, causing us sorrow and disappointment
- become afraid to let other people be who they are and allow events to happen naturally
- don't see or deal with our fear of loss of control
- think we know best how things should turn out and how people should behave
- try to control events and people through helplessness, guilt, coercion, threats, giving advice, manipulation, or domination
- eventually fail in our efforts or provoke people's anger
- get frustrated and angry
- feel controlled by events and people

DENIAL

Codependents tend to:

- ignore problems or pretend they aren't happening
- pretend circumstances aren't as bad as they are
- tell ourselves things will be better tomorrow

- stay busy so we don't have to think about things
- get confused
- get depressed
- get sick
- go to doctors and get tranquilizers
- become workaholics
- spend money compulsively
- overeat
- pretend those things aren't happening either
- watch problems get worse
- believe lies
- lie to ourselves
- wonder why we feel like we're going crazy

DEPENDENCY/ATTACHMENT

Many codependents:

- don't feel happy, content, or peaceful with ourselves
- look for happiness outside ourselves
- latch onto whoever or whatever we think can provide happiness
- feel terribly threatened by the loss of any thing or person we think provides our happiness
- didn't feel love and approval from our parents

- don't love ourselves
- believe other people can't or don't love us
- desperately seek love and approval
- often seek love from people incapable of loving
- believe other people are never there for us
- equate love with pain
- believe we want/need/love people more than they want/need/love us
- try to prove we're good enough to be loved
- don't take time to see if other people are good for us
- worry whether other people love or like us
- don't take time to figure out if we love or like other people
- center our lives around other people
- look to relationships to provide all our good feelings
- lose interest in our own lives when we love
- worry other people will leave us
- don't believe we can take care of ourselves
- stay in relationships that don't work
- tolerate abuse to keep people loving us
- feel trapped in relationships
- leave bad relationships and form new ones that don't work either
- wonder if we'll ever find love

POOR COMMUNICATION

Codependents frequently:

- blame

- threaten

- coerce

- beg

- bribe

- advise

- don't say what we mean

- don't mean what we say

- don't know what we mean

- don't take ourselves seriously

- think other people don't take us seriously

- take ourselves too seriously

- ask for what we want and need indirectly—by sighing, for example

- find it difficult to get to the point

- aren't sure what the point is

- gauge our words carefully to achieve a desired effect

- try to say what we think will please people

- try to say what we think will provoke people

- try to say what we hope will make people do what we want them to do

- eliminate the word *no* from our vocabulary

- talk too much

- talk about other people

- avoid talking about ourselves, our problems, feelings, and thoughts

- say everything is our fault

- say nothing is our fault

- believe our opinions don't matter

- wait to express our opinions until we know other people's opinions

- lie to protect and cover for people we love

- lie to protect ourselves

- have a difficult time asserting our rights

- have a difficult time expressing our emotions honestly, openly, and appropriately

- think most of what we have to say is unimportant

- begin to talk in cynical, self-degrading, or hostile ways

- apologize for bothering people

WEAK BOUNDARIES

Codependents frequently:

- say we won't tolerate certain behaviors from other people
- gradually increase our tolerance until we can tolerate and do things we said we never would
- let others hurt us
- keep letting people hurt us
- wonder why we hurt so badly
- complain, blame, and try to control while we continue to stand there hurting
- finally get angry
- become totally intolerant

LACK OF TRUST

Codependents:

- don't trust ourselves
- don't trust our feelings
- don't trust our decisions
- don't trust other people
- try to trust untrustworthy people
- think our Higher Power has abandoned us
- lose faith and trust in a Higher Power

ANGER

Many codependents:

- feel very scared, hurt, and angry
- live with people who are very scared, hurt, and angry
- are afraid of our own anger
- are afraid of other people's anger
- think people will go away if anger enters the picture
- think other people make us feel angry
- are afraid to make other people feel anger
- feel controlled by other people's anger
- repress angry feelings
- react to our anger by crying, getting depressed, overeating, getting sick, doing mean and nasty things to get even, acting hostile, or having violent outbursts
- punish other people for making us angry
- feel ashamed for feeling angry
- shame ourselves for feeling angry
- feel increasing amounts of anger, resentment, and bitterness
- feel safer with our anger than with hurt feelings
- wonder if we'll ever not be angry

SEX/INTIMACY PROBLEMS

Some codependents:

- are caretakers in the bedroom
- have sex when we don't want to
- have sex when we'd rather be held, nurtured, and loved
- try to have sex when we're angry or hurt
- refuse to enjoy sex because we're so angry at our partners
- fear losing control
- have a difficult time asking for what we need in bed
- withdraw emotionally from our partners
- feel sexual revulsion toward our partners
- don't talk about it
- reduce sex to a technical act
- wonder why we don't enjoy sex
- lose interest in sex
- make up reasons to abstain
- wish our sex partners would die, go away, or sense our feelings
- have strong sexual fantasies about other people
- consider or have an extramarital affair

MISCELLANEOUS

Codependents tend to:

- be extremely responsible

- be extremely irresponsible

- become martyrs, sacrificing our happiness and that of others for causes that don't require sacrifice

- find it difficult to feel close to people

- find it difficult to have fun and be spontaneous

- have an overall passive response to codependency—crying, hurt, helplessness

- have an overall aggressive response to codependency—violence, anger, dominance

- combine passive and aggressive responses

- vacillate in decisions and emotions

- laugh when we feel like crying

- stay loyal to our compulsions and people even when it hurts

- feel ashamed about family, personal, or relationship problems

- feel confused about the nature of the problem

- cover up, lie, and protect the problem

- avoid seeking help because we tell ourselves the problem isn't bad enough or we aren't important enough

- wonder why the problem doesn't go away

PROGRESSIVE CODEPENDENCY

In the later stages of codependency, we may:

- feel lethargic
- feel depressed
- become withdrawn, isolated, or disenfranchised
- experience a complete loss of daily routine and structure
- abuse or neglect our children and other responsibilities
- feel hopeless
- begin to plan our escape from a relationship we feel trapped in
- think about suicide
- become violent
- become seriously emotionally, mentally, or physically ill
- experience an eating disorder
- become addicted to alcohol and other drugs

• • •

The preceding checklists are long but not all-inclusive. Like all people, codependents do, feel, and think many things. There is not a certain number of traits that guarantees whether a person is or isn't codependent. Each of us is different; each of us has our own way of doing things. What's most important is that we first identify behaviors or areas that cause us problems and then decide what we want to do.

At the end of chapter 3, I asked which definition of codependency resonated with you. As Earnie Larsen says, if you defined your problem as "living with an alcoholic," you may think *not* living with an alcoholic is the solution to your problem. That may be partially correct. But our real problems as codependents are our own characteristics—our codependent behaviors.

Who's codependent? I am.

In a 2019 Gallup poll, 46 percent of US adults reported having dealt with substance abuse in their families.[3] They are probably codependent.

People who love, care about, or work with troubled people may be codependent.

People who care about people with eating disorders are probably codependent. In her book *Fat Is a Family Affair*, Judi Hollis writes that one person suffering from an eating disorder can keep fifteen to twenty codependents busy.[4] Many people with eating disorders are codependents too. "In an informal survey, I discovered at least 40 percent of the wives of alcoholics were obese," Hollis says.[5]

People who care about people with any kind of mental illness or compulsive disorder—from agoraphobia and depression to hoarding and obsessive compulsive disorder (OCD)—may be codependent.

You may be reading this book for yourself; you may be codependent. Or you may be reading this book to help someone else; if so, you probably are codependent. If concern has turned into obsession; if compassion has turned into caretaking; if you are taking care of other people and not taking care of yourself—you may be in trouble with codependency. Each of us must decide for ourselves if codependency is a problem. Each of us must decide for ourselves what needs to be changed and when that should happen.

Codependency is many things. It's a dependency on people—on their moods, behaviors, sickness or well-being, and their love. It's a "paradoxical dependency."[6] Codependents appear to be depended upon, but they are dependent on. We look strong but feel helpless. We appear controlling, but in reality we are controlled ourselves, sometimes by an illness such as alcoholism.

These are the issues that dictate recovery. Solving these problems makes recovery fun. Many recoveries from problems that involve a person's mind, emotions, and spirit are long and grueling. Not so here. Except for healthy human emotions we would be feeling anyway and twinges of discomfort as we begin to behave differently, recovery from codependency is exciting. It's liberating. It lets us be who we are. It lets other people be who they are. It helps us own our innate power to think, feel, and act. It feels good. It brings peace. It enables us to love ourselves and others. It allows us to receive love—some of the good stuff we've all been looking for. It provides an optimum environment for the people around us to get and stay healthy. And recovery helps stop the unbearable pain many of us have been living with.

Recovery is not only fun, it's simple. It's not always easy, but it is simple. It's based on a premise many of us have forgotten or never learned: we're all responsible for ourselves. It involves learning one new behavior that we will devote ourselves to: taking care of ourselves. In the second part of this book, we'll discuss specific ideas for doing that.

··· ACTIVITY ···

1. Go through the lists in this chapter. Mark each characteristic with a 0 if it's never a problem for you. Mark the characteristic with a 1 if it's occasionally a problem. And mark it with a 2 if it's frequently a problem. Later, in chapter 16, "Set Your Intention," you can use this report to establish goals.

2. How do you feel about changing yourself? What do you think would happen if you began to change? Do you think you can change? Why or why not? Write several paragraphs answering these questions.

PART II

The Basics of Self-Care

5

Detachment

Detachment is not detaching from the person we care about but from the agony of involvement.

—AL-ANON MEMBER

When I was trying to choose the topic for the first chapter in this section of the book, many subjects competed for first place. I chose detachment not because it's significantly more important than the other concepts. I selected it because it is an *underlying* concept. It's something we need to do frequently as we strive to live happy lives. It's the goal of most recovery programs for codependents. And it's also something we must do first—before we can do the other things we need to do. We cannot begin to work on ourselves, to live our own lives, feel our own feelings, and solve our own problems, until we have detached from the object of our obsession. From my experiences (and those of others), it appears that even our Higher Power can't do much with us until we have detached.

ATTACHMENT

When a codependent says, "I think I'm getting attached to you," look out! They probably mean it.

Most people with codependency issues are attached to the people and problems in their environments. By "attached," I don't mean they experience average feelings of liking people, concern about problems, or connection to the world. In this case, attachment means becoming overly involved and sometimes hopelessly entangled.

Attachment can take several forms:

- We may become excessively worried about and preoccupied with a problem or person (our mental energy is attached).

- We may graduate to becoming obsessed with and controlling of the people and problems in our environment (our mental, physical, and emotional energy is directed at the object of our obsession).

- We may become reactionaries instead of acting authentically of our own volition (our mental, emotional, and physical energy is attached).

- We may become emotionally dependent on the people around us (now we're really attached).

- We may become caretakers (rescuers, enablers) to the people around us (firmly attaching ourselves to their need for us).

The problems with attachment are many. (In this chapter I will focus on worry and obsession. In following chapters I will cover the other forms of attachment.) Overinvolvement of any sort can keep us in a state of chaos; it can keep the people around us in a state of chaos. If we're focusing all our energies on people and problems, we have little left for the business of living our own lives. And there is just so much worry and responsibility in the air. If we take it all on ourselves, there is none left for the people around us. It overworks us and underworks them. Furthermore, worrying about people and problems doesn't help. It doesn't solve problems, it doesn't help other people, and it doesn't help us. It is wasted energy.

There's a saying often attributed to philosopher William James: "If you believe that feeling bad or worrying long enough will change a fact, then you are residing on another planet with a different reality system."[1]

Worrying and obsessing keep us so mentally entangled that we can't solve our problems. Whenever we become *attached* in these ways to someone or something, we become *detached* from ourselves. We lose touch with ourselves. We forfeit our power and ability to think, feel, act, and take care of ourselves. We lose control.

Have you ever seen someone who is obsessed with someone or something? That person can talk about nothing else, can think of nothing else. Even if they appear to be listening when you talk, you know they don't hear you. Their mind is tossing and turning, crashing and banging, around and around on an endless racetrack of compulsive thought. They are preoccupied. They relate whatever you say, no matter how unrelated it actually is, to the object of their obsession. They say the same things over and over, sometimes changing the wording slightly, sometimes using the same words. Nothing you say makes any difference. Even telling them to stop doesn't help. They probably would if they could. The problem is they can't (at the moment). They are bursting with the jarring energy of obsession.

Many of the people I've worked with in family groups have been *that* obsessed with those they care about. When I asked them what they were feeling, they told me what another person was feeling. When I asked what they did, they told me what another person had done. Their entire focus was on someone or something other than themselves. Some of them had spent years of their lives doing this—worrying about, reacting to, and trying to control other human beings. They were shells, sometimes almost invisible shells, of people. Their energy was depleted—directed elsewhere. They couldn't tell me what they were feeling and thinking because they didn't know.

Maybe you've been obsessed with someone or something. Someone does or says something. A thought occurs to you. Something reminds you of a past event. A problem enters your awareness. Something happens or doesn't happen. Or you sense something's happening, but you're not sure what. Someone who usually calls doesn't call. They don't answer the phone, and they should. It's payday. In the past they always got wasted on payday. They've only been clean three months. You wonder, *Will it happen again today?*

You may not know what, you may not know why, and you're not sure when, but you know something bad—something terrible—has happened, is happening, or is about to happen.

It hits you in the stomach. The feeling fills you up—that gut-twisting, hand-wringing anxiety that is so familiar to codependents. It's what causes us to do much of what we do that hurts ourselves; it's the substance worry and obsession feed on. It's fear at its worst. Fear usually comes and goes, leaving us in flight, ready to fight, or just temporarily frightened. But anxiety hangs in there. It grips the mind, paralyzing it for all but its own purposes—an endless rehashing of the same useless thoughts. It's the fuel that propels us into controlling behaviors of all sorts. We can think of nothing but keeping a lid on things, controlling the problem, and making it go away; it's the stuff codependency is made of.

When you're obsessed, you can't get your mind off that person or that problem. You don't know what you are feeling. You don't know what you were thinking. You're not even sure what you should do, but oh my God, you should do something! And fast!

Worrying, obsessing, and controlling are illusions. They are tricks we play on ourselves. We feel like we're doing something to solve our problems, but we're not. Many of us have reacted this way with justifiably good reason. We may have lived with serious, complicated problems that have disrupted our lives, and they would provoke any normal person to become anxious, upset, worried, and obsessed. We may love someone who is in trouble—someone who's out of control. Their problem may be substance abuse, an eating disorder, gambling, a mental or emotional issue, anger management, or any combination of these.

Some of us may be living with less-serious problems, but they concern us anyway. People we love or care about may have mood swings. They may do things we wish they wouldn't do. We may think they should do things differently, a better way, a way that we believe wouldn't cause so many problems.

Out of habit, some of us may have developed an attitude of attachment—of worrying, reacting, and obsessively trying to control. Maybe we have lived with people and through events that were out of control. Maybe obsessing and controlling is the way we kept things in balance or temporarily kept things from getting worse. And then we just kept on doing it. Maybe we're afraid to let go because when we let go in the past, terrible, hurtful things happened.

Maybe we've been attached to people—living their lives for and through them—for so long that we don't have any life of our own left to live. It's safer to stay attached. At least we know we're alive if we're reacting. At least we've got something to do if we're obsessing or controlling. For various reasons, codependents tend to attach themselves to problems and people. Never mind that worrying isn't solving anything. Never mind that those problems rarely have solutions. Never mind that we're so obsessed we can't read a book, watch television, or go for a walk. Never mind that our emotions are constantly in turmoil over what someone said or didn't say, what they did or didn't do, or what they will do next. Never mind that the things we're doing aren't helping anyone. No matter the cost, we will hang on. We will grit our teeth, clutch the rope, and grab more tightly than ever.

Some of us may not even be aware we've been holding on so tightly. We may have convinced ourselves that we have to hang on this tightly. We believe there is simply no other choice but to react to this particular problem or person in this obsessive manner. Frequently, when I suggest to people that they detach from a person or problem, they recoil in horror. "Oh, no!" they say. "I could never do *that*. I love them too much. I care too much to do that. This problem or person is too important to me. I *have* to stay attached!"

My answer to that is, "Who says you have to?"

I've got news—good news. We don't "have to." There's a better way. It's called detachment.[2] It may be scary at first, but it will ultimately work better for everyone involved.

A BETTER WAY

Exactly what is detachment? (The term, as you may have guessed, is more jargon.)

First, let's discuss what detachment isn't. Detachment is not a cold, hostile withdrawal; a resigned, despairing acceptance of anything life and people throw our way; a robotic walk through life oblivious to, and totally unaffected by, people and problems; a Pollyannaish, ignorant bliss; a shirking of our *true* responsibilities to ourselves and others; a severing of our relationships. Nor is it a removal of our love and concern, although sometimes these ways of detaching might be the best we can do, for the moment.

Ideally, detachment is releasing, or detaching from, a person or problem *in love*. We mentally, emotionally, and sometimes physically disengage ourselves from unhealthy (and frequently painful) entanglements with others' lives and responsibilities and from problems we cannot solve, according to a handout titled "Detachment" that has been passed around Al-Anon groups for years.

Detachment is based on the premises that everyone is responsible for themselves, that we can't solve problems that aren't ours to solve, and that worrying doesn't help. We adopt a policy of keeping our hands off other people's responsibilities and tending to our own responsibilities instead. If people have created some disasters for themselves, we allow them to face their own proverbial music. We allow people to be who they are. We give them the freedom to be responsible and to grow. And we give ourselves that same freedom. We live our own lives to the best of our abilities. We strive to ascertain what we can change and what we cannot change. Then we stop trying to change the things we can't. We do what we can to solve problems, and then we stop fretting and stewing. If we cannot solve a problem and we have done what we can, we learn to live with, or in spite of, that problem. And we try to live happily—focusing heroically on what is good in our lives today and feeling grateful for that. We learn the magical lesson that making the most of what we have turns it into more.

Detachment involves living in the here and now. We allow life to happen instead of forcing and trying to control it. We relinquish regrets over the past and fears about the future. We make the most of each day. We live freely.

Detachment also involves accepting reality—the facts. It requires faith—in ourselves, in a Higher Power, in other people, and in the natural order and destiny of things in this world. We believe in the rightness and appropriateness of each moment. We release our burdens and cares and give ourselves the freedom to enjoy life in spite of our unsolved problems. We trust that all is well despite the conflicts. We trust that someone or something greater than ourselves knows, has ordained, and cares about what is happening. We understand that this someone (or something) can do much more to solve a problem than we can. So we try to stay out of the way and let it be. In time, we know that all is well because we see how the strangest (and sometimes most painful) things work out for the best and for the benefit of everyone.

Judi Hollis writes of codependency detachment in her book *Fat Is a Family Affair*. She describes it as a "healthy neutrality."[3]

Detaching does not mean we don't care. It means we learn to love, care, and be involved without going crazy. We stop creating all this chaos in our minds and environments. When we are not anxiously and compulsively thrashing about, we become able to make good decisions about how to love people and how to solve our problems. We become free to care and to love in ways that help others and don't hurt ourselves.[4]

The rewards from detachment are great: serenity; a deep sense of peace; the ability to give and receive love in self-enhancing, energizing ways; and the freedom to find real solutions to our problems. We find the freedom to live our own lives without excessive feelings of guilt about or responsibility toward others.[5] Sometimes detachment even motivates and frees people around us to begin to solve their problems. We stop worrying about them, and they pick up the slack and finally start worrying about themselves. What a grand plan! We each mind our own business.

Earlier, I described a person caught in the entanglement of obsessions and worry. I've known many people who have had to (or have chosen to) live with serious problems such as an alcoholic spouse who never sobered up, a child with severe disabilities, or a teenager hell-bent on self-destruction through drugs and criminal behavior. These people learned to live with, and in spite of, their problems. They grieved for their losses, then found a way to live— not in resignation, martyrdom, and despair but with enthusiasm, peace, and a true sense of gratitude for that which was good. They took care of their actual responsibilities. They gave to people, they helped people, and they loved people. But they also gave to and loved themselves. They held themselves in high esteem. They didn't do these things perfectly or without effort or instantly. But they strived to do these things, and they learned to do them well.

I owe a debt of gratitude to these people. They taught me that detachment was possible. They showed me it could work. I would like to pass that same hope on to you. It is my wish that you will find other people to pass that hope on to, for detachment is real and thrives with reinforcement and nurturing.

Detachment is both an act and an art. It's a way of life. I believe it's also a gift. And it will be given to those who seek it.

How do we detach? How do we extricate our emotions, minds, bodies, and spirits from the agony of entanglement? As best we can. And probably a bit clumsily at first. An old AA and Al-Anon saying suggests a three-part formula that uses the acronym "HOW": honesty, openness, and willingness to try.[6]

In the chapters ahead, I will discuss some specific concepts for detaching from certain forms of attachment. Many of the other concepts I discuss later can lead to detachment. You will have to decide how these ideas apply to you and your particular situation and then find your own path to well-being. With a little humility, surrender, and effort, I believe you can do it. I believe detachment can become a habitual response, in the same manner that obsessing, worrying, and controlling became habitual responses—by practice. You may not do it perfectly, but no one has. However, and at whatever pace you practice detachment in your life, I believe it will be right for you. I hope you will be able to detach with love for the person or persons you are detaching from. I think it is better to do everything with an attitude of love. However, for a variety of reasons, we can't always do that. If you can't detach in love, it's my opinion that it's better to detach in anger than to stay attached. If we are detached, we're in a better position to work on (or through) our resentful emotions. If we're attached, we probably won't do anything other than stay upset.

When should we detach? When we can't stop thinking, talking about, or worrying about someone or something; when our emotions are churning and boiling; when we feel like we *have* to do something about someone because we can't stand it another minute; when we're hanging on by a single thread that's starting to feel frayed; and when we believe we can no longer live with the problems we've been trying to live with. It is time to detach! You will learn to recognize when detachment is advisable. A good rule of thumb is: you need to detach most when it seems the least likely or possible thing to do.

I'll close this chapter with a true story. One night about midnight my telephone rang. I was in bed and wondered, as I picked up the receiver, who was calling me at that hour. I thought it had to be an emergency.

In a way it was an emergency. It was a stranger. She had been calling various friends all evening, trying to find some kind of consolation. Apparently, she hadn't been able to find it. Someone had given her someone else's phone number, that person had given her someone else's phone number, and the last person had suggested she call me.

Immediately upon introducing herself, the woman exploded in a tirade. Her husband used to go to Alcoholics Anonymous. He had separated from her, and now he was seeing another woman because he wanted to "find himself." Furthermore, before he left her, he had been acting crazy and stopped going to meetings. And she wondered, "Isn't he acting crazy now by dating a woman who is *that much younger than him?*"

I was speechless at first, then barely could get a word in. She went on and on. Finally she asked, "Don't you think he's sick? Don't you think he's acting crazy? Don't you think something should be done about him?"

"That could be," I replied. "But obviously I can't do it, and neither can you. I'm more concerned about you. What are *you* feeling? What do *you* think? What do you need to do to take care of *yourself?*"

I'd say the same thing to you, dear reader. I know you have problems. I understand that many of you are in deep grief over, and concerned about, certain people in your lives. Many of them may be destroying themselves, you, and your family right before your eyes. But I can't do anything to control those people, and you probably can't either. If you could, you would have done it by now.

Detach. Detach in love or detach in anger, but strive for detachment. I know it's difficult, but it will become easier with practice. If you can't let go completely, try to hang on loosely. Relax. Sit back. Now, take a deep breath. The focus is on you.

··· ACTIVITY ···

1. Is there a problem or person in your life that you are excessively worried about? Write about that person or problem. Write as much as you need to write to get it out of your system. When you have written all you need to write about that person or problem, focus on yourself. What are you thinking? What are you feeling?

2. How do you feel about detaching from that person or problem? What might happen if you detach? Will that probably happen anyway? How has staying attached—worrying, obsessing, trying to control—helped so far?

3. If you did not have that person or problem in your life, what would you be doing that's different from what you're doing now? How would you be feeling and behaving? Spend a few minutes visualizing yourself living, feeling, and behaving that way—in spite of your unsolved problem. All is as it should be and as it needs to be for this moment.

Don't Be Blown About
by Every Wind

Easy does it.

I am a reactionary.

That thought burned deeply into my consciousness one day while I was sitting in my office. I had heard people discuss reacting, but until that moment, I hadn't understood *how much* I reacted.

I reacted to other people's feelings, behaviors, problems, and thoughts. I reacted to what they *might* be feeling, thinking, or doing. I reacted to my own feelings, my own thoughts, my own problems. My strong point seemed to be reacting to crises—I thought almost everything was a crisis. I overreacted. Hidden panic (which bordered on hysteria) brewed in me much of the time. I sometimes underreacted. If the problem I faced was significant, I often used the tool of denial. I reacted to almost everything that came into my awareness

and environment. My entire life had been a reaction to other people's lives, desires, problems, faults, successes, and personalities. Even
my low self-worth, which I dragged around like a bag of stinking
garbage, had been a reaction. I was like a puppet with strings hanging out, inviting and allowing anyone or anything to yank them.

Most codependents are reactionaries. We react with anger, guilt,
shame, self-hate, worry, hurt, controlling gestures, caretaking acts,
depression, desperation, and fury. We react with fear and anxiety.
Some of us react so much it's painful to be around people and tor-
turous to be in large groups. It's normal to react and respond to our
environment. Reacting is part of life. It's part of interacting, and it's
part of being alive and human. But those of us who struggle with
codependency allow ourselves to get so upset—and so distracted.
Little things, big things—anything has the power to throw us off
track. And the way we respond after we react is frequently not in
our best interests.

We may have started reacting and responding urgently and
compulsively in patterns that hurt us. Just *feeling* urgent and compulsive is enough to hurt us. We keep ourselves in a crisis state—
adrenaline flowing and muscles tensed, ready to react to emergencies
that usually aren't emergencies. Someone does something, so we
must do something back. Someone says something, so we must say
something back. Someone feels a certain way, so we must feel a
certain way. We jump into the first feeling that comes our way and
then wallow in it. We think the first thought that comes into our
heads and then elaborate on it. We say the first words on our
tongues and sometimes regret them. We do the first thing that
comes to mind, usually without thinking about it. That is the problem: we are reacting without thinking—without honest thought

about what we need to do and how we want to handle any given situation. Our emotions and behaviors are being controlled—triggered—by everyone and everything in our environments. We are indirectly allowing others to tell us what to do. That means we have lost control. We are being controlled.

When we react we forfeit our personal power to think, feel, and behave *in our best interests*. We give up agency over ourselves. We allow others to determine when we will be happy; when we will be peaceful; when we will be upset; and what we will say, do, think, and feel. We forfeit our right to feel peaceful at the whim of our environments. We are like a wisp of paper in a thunderstorm, blown about by every wind.

Here is an example of a way I tended to react (one of many) when I was younger: My office was in my home, and I had two young children. Sometimes when I was working, they'd start to go wild in the other rooms—fighting, running, messing up the house, and eating and drinking everything in the kitchen. My first, instinctive reaction was to screech at them to "Stop that!" My second reaction was to holler some more. It came naturally. Reacting that way appeared to be easier than leaving my office, working my way through the laundry room, and walking upstairs. It also appeared easier than taking the time to think about how I wanted to handle the situation. But bellowing and screaming didn't work. It wasn't easier. It made my throat sore and taught the children how to make me sit in my office and screech.

Reacting usually doesn't work. We react too quickly, with too much intensity and urgency. Rarely can we do our best at anything in this state of mind. The irony is that we are not called upon or required to do things in this state of mind. There is little in our lives we need to do that we cannot do better if we respond from a place of peace. Few situations—no matter how greatly they appear to demand it—can be bettered by us going berserk.

Why do we do it, then?

We react because we're anxious and afraid of what has happened, what is happening, and what might happen.

Many of us react as though everything is a crisis because we have lived with so many crises for so long that our reactions have become habitual.

We react because we think things *shouldn't* be happening the way they are.

We react because we don't feel good about ourselves.

We react because most people react.

We react because we think we have to react.

We don't have to.

We don't have to be so afraid of people. They are just people like us.

We don't have to forfeit our peace. It doesn't help. We have the same facts and resources available to us when we're peaceful that are available to us when we're frantic and chaotic. We actually have more resources available because our minds and emotions are free to perform at peak level.

We don't have to forfeit our power to pause, think, and feel in any situation. That's also not required of us.

We don't have to take things so seriously (ourselves, events, and other people). We blow things out of proportion—our feelings, thoughts, actions, and mistakes. We do the same thing with other people's feelings, thoughts, and actions. We tell ourselves things are awful, terrible, a tragedy, and the end of the world. Many things might be sad, too bad, and unpleasant—but the only thing that's the end of the world is the end of the world. Feelings are important, but they're only feelings. Thoughts are important, but they're only thoughts—and we all think a lot of different things. Plus our thoughts are subject to change. What we say and do is important, what others say and do is important, but the world doesn't hinge on any particular speech or action. And if it is particularly important that something gets done or said, don't worry: it'll happen. Lighten up. Give yourself and others room to move, to talk, to be who they are—to be human. Give life a chance to happen. Give yourself an opportunity to enjoy it.

We don't have to take other people's behaviors as reflections of our self-worth. We don't have to be embarrassed if someone we love chooses to behave inappropriately. It's normal to react that way, but we don't have to continue to feel embarrassed and less than if someone else continues to behave inappropriately. People are responsible for their own behaviors. If another person behaves inappropriately, let them feel embarrassed. If you have done nothing to feel embarrassed about, don't feel embarrassed. I know this is a tough concept, but it can be mastered.

We don't have to take rejection as a reflection of our self-worth. If somebody who is important (or even someone unimportant) to you rejects you or your choices, you are still real, and you are still worth every bit as much as you would be if you had not been rejected. Feel any feelings that go with rejection. Talk about your thoughts. But don't forfeit your self-esteem to another's disapproval or rejection of who you are or what you've done. Even if the most important person in your world rejects you, you are still real, and you are still okay. If you've done something inappropriate or you need to solve a problem or change a behavior, then take appropriate steps to take care of yourself. But don't reject yourself, and don't give so much power to other people's rejection of you. It isn't necessary.

We don't have to take things so personally. We take things to heart that we have no business taking to heart. For instance, saying, "If you loved me you wouldn't drink" to someone struggling with alcoholism makes as much sense as saying, "If you loved me, you wouldn't cough" to someone with pneumonia. A person with pneumonia will cough until they get appropriate treatment for their illness. A person struggling with alcoholism will drink until they get the same. When people with compulsive disorders do whatever it is they're compelled to do, they're not saying they don't love you—they're saying they don't love themselves.

We don't have to take little things personally either. If someone has a bad day or gets angry, don't assume it has something to do with you. It may or may not have anything to do with you. If it does, you'll find out. Usually things have far less to do with us than we think.

Someone else's bad mood, sharp tongue, bad day, negative thoughts, social media rant, or active substance abuse does not have to run or ruin our lives, days, or even an hour of our time. If people don't want to be with us or act healthy, it's not a reflection on *our* self-worth. It reflects *their* present circumstances. By practicing detachment, we can lessen our destructive reactions to the world around us. Separate yourself from things. Leave things alone, and let people be who they are. Who are you to say that the interruption, mood, word, comment, bad day, or problem is not an important and necessary part of life? Who are you to say that this problem won't ultimately be beneficial to you or someone else?

We don't have to react. We have options. That's another joy of recovery from codependency. And each time we exercise our right to choose how we want to act, think, feel, and behave, we feel better and stronger.

"But," you might protest, "why shouldn't I react? Why shouldn't I say something back? Why shouldn't I be upset? They deserve to bear the brunt of my turmoil." That may be, but *you* don't. We're talking about your lack of peace here, your lack of serenity, your wasted moments. This is your life. How do you want to spend it? You're not detaching for them. You're detaching for *you*. Chances are everyone will benefit from it.

We're like singers in a large chorus. If the person next to us goes off-key, must we also? Wouldn't it help them, and us, if we strived to stay on key? We can learn to hold our part.

We don't need to eliminate all our reactions to people and problems. Reactions can be useful. They help us identify what we like and what feels good. They help us identify problems in and around us. But most of us react too much. And much of what we react to is nonsense. It isn't all that important, and it doesn't merit the time and attention we give it. Some of the things we react to are other people's reactions to us. (I'm mad because they're mad; they're mad because I was angry; I was angry because I thought they were angry with me; they weren't angry, they were hurt because . . .) Our reactions can be such a chain reaction that frequently, everyone's upset, and nobody knows why. Then everyone's out of control and being controlled. Sometimes people behave in certain ways to provoke us to react in certain ways. If we stop reacting in these ways, we take all the fun out of their provocation. We remove ourselves from their control and take away their power over us.

Sometimes our reactions provoke other people to react in certain ways. We help them justify certain behaviors. (We don't need any more of that, do we?) Sometimes reacting narrows our vision so much that we get stuck reacting to symptoms of problems. We may stay so busy reacting we never have the time or energy to identify the real problem, much less figure out how to solve it. We can spend years reacting to each drinking incident and resulting crisis, completely failing to recognize that the true problem is alcoholism! Learn to stop reacting in ways that aren't necessary and don't work. Eliminate the reactions that hurt *you*.

Some suggestions follow to help you detach from people and your destructive reactions to them. These are only suggestions. There is no precise formula for detachment. You need to find your own way, a way that works for you.

1. *Learn to recognize when you're reacting, when you're allowing someone or something to yank your chain.* Usually when you start to feel anxious, afraid, indignant, outraged, rejected, sorry for yourself, ashamed, worried, or confused, something in your environment has snagged you. (I'm not saying it's wrong to feel these feelings. Probably anybody would feel that way. The difference is, we're learning to decide *how long* we want to feel that way, and what we want to do about it.) When we say someone "made me feel," it often indicates that we're reacting. Losing our sense of peace and serenity is probably the strongest indication that we are caught up in some sort of reaction.

2. *Make yourself comfortable.* When you recognize that you're having a chaotic reaction, say or do as little as possible until you can restore your level of serenity and peace. Do whatever you need to do (that is not self- or other-destructive) to help yourself relax.

Take a few deep breaths. Go for a walk. Clean the kitchen. Go sit in the bathroom. Go to a friend's house. Go to an Al-Anon meeting. Read a meditation book. Take a trip to Florida. Watch a television program. Find a way to emotionally, mentally, and (if necessary) physically separate yourself from whatever you're reacting to. Find a way to ease your anxiety; don't take a drink or drive the car down a side street at eighty-five miles per hour. Do something safe that will help restore your balance and ground you in your self and your life.

3. *Examine what happened.* If it was a minor incident, you may be able to sort through it yourself. If you're facing a serious problem, or if it's seriously upsetting you, you may want to discuss it with a friend to help clear your thoughts and emotions. Troubles and feelings go wild when we try to keep them caged inside. Talk about your feelings. Take responsibility for them. Feel whatever feeling you have. Nobody made you feel. Someone might have helped you feel a particular way, but you did your feeling all by yourself. Accept it. Then, tell yourself the truth about what happened.[1] Was someone trying to insult you? (If in doubt about whether to interpret something as an insult or rejection, I prefer to believe it had nothing to do with me. It saves time and helps me feel good about myself.) Were you trying to control someone or some event? How serious is the problem or issue now? Are you taking responsibility for someone else? Are you angry because someone didn't guess what you really wanted or what you were really trying to say? Are you taking someone's behavior too personally? Did someone push your insecurity or guilt buttons? Is it truly the end of the world, or is it merely sad and disappointing?

4. *Figure out what you need to do to take care of yourself.* Make your decisions based on reality, and make them from a peaceful state. Do you need to apologize? Do you want to let it go? Do you need to have a heart-to-heart talk with someone? Do you need to make some other decision to take care of yourself? When you make your decision, keep in mind what your responsibilities are. You are not responsible for making other people "see the light," and you do not need to "set them straight." You are responsible for helping yourself see the light and for setting yourself straight. If you can't get peaceful about a decision, let it go. It's not time to make it yet. Wait until your mind is consistent and your emotions are calm.

Slow down. You don't have to feel so frightened. You don't have to feel so frantic. Keep things in perspective. Make life easier for *you*.

••• ACTIVITY •••

1. Pay attention to what triggers you in your environment. Are you spending too much time reacting to someone or something? Who or what? Are you spending too much time on social media? How are you reacting? Is that how you would choose to behave or feel if you had a choice?

2. Go through the previous steps on detachment for whatever or whoever is bothering you the most. If you need to talk to someone, select a trusted friend. If necessary, seek professional help.

3. What activities help you feel peaceful and comfortable? (A Twelve Step meeting, a steaming hot shower, a good movie, and dancing are my favorites.)

7

Set Yourself Free

Let go and let God.

—TWELVE STEP PROGRAM SLOGAN

People say codependents are controllers.

We nag; lecture; scream; holler; cry; beg; bribe; coerce; hover over; protect; accuse; chase after; run away from; try to talk into; try to talk out of; attempt to induce guilt in; seduce; entrap; snoop; check on; demonstrate how much we've been hurt; hurt people in return so they'll know how it feels; threaten to hurt ourselves; pull power plays; deliver ultimatums; do things for; refuse to do things for; get even with; whine; vent fury on; act helpless; suffer in loud silence; try to please; lie; do sneaky little things; do sneaky big things; clutch at our hearts and threaten to die; grab our heads and threaten to go crazy; beat on our chests and threaten to kill; enlist the aid of supporters; gauge our words carefully; sleep with; refuse to sleep with; have children with; bargain with; drag to counseling; drag out of counseling; talk mean about; talk mean to;

insult; condemn; pray for miracles; pay for miracles; go to places we don't want to go; stay nearby; supervise; dictate; command; complain; write letters about; write letters to; stay home and wait for; go out and look for; call all over looking for; drive down dark alleys at night hoping to see; chase down dark alleys at night hoping to catch; run down alleys at night to get away from; bring home; keep home; lock out; move away from; move with; scold; impress upon; advise; teach lessons to; set straight; insist; give in to; placate; provoke; try to make jealous; try to make afraid; remind; inquire; hint; look through pockets; scroll through cell phones; peek in wallets; search dresser drawers; dig through glove boxes; look in toilet tanks; try to look into the future; search through the past; call relatives about; reason with; settle issues once and for all; settle them again; punish; reward; almost give up on; then try even harder; and a list of other handy maneuvers I've either forgotten or haven't tried yet.

We aren't the people who "make things happen." Codependents are the people who consistently, and with a great deal of effort and energy, try to force things to happen.

We control in the name of love.

We do it because we're "only trying to help."

We do it because we know best how things should go and how people should behave.

We do it because we're right and they're wrong. We control because we're afraid not to do it.

We do it because we don't know what else to do. We do it to stop the pain.

We control because we think we have to. We control because we don't think.

We control because controlling is all we can think about.

Ultimately, we may control because that's the way we've always done things.

Tyrannical and dominating, some rule with an iron hand from a self-appointed throne. They are powerful. They know best. And by God, it will be done this way. They will see to it.

Others do their dirty work undercover. They hide behind a costume of sweetness and niceties and secretly go about their business—other people's business.

Others, sighing and crying, claim inability, proclaim their dependence, announce their overall victimization, and successfully control through weakness. They are so helpless. They need your cooperation so badly. They can't live without it. Sometimes the weak are the most powerful manipulators and controllers.[1] They have learned to tug at the guilt and pity strings of the world.

Many codependents combine tactics, using a variety of methods. Whatever works! (Or, more accurately, whatever doesn't work, although we continue to hope it will.)

Regardless of the tactics, the goals remain the same. Make other people do what you want them to. Make them behave as you think they should. Don't let them behave in ways you think they shouldn't, but probably would, without your "assistance." Force life's events to unravel and unfold in the manner and at such times as you have designated. Do not let what's happening, or what might happen, occur. Hold on tightly and don't let go. We have written the play, and we will see to it that the actors behave and the scenes unfold exactly as we have decided they should. Never mind that we continue to buck reality. If we charge ahead insistently enough, we can (we believe) stop the flow of life, transform people, and change things to our liking.

We are fooling ourselves.

Let me tell you about Maria. She married a man who turned out to be an alcoholic. He was a binge drinker. He didn't drink every day, every weekend, or every month, but when he did—look out. He stayed drunk for days, sometimes weeks. He started drinking at eight in the morning and drank until he passed out. He vomited all over, devastated the family's finances, got fired from jobs, and created unbearable chaos each time he drank.

Life wasn't perfect between binges either. A sense of impending doom and unresolved feelings filled the air. Other problems, residues from the drinking, cluttered their lives. They could never get ahead of the disasters. They were always starting over with a dirty slate. But it was better—for Maria and her three children—when her husband wasn't drinking. There was hope, too, that this time it would be different.

It never was different. For years, each time Maria turned around or turned her back, her husband went on a binge. Whenever she left home—when she went to the hospital to deliver her babies, when her husband left town on a trip, or when he was out of her sight for any reason—he drank.

Whenever Maria returned or retrieved him from wherever he was drinking, he would abruptly quit drinking. Maria decided that the key to her husband's sobriety was her presence. She could control the drinking (and all the pain it caused) by sticking close to home and standing guard over her husband. Because she learned this method of control, and because of increasing feelings of shame, embarrassment, anxiety, and the overall trauma that accompanies codependency, Maria became a recluse. She turned down opportunities to travel, and she refused to attend conferences that interested her. Even leaving the house for more than a trip to the grocery store began to threaten the delicate balance she'd created—or thought she had created. Despite her determined and desperate efforts, her husband still found opportunities to drink. He found ways to drink at home without her knowing about it, and he drank when she had no choice but to spend the night away from home.

After one particularly disruptive bout, Maria's husband informed her that the impossible financial predicament they were in caused him to drink. (He neglected to mention that his drinking had caused the impossible financial predicament.) He said that if she would take a job and help out financially, he would not feel like he had to drink anymore. The pressure would be off. Maria thought about his request, then reluctantly agreed. She was afraid to leave home and felt concerned about setting up appropriate childcare arrangements. She didn't feel emotionally or mentally able to work. She especially resented taking a job to earn extra money when her husband was so financially irresponsible. But it was worth a try. Anything to keep this man sober!

Before long Maria found a job as an administrative assistant. She did well—better than she thought she would. People with codependency issues make great employees. They don't complain; they do more than their share; they do whatever is asked of them; they please people; and they try to do their work perfectly—at least for a while, until they become angry and resentful.

Maria started feeling a little better about herself. She enjoyed her contact with people—something that had been missing in her life. She liked the feeling of independence, of earning her own money. And her employers appreciated her. They gave her increasing amounts of responsibility and were on the verge of promoting her. But about that time Maria began to feel that old familiar anxiety—her cue that her husband was about to binge again.

The feeling came and went for days. Then one day, it slammed her. That hand-wringing, gut-twisting anxiety came back in full force. Maria started calling her husband, but he didn't answer his phone. He wasn't at work. His coworkers didn't know where he was. She made more calls. Nobody knew where he was. She spent the day biting her nails, making frantic phone calls, and hoping her fellow employees wouldn't see through her "everything's fine—no problem" veneer. The daycare center called and reported that her husband hadn't picked up the children. She apologized and left work early to pick up her kids. Her husband finally strolled in at one in the morning, drunk. The next day, she quit her job—walked out with no appropriate notice. She was back at home, guarding her husband.

Years later she said, "I felt like I had to do this. I had to get things under control—*my control.*"

My question is this: Who's controlling whom?

Maria learned she was not controlling her husband or his drinking at all. He and his alcoholism were controlling her.

This point was further clarified for me one evening when, during a family group facilitation I had at a treatment center, the wife of an alcoholic talked openly to her husband—a man who had spent many years of their marriage drinking, unemployed, and in prison.

"You accuse me of trying to control you, and I guess I have," she said. "I've gone to bars with you so you wouldn't drink so much. I've let you come home when you were abusive and drunk so you wouldn't drink anymore or hurt yourself. I've measured your drinks, drank with you (and I hate drinking), hid your bottles, and taken you to AA meetings."

"But the truth is," she said, "you've been controlling me. All those letters from prison telling me what I've wanted to hear. All those promises, all those words. And every time I'm ready to leave you—to walk out for good—you do or say just the right thing to keep me from leaving. You know just what I want to hear, and that's what you tell me. But you never change. You've never intended to change. You just want to control me."

He offered a half smile and nodded when she said that. "Yes," he said, "I have been trying to control you. And I've been doing a pretty good job of it."

When we attempt to control people and things that we have no business controlling, we are controlled. We forfeit our power to think, feel, and act in accordance with our best interests. We frequently lose control of ourselves. Often, we are being controlled not just by people but by diseases such as alcoholism and other compulsive disorders. These are powerful forces. Never forget that addicts are expert controllers. We have met our match when we attempt to control them or their disease. We lose the battles. We lose the wars. We lose ourselves—our lives. Borrowing a phrase from Al-Anon: you didn't cause it; you can't control it; and you can't cure it.

Stop trying! We become utterly frustrated when we try to do the impossible. And we usually prevent the possible from happening. I believe that clutching tightly to a person or thing or forcing my will on any given situation eliminates the possibility of doing anything constructive about that situation, the person, or me. My controlling blocks access to my higher self. It blocks other people's ability to grow. It stops events from happening naturally. It prevents me from enjoying people or events.

Control is an illusion. It doesn't work. We cannot control alcoholism. We cannot control anyone's compulsive behaviors. We cannot (and have no business trying to) control anyone's emotions, thoughts, or choices. We cannot control the outcome of events. We cannot control life. Some of us can barely control ourselves.

People ultimately do what they want to do. They feel how they want to feel (or how they are feeling); they think what they want to think; they do the things they believe they need to do; and they will change only when they're ready to change. It doesn't matter if they're wrong and we're right. It doesn't matter if they're hurting themselves. It doesn't matter that we could help them if they'd only listen to and cooperate with us.

It doesn't matter, doesn't matter, doesn't matter, doesn't matter.

We cannot change people. Any attempts to control them are a delusion as well as an illusion. People will either resist our efforts or redouble their efforts to prove we can't control them. They may temporarily adapt to our demands, but the moment we turn our backs, they will return to their natural state. Furthermore, people will punish us for making them do something they don't want to do or be something they don't want to be. No amount of control will effect a permanent or desirable change in another person. We can sometimes do things that increase the probability that people will want to change, but we can't even guarantee or control that.

And that's the truth. It's too bad. It's sometimes hard to accept, especially if someone you love is self-harming and hurting you. But that's the way it is. The only person you can now or ever change is yourself. The only person who it is your business to control is you.

Detach. Surrender. Sometimes when we do, the result we have been waiting and hoping for happens quickly, almost miraculously. Sometimes it doesn't. Sometimes it never happens. But you will benefit. You don't have to stop caring or loving. You don't have to tolerate abuse. You don't have to abandon constructive problem-solving methods such as professional intervention. You only need to put your emotional, mental, spiritual, and physical hand back in your own pocket and leave things and people alone. Let them be. Make any decisions you need to make to take care of yourself, but don't make them to control other people. Start taking care of yourself!

"But this is so important to me," many people protest. "I can't detach."

If it's that important to you, that's all the more reason to detach.

I heard some wisdom on detachment out of the mouths of babes—my babies. Sometimes, my youngest son, Shane, would hang on too tightly and too long after a hug. He'd start to tip me over. I'd lose my balance and become impatient for him to stop hugging me. I began to resist him. Perhaps he did it to keep me close to him a little longer. Maybe it was a form of control. I don't know. One night when he did this, my daughter watched until even she became frustrated and impatient.

"Shane," she said, "there comes a time to let go."

For each of us, there comes a time to let go. You will know when that time has come. When you have done all you can do, it's time to detach. Deal with your feelings. Face your fears about losing control. Gain control of yourself and your responsibilities. Free others to be who they are. In so doing, you will set yourself free.

1. Is there an event or person in your life that you're trying to control? Explain this. Write a few paragraphs about it to gain understanding.

2. In what ways (mentally, physically, emotionally, etc.) are you being controlled by whatever or whomever you are attempting to control?

3. What would happen (to you and the other person) if you detached from this situation or person? Will that probably happen anyway, despite your attempts at control? How are you benefiting by attempting to control the situation? How is the other person benefiting by your attempts to control? How effective are your attempts at controlling the outcome of events?

4. Keep a control journal. Get to know what triggers your need to control.

8

Remove the Victim

We're so careful to see that no one gets hurt.
No one, that is, but ourselves.

—ANONYMOUS

About a year into my recovery from codependency, I realized I was still doing something over and over that caused me pain. I sensed this pattern had something to do with why many of my relationships went sour. But I didn't know what "it" was that I was doing, so I couldn't stop doing it.

One sunny day, as I was walking down the sidewalk with my friend Scott, I stopped, turned to him, and asked, "What is the one thing codependents do over and over? What is it that keeps us feeling so bad?"

He thought about my question for a moment before answering. "Codependents are caretakers—rescuers. They rescue, then they persecute, then they end up victimized. Study the Karpman Drama Triangle," he said.

The Karpman Drama Triangle and the accompanying roles of rescuer, persecutor, and victim are the work and observation of Stephen B. Karpman.[1] What Scott said didn't make sense at the time, but I went home, dragged out some therapy books that were collecting dust on my shelves, and studied. After a while, a light went on in my head. I saw. I understood. And I felt like I had discovered fire.

This was it. This was my pattern. This is our pattern. This is what we repeatedly do with friends, family, acquaintances, clients, or anybody around us. As codependents, we may do many things, but this pattern is what we do best and most often. This is our favorite reaction.

We are the rescuers, the enablers. We are the great godparents to the entire world, as Earnie Larsen says. We not only meet people's needs, we anticipate them. We fix, nurture, and fuss over others. We make better, solve, and attend to. And we do it all so well. "Your wish is my command" is our theme. "Your problem is my problem" is our motto. We are the caretakers.

WHAT'S A RESCUE?

Rescuing and *caretaking* mean almost what they sound like. We rescue people from their responsibilities. We take care of people's responsibilities for them. Later we get mad at *them* for what *we've* done. Then we feel used and sorry for ourselves. That's the pattern, the triangle.

Rescuing and caretaking are synonymous. Their definitions are closely connected to enabling. *Enabling* is therapeutic jargon that means a destructive form of helping. Any acts that help a substance abuser continue abusing, prevent the abuser from suffering consequences, or in any way make it easier for a substance abuser to continue abusing are considered enabling behaviors.

As counselor Scott Egleston says, we rescue anytime we take responsibility for another human being—for that person's thoughts, feelings, decisions, behaviors, growth, well-being, problems, or destiny. The following acts constitute a rescuing or enabling move:

- doing something we really don't want to do

- saying yes when we mean no

- doing things for people who should be doing those things for themselves

- meeting people's needs without being asked and before we've agreed to do so

- doing more than a fair share of work after our help is requested

- consistently giving more than we receive in a particular situation

- fixing people's feelings

- doing people's thinking for them

- speaking for another person

- suffering people's consequences for them

- solving people's problems for them

- putting more interest and activity into a joint effort than the other person does

- not asking for what we want, need, and desire

We rescue whenever we take care of other people.

At the time we rescue or caretake, we may experience one or more of the following feelings: discomfort and awkwardness about the other person's dilemma; urgency to do something; pity; guilt; saintliness; anxiety; extreme responsibility for that person or problem; fear; a sense of being forced or compelled to do something; mild or severe reluctance to do anything; more competency than the person we are "helping"; or occasional resentment at being put in this position. We also think the person we are taking care of is helpless and unable to do what we are doing for them. We feel needed temporarily.

I am not referring to acts of love, kindness, compassion, and true helping—situations where our assistance is legitimately wanted and needed and we want to give that assistance. These acts are the good stuff of life. Rescuing and caretaking aren't.

Caretaking looks like a much friendlier act than it is. It requires incompetency on the part of the person being taken care of. We rescue "victims"—people who we believe are not capable of being responsible for themselves. The victims are capable of taking care of themselves, even though we and they don't admit it. Usually, our victims are just hanging around that corner of the triangle, waiting for us to make our move and jump on the triangle with them.

After we rescue, we will inevitably move to the next corner of the triangle: persecution. We become resentful and angry at the person we have so generously "helped." We've done something we didn't want to do, we've done something that was not our responsibility to do, we've ignored our own needs and wants, and we get angry about it. To complicate matters, this victim, this poor person we've rescued, is not grateful for our help. They are not appreciative enough of the sacrifice we have made. The victim isn't behaving the way they should. This person is not even taking our advice, which we offered so readily. This person is not letting us fix that feeling. Something doesn't work right or feel right, so we rip off our halos and pull out our pitchforks.

Sometimes people don't notice, or they choose not to notice, our peeved moods. Sometimes we do our best to hide those feelings. Sometimes we let loose with the full force of our fury; we particularly do this with family members. Something about family tends to bring out the *real* us. Whether we show, hide, or partially hide our agitation and resentment, *we know* what's going on.

Most of the time, the people we rescue immediately sense our shift in mood. They saw it coming. It's just the excuse they needed to turn on us. It's *their* turn in the persecution corner. This may precede, happen at the same time as, or follow our feelings of anger. Sometimes, the victims respond to our anger. Usually, theirs is a response to our taking responsibility for them, which directly or indirectly tells them how incapable we believe they are. People resent being told or shown they are incompetent, no matter how loudly they plead incompetency. And they resent us for adding insult to injury by becoming angry with them after we point out their incompetency.

Then it's time for our final move. We head right for our favorite spot: the victim corner on the *bottom*. This is the predictable and unavoidable result of a rescue. Feelings of helplessness, hurt, sorrow, shame, and self-pity abound. We have been used—again. We have gone unappreciated—again. We've tried so hard to help people, to be good to them. We moan, "Why? Why does this *always* happen to me?" Another person has trampled on us, taken advantage of us. We wonder, Are we destined always to be victims? Probably, if we don't stop rescuing and caretaking.

Many codependents, at some time in their lives, *were* true victims—of someone's abuse, neglect, abandonment, alcoholism, or any number of situations that can victimize people. We were, at some time, truly helpless to protect ourselves or solve our problems. Something came our way, something we didn't ask for, and it hurt us terribly. That is sad, truly sad. But an even sadder fact is that many of us codependents began to see ourselves as victims. Our painful history repeats itself. As caretakers, we allow people to victimize us, and we participate in our victimization by perpetually rescuing people. Rescuing or caretaking is not an act of love. The Drama Triangle is a hate triangle. It fosters and maintains self-hate, and it hinders our feelings for other people.

The triangle and the shifting roles of rescuer, persecutor, and victim are a visible process we go through. The role changes and the emotional changes come over us as certainly and as intensely as if we were reading a script. We can complete the process in seconds, experiencing only mild emotions as we shift roles. Or we can take years to complete the triangle and really work up to a major explosion. We can, and many of us do, rescue twenty times in one day.

Let me illustrate a rescue. A friend of mine was married to an alcoholic. Whenever he got drunk, she would drive all over town, enlist the aid of friends, and relentlessly pursue her husband until she found him. She usually felt benevolent, concerned, and sorry for him—a warning that a rescue was about to take place—until she got him home and tucked into bed, taking responsibility for him and his sobriety. When his head hit the pillow, things changed. She charged into the persecutor position. She didn't want this man in her home. She expected him to whine for days about how sick he was. He would be unable to assume his responsibilities in the family and would act pitifully. He had done this so many times! So, she would start in on him, beginning with little snipes and working up to a full-blown blast. He would briefly tolerate her persecution before switching from a helpless victim to vengeful persecutor. She'd then take a downward dip into the victim role. Self-pity, feelings of helplessness, shame, and despair would set in. This was the story of her life, she would moan. After all she had done for him, how could he treat her this way? Why did this always happen to her? She felt like a victim of circumstance, a victim of her husband's outrageous behavior, a victim of life. It never occurred to her that she was also a victim of herself and her own behavior.

Here's another illustration of a rescue. One autumn, a friend wanted me to take her apple picking. Originally, I wanted to go, and we set a date. By the time that date came, however, I was extremely busy. I called her and instead of telling her I wasn't able to go, I asked to postpone it. I felt guilty and responsible for her feelings—another rescue on the way. I couldn't disappoint her because I thought she couldn't handle or be responsible for her feelings. I couldn't tell her the truth because I thought she might be angry with me (more emotional responsibility)—as if someone else's anger is my business. The next weekend rolled around, and I squeezed the trip into my even busier schedule. I didn't need any apples; I had two drawers in my refrigerator crammed with apples. Before I pulled up at her house, I had already switched into the persecuting role. I could feel resentment brewing in me as we drove to the apple orchard. When we arrived at the orchard and began tasting and looking at apples, it became apparent neither of us was enjoying herself. After a few minutes, my friend turned to me. "I really don't want any apples," she said. "I bought some last week. I only came because I thought you wanted to, and I didn't want to hurt your feelings."

This example is only one of the thousands of rescues I have devoted my life to performing. When I began to understand this process, I realized that I spent most of my waking moments flipping around the jagged edges of this triangle, taking responsibility for anybody and everybody besides myself. Sometimes I managed big rescues; sometimes I managed little rescues. My friendships were initiated, maintained, and ultimately discontinued according to the rescue progression. Rescuing infiltrated my relationships with family members and clients. It kept me in a tizzy most of the time.

Two codependents in a relationship can really wreak havoc on each other. Consider two people pleasers in a relationship with each other. Now consider two people pleasers in a relationship with each other when they both want out of the relationship. They will do horrid things. They'll nearly destroy each other and themselves before one will stop rescuing and say, "I want out."

As codependents, we spend much of our time rescuing. I can usually spot a codependent within the first five minutes of meeting and talking. They will either offer me unrequested help or they'll keep talking to me although they are obviously uncomfortable and want to end the conversation. They begin the relationship by taking responsibility for me and not taking responsibility for themselves.

Some of us become so tired from the enormous burden—total responsibility for other human beings—that we may skip the feelings of pity and concern that accompany the rescue act and move ahead to anger. We're angry all the time; we feel anger and resentment toward potential victims. A person with a need or problem provokes us to feel we must act or experience guilt. After a rescue, we make no bones about our hostility toward this uncomfortable predicament. I have frequently seen this happen to people in helping professions. After so many years of rescuing—giving so much and receiving far less in return—many professional helpers adopt a hostile attitude toward their clients. They may continue to hang in there and keep "helping" them anyway, but they will usually leave their profession feeling terribly victimized, according to some counselors.

Caretaking doesn't help; it causes problems. When we take care of people and do things we don't want to do, we ignore personal needs, wants, and feelings. We put *ourselves* aside. Sometimes, we get so busy taking care of people that we put our entire lives on hold. Many caretakers are harried and overcommitted; they enjoy none of their activities. Caretakers look so responsible, but we aren't. We don't assume responsibility for our highest responsibility—ourselves.

We consistently give more than we receive, then feel abused and neglected because of it. We wonder why, when we anticipate the needs of others, no one notices *our* needs. We may become seriously depressed as a result of not getting our needs met. Yet a good caretaker feels safest when giving; we feel guilty and uncomfortable when someone gives to us or when we do something to meet our needs. Sometimes, codependents may become so locked into a caretaker role that we feel dismayed and rejected when we can't caretake or rescue someone—when someone refuses to be "helped."

The worst aspect of caretaking is that we become and stay victims. I believe many serious self-destructive behaviors—substance abuse, eating disorders, sexual disorders—are developed through this victim role. As victims, we attract perpetrators. We believe we need someone to take care of us because we feel helpless. Some caretakers will ultimately present themselves to somebody or some institution, needing to be taken care of mentally, physically, financially, or emotionally. *Being a victim becomes our story.*

Why, you might ask, would apparently rational people do this rescuing? Many reasons. Most of us aren't even aware of what we're doing. Most of us truly believe we're helping. Some of us believe we *have to* rescue. We have confused ideas about what constitutes help and what doesn't. Many of us are convinced that rescuing is a charitable deed. We may even think it cruel and heartless to allow someone to work through or face a legitimate feeling, suffer a consequence, be disappointed by hearing no, respond to our needs and wants, and generally be held responsible and accountable. Never mind that they will certainly pay a price for our "helping"—a price that will be as harsh as or more severe than any feeling they may be facing.

Many of us do not understand what we are responsible for and what we are not responsible for. We may believe we have to work ourselves into a frenzy when someone has a problem because it's our responsibility to do that. Sometimes, we become sick of feeling responsible for so much that we reject all responsibility and become totally irresponsible.

However, at the heart of most rescues is a demon: low self-worth. We rescue because we don't feel good about ourselves. Although the feelings are transient and artificial, caretaking provides us with a temporary hit of good feelings, self-worth, and power. Just as a drink helps an alcoholic momentarily feel better, a rescue move momentarily distracts us from the pain of being who we are. We don't feel lovable, so we settle for being needed. We don't feel good about ourselves, so we feel compelled to do a particular thing to *prove* how good we are.

We rescue because we don't feel good about other people either. Sometimes with justification, sometimes without, we decide other people cannot be held responsible for themselves. Although this may appear to be true, it isn't accurate. Unless a person has brain damage, a serious physical impairment or disability, or is an infant, they can be responsible for themselves.

Sometimes we rescue because it's easier than dealing with the discomfort and awkwardness of facing other people's unsolved problems. We haven't learned to say, "It's too bad you're having that problem. What do you need from me?" We've learned to say, "Here. Let me do that *for* you."

Some of us learned to be caretakers when we were children. Perhaps we were almost forced to as a result of living with the family dynamics of alcoholism. Some of us may have started caretaking later in life due to being in a committed relationship with someone who refused and appeared unable to take care of themselves. We decided to cope by picking up the slack and assuming other people's responsibilities.

Many codependents have been taught other ways to be caretakers. Maybe we believed these common lies: don't be selfish, always be kind and help people, never hurt other people's feelings, never say no, and don't mention personal wants and needs because it's not polite.

We may have been taught to be responsible for other people but not responsible for ourselves. Some women were taught that good, desirable wives and mothers were caretakers. Caretaking was expected and required of them. It was their duty. Some men believe good husbands and fathers are caretakers—superheroes responsible for meeting every need of each family member.

Sometimes a state resembling codependency sets in when a person is taking care of infants, young children, or people of any age with special needs. Taking care of infants requires a person to forfeit their needs, to do things they don't want to do, to squelch their feelings and desires (four o'clock in the morning feedings usually only meet the needs of the person being fed), and to assume total responsibility for another human being. Taking care of children is not rescuing. That is an actual responsibility and is not the kind of caretaking I'm talking about. But if caretakers don't take care of themselves, they may begin to feel the codependent blues.

Others may have interpreted religious beliefs as a mandate to caretake. Be cheerful givers, we are told. Go the extra mile. Love our neighbors. And we try; we try so hard. We try too hard. And then we wonder what's wrong with us because our religious beliefs aren't working. Our lives aren't working either.

Religious beliefs work just fine. Your life can work just fine. It's rescuing that doesn't work. "It's like trying to catch butterflies with a broomstick," a friend observed. Rescuing leaves us bewildered and befuddled every time. It's a self-destructive reaction, another way codependents attach themselves to people and become detached from themselves. It's another way we attempt to control but instead become controlled by people. Caretaking is an unhealthy parent-child relationship—sometimes between two consenting adults, sometimes between an adult and a child.

Caretaking breeds anger. Caretakers become angry parents, angry children, angry friends, angry lovers. We may become unsatisfied, frustrated, and confused. The people we help either are or they become helpless, angry victims. Caretakers, too, become victims.

Most of us have heard the biblical parable about Mary and Martha as told in chapter 10 of the gospel of Luke. While Mary sat and talked with Jesus and his friends, Martha cleaned and cooked. Before long, the story goes, Martha started banging pans, accusing Mary of being lazy. Martha complained that she had to do everything while Mary relaxed and enjoyed herself. Does this sound familiar? Jesus didn't let this one go by. He told Martha to hush. Mary knew what was important, he said. Mary made the right decision.

The message here might be that Mary made the right choice because it's more important to enjoy people than it is to cook and clean. But I also believe there's a message about taking responsibility for our choices, doing what we *want* to be doing, and realizing how we become angry when we don't. Maybe Mary's choice was right because she acted as she wanted to. Jesus helped many people, but he was honest and straightforward about it. He didn't persecute people after he helped them. And he *asked* them what they wanted from him. Sometimes he asked why too. He held people responsible for their behavior.

I think caretaking perverts religious messages about giving, loving, and helping. Nowhere in the Bible are we instructed to do something for someone and then scratch their eyes out. Nowhere are we told to walk the extra mile with someone and then grab the person's cane and beat them with it. Caring about people and giving are good, desirable qualities—something we need to do—but many codependents have misinterpreted the suggestions to "give until it hurts." We continue giving long after it hurts, usually until we are doubled over in pain. It's good to give, but we don't have to give it all away. It's okay to keep some for ourselves.

I believe helping people and sharing our time, talents, and money are worthy endeavors. But I also believe that our giving should come from a place of high self-esteem. I believe acts of kindness are not kind unless we feel good about ourselves, what we are doing, and the person we are doing it for. A higher self is there to guide each of us—if we listen. If we absolutely can't feel good about something we're doing, then we shouldn't do it—no matter how charitable it seems. We also shouldn't do things for others that they ought to and are capable of doing for themselves. Other people aren't helpless. Neither are we.

Giving to and doing things for and with people are essential parts of healthy living and healthy relationships. But learning when not to give, when not to give in, and when not to do things for and with people are also essential parts of healthy living and healthy relationships. It is not good to take care of people who take advantage of us to avoid responsibility. It hurts them, and it hurts us. There is a thin line between helping and hurting people, between beneficial giving and destructive giving. We can learn to make that distinction.

Caretaking is an act and an attitude. For some of us, it becomes a role, an approach to our entire lives and to all the people around us. Caretaking is closely associated with martyrdom (a state co-dependents are frequently accused of being in), and people pleasing (another accusation hurled at us). Martyrs, according to Earnie Larsen, "screw things up." We need to keep sacrificing our happiness as well as others' for the good of some unknown cause that doesn't demand sacrifice. People pleasers, Larsen says, can't be trusted. We lie. And as caretakers, we don't take care of ourselves.

The most exciting thing about caretaking is learning to understand what it is and when we are doing it so we can stop doing it.

We can learn to recognize a rescue. Refuse to rescue. Refuse to let people rescue us. Take responsibility for ourselves, and let others do the same. Whether we change our attitudes, our circumstances, our behavior, or our minds, the kindest thing we can do is remove the victims—ourselves.

1. This assignment may take some time, but if caretaking/rescuing/ enabling is causing problems, it may be a breakthrough experience for you. Become familiar with the Karpman Drama Triangle and how you go through the process in your life. Keep a rescue journal. Focus on the relationships that are troubling you. Record your interactions with the people you identify as causing you stress, anxiety, or concern. Observe when you get angry. Observe when you feel victimized. Observe when you feel confused. The point here is to develop awareness of yourself and your participation in rescuing/caretaking and how that results in you feeling victimized. Watch for the role and mood shifts. When you catch yourself feeling resentful or used, write down how you rescued.

2. Practice non-rescuing behaviors: Set boundaries. Say no when you want to say no. Do things you want to do. Refuse to guess what people want and need; instead insist that others ask you directly for what they want and need from you. Begin asking directly for what you want and need. Refuse to assume other people's responsibilities. When you initially stop taking care of people who are used to you taking care of them, they may become angry or frustrated. You've changed the system, rocked the boat. It means more work for them, and they can't use you anymore. Explain to them what you are doing and allow them to be responsible for their feelings. They may thank you later. They may even surprise you—sometimes the people we thought least able to take care of themselves can do so successfully when we stop taking care of them.

9

Undependence

"What is it about me?" she asked. "Do I need a dead body lying in my bed in order to feel good about myself?"

—ALICE B., A CODEPENDENT WHO HAS BEEN
MARRIED TO TWO ALCOHOLICS

I'm real independent—as long as I'm in a relationship," announced a police officer who has been involved with several emotionally troubled men.

"My husband has been lying on the couch drunk and hasn't brought home a paycheck in ten years," said another woman, the director of a large human services organization. "Who needs this? I must," she said, answering her own question. "But why? And for what?"

A woman who had recently joined Al-Anon called me one afternoon. This married woman worked part-time as a registered nurse, had assumed all the responsibility for raising her two children, and took care of everything relating to the house, including repairs and finances. "I want to separate from my husband," she said. "I can't stand him or his abuse any longer. But please tell me . . . do you think I can take care of myself?"

The words vary, but the thought is the same: *I'm unhappy living with this person, but I don't think I can live without them. I cannot, for some reason, find it within myself to face the stark truth that every human being must face or continue to run from—that of being ultimately and solely responsible for taking care of myself. I don't believe I can take care of myself. I'm not sure I want to be this alone. I need a person, any person, to buffer the shock of my solitary condition. No matter the cost.*

Colette Dowling wrote about this thought pattern in *The Cinderella Complex*. Penelope Russianoff discussed it in *Why Do I Think I Am Nothing Without a Man?* I've said it many times.

Whether codependents appear fragile and helpless or sturdy and powerful, most of us are frightened, needy, vulnerable children who are aching and desperate to be loved and cared for.

This child in us believes we are unlovable and will never find the comfort we are seeking; sometimes this vulnerable child becomes too desperate. People have abandoned us, emotionally and physically. People have rejected us. People have abused us, let us down. People have never been there for us; they have not seen, heard, or responded to our needs. We may come to believe that people will never be there for us. For many of us, even our faith is challenged.

We've been there for so many people. Most of us want someone (finally) to be there for us. We need someone, anyone, to rescue us from the stark loneliness and alienation. We want some of life's good stuff. But all that's around us—inside us—is pain. We feel so helpless and uncertain. Others look so powerful and assured. We're convinced that the magic is in them.

So we become dependent on them. We can become dependent on lovers, spouses, friends, parents, or our children. We become dependent on their approval. We become dependent on their presence. We become dependent on their need for us. We become dependent on their love, even though we believe we'll never receive their love because we believe we're unlovable. Nobody has ever loved us in a way that met our needs.

I'm not saying codependents are peculiar ducks because they want and need love and approval. Most people want to be in loving relationships. They want a special person in their lives. Most people want and need friends. Most people want the people in their lives to love and approve of them. These are natural, healthy desires. A certain amount of emotional dependency is present in most relationships, including the healthiest ones.[1] But many of us don't just want people—we need people. We may become driven, controlled by this need.

Needing people too much can cause problems. Other people become the key to our happiness. I believe much of this centering our lives around other people goes hand in hand with codependency and springs out of our emotional insecurity. I believe much of this incessant approval seeking also comes from insecurity. The magic is in others, not us, we believe. The good feelings are in them, not us. The less good stuff we find in ourselves, the more we seek it in others. *They* have it all; we have nothing. *Our* existence is not important. We have been abandoned and neglected so often that we also abandon ourselves.

Needing people so much, yet believing we're unlovable and people will never be there for us, can become a deeply ingrained belief and a source of inner conflict. Sometimes, we think people aren't there for us when they really are. This dysfunctional belief may block our vision, preventing us from seeing the love that is there.

Sometimes, no human being could be there for us the way we need them to be—to absorb and care for us, and make us feel good, complete, and safe.

Many of us expect and need other people so much that we settle for too little. We may become dependent on troubled people. We can become dependent on people we don't particularly like or love. Sometimes, we need people so badly we settle for nearly anyone. We may need people who don't meet our needs. Again, we may find ourselves in situations where we need someone to be there for us but the person we have chosen cannot or will not do that.

We may even convince ourselves that we can't live without someone and will wither and die if that person isn't in our lives. If that person is troubled, we may tolerate abuse and insanity to keep them in our lives, to protect our source of emotional security. Our need becomes so great that we settle for too little. Our expectations drop below normal, below what we ought to expect from our relationships. Then, we become trapped, stuck. And the object of our obsession can sense this and may begin to feel suffocated.

As Janet Geringer Woititz writes in *The Complete ACOA Sourcebook*:

> It is no longer Camelot. It is no longer even person-to-person. The distortion is bizarre. I will stay because "He doesn't beat me." "She doesn't run around." "He hasn't lost his job." Imagine getting credit for the behaviors we ordinary mortals do as a matter of course. Even if the worst is true—even if he does beat you; even if she does run

around; even if he is no longer working—even with all this, you will then say, "But I love him/her!" When I respond, "Tell me, what is so lovable?" there is no response. The answer doesn't come, but the power of being emotionally stuck is far greater than the power of reason.[2]

I am not suggesting all our intimate relationships are based on insecurities and dependencies. Certainly the power of love overrides common sense, and perhaps that's how it should be at times. By all means, if we love an alcoholic and want to stick with them, we should continue loving that person. But the driving force of emotional insecurity can also become far greater than the power of reason or love. Not being centered in ourselves and not feeling emotionally secure with ourselves may trap us.[3] We may become afraid to terminate relationships that are dead and destructive. We may allow people to hurt and abuse us, and that's *never* in our best interest.

People who feel trapped look for escapes. Codependents who feel stuck in a relationship may begin planning an escape. Sometimes our escape route is a positive, healthy one; we begin taking steps to become undependent, financially and emotionally. "Undependence" is a term Penelope Russianoff uses to describe that desirable balance wherein we acknowledge and meet our healthy, natural needs for people and love, yet we don't become overly or harmfully dependent on them.[4]

We may go back to school, get a job, or set other goals that will bring freedom. And we usually begin setting those goals when we are sick enough of being trapped. Some codependents, however, plan destructive escapes. We may try to escape our prison by using alcohol or drugs. We may become workaholics. We may seek escape by becoming emotionally dependent on another person who is like the person we were attempting to escape—another alcoholic, for example. Many codependents begin to contemplate suicide. For some, ending their lives appears to be the only way out of this terribly painful situation.

Emotional dependency and feeling stuck can also cause problems in salvageable relationships. If we are in a relationship that is still good, we may be too insecure to detach and start taking care of ourselves. We may stifle ourselves and smother or drive away the other person. That much need becomes obvious to other people. It can be sensed, felt.

Ultimately, too much dependency on a person can kill love. Relationships based on emotional insecurity and need, rather than on love, can become self-destructive. They don't work. Too much need smothers love. It drives people away. It attracts the wrong kind of people. And our real needs don't get met. Our real needs become greater, and so does our despair. We center our lives around this person, trying to protect our source of security and happiness. We forfeit our lives to do this. And we become angry at this person. We're being controlled by them. We're dependent on them. We ultimately become angry and resentful at what we're dependent on and controlled by because we have given our personal power and rights—our agency—away.[5]

Feeling desperate or dependent can expose us to other risks too. If we let the desperate part of us make our choices, we may unwittingly put ourselves in situations where we expose ourselves to sexually transmitted diseases, abuse, and worse. It is not safe to be that needy in intimate relationships.

Sometimes, we may play tricks on ourselves to disguise our dependency. Some of these tricks, according to Colette Dowling, are making someone more than they are ("He's such a genius; that's why I stick with him"), making someone less than they are ("Men are such babies; they can't take care of themselves"), and—the favorite trick of codependents—caretaking. Dowling demonstrates these characteristics in *The Cinderella Complex*, where she cites the case history of Madeleine, a woman who was extricating herself from a destructive relationship with Manny, her alcoholic husband.

> That is the last trick of the dependent personality—believing that you're responsible for "taking care of" the other one. Madeleine had always felt more responsible for Manny's survival than for her own. As long as she was concentrating on Manny—*his* passivity, *his* indecisiveness, *his* problems with alcohol—she focused all her energy on devising solutions for him, or for "them," and never had to look inside herself. It was why it had taken twenty-two years for Madeleine to catch on to the fact that if things continued as they had always been, she would end up shortchanged. She would end up *never having lived a life*.
>
> . . . From the time she was eighteen until she was forty—years when people are supposed to reap, and grow, and experience the world—Madeleine Boroff had been hanging on, pretending to herself that life was not what it was, that her husband would get his bearings before long, and that she would one day spring free to live her own inner life—peacefully, creatively.

For twenty-two years she had not been able to cope with what it would mean to face down the lie, and so, without intending any harm, but too frightened to live authentically, she turned her back on truth.

It may seem dramatic in its surface details, but in its fundamental dynamic Madeleine's story is not so unusual. The go-along quality she exhibited, the seeming inability to extricate herself, or even *think* of extricating herself, from an utterly draining relationship—these signs of helplessness are characteristic of women who are psychologically dependent.[6]

Why do we do this to ourselves? Why do we feel so uncertain and insecure that we can't go about the business of living our lives? Why, when we have proved we are so strong and capable by the sheer fact that many of us have endured and survived what we have, can't we believe in ourselves? Why, when we are experts at taking care of everybody around us, do we doubt our ability to take care of ourselves? What is it about us?

Many of us learned these things because when we were children, someone very important to us was unable to give us the love, approval, and emotional security we needed. So we've gone about our lives the best way we could, still looking vaguely or desperately for something we never got. Some of us are still beating our heads against the cement trying to get this love from people who, like Mom or Dad, are unable to give us what we need. The cycle repeats itself until it is interrupted and stopped. It's called unfinished business.

Maybe we've been taught not to trust ourselves. This happens when we have a feeling and we're told it's wrong or inappropriate. Or when we confront a lie or an inconsistency and we're told we're crazy. We lose faith in that deep, important part of ourselves that feels appropriate feelings, senses truth, and has confidence in its ability to handle life's situations. Pretty soon, we may believe what we are told about ourselves—that we're off, a tad crazy, not to be trusted. We look at the people around us—sometimes sick, troubled, out-of-control people—and we think, "They're okay. They must be. They told me so. So it must be me. There must be something fundamentally wrong with me."

Some of us may have entered an adult relationship with our emotional security intact, only to discover we were in a relationship with a troubled person. Nothing will destroy emotional security more quickly than loving someone who has a substance abuse problem or any other compulsive disorder. These diseases demand that we center our lives around them. Confusion, chaos, and despair reign. Even the healthiest of us may begin to doubt ourselves after living with an addict. Needs go unmet. Love disappears. The needs become greater, and so does the self-doubt. Substance abuse creates emotionally insecure people. Substance abuse creates victims of us—addicts and nonaddicts alike—and we doubt our ability to take care of ourselves.

If we have decided, for whatever reason, that we can't take care of ourselves, I have good news. We aren't helpless. Being ourselves and being responsible for ourselves does not have to be painful and scary. We can handle whatever life brings our way. We don't have to be so dependent on the people around us. We can live without any particular human being. As one woman put it: "For years, I kept telling myself I couldn't live without a man. I was wrong. I've had four husbands. They're all dead, and I'm still living." Knowing we can live without someone doesn't mean we have to live without that person, but it may free us to love and live in ways that work.

But here's the rest of the news: there is no magic bullet, no shortcut to becoming instantly undependent. It's a process, but we can strive to become *less* dependent.

Here are some ideas that may help:

1. *Finish emotional business from your childhood as best as you can.* Grieve. Get some perspective. Figure out how events from childhood are affecting—even driving—what you're doing now.

My dad left home when I was two years old. He had been drunk for those years, or so Mom said. I rarely saw him after he moved out. He visited a few times after the divorce, but there was no substance to the relationship. As I grew up, I called my dad from time to time. He had a new family and seemed to be stable. I'd tell him about important events in my life: high school graduation, marriage, the births of Nichole and Shane. Each time, we'd talk for five minutes. He'd mention seeing me sometime, then hang up. I didn't feel particularly hurt or angry; I expected this from him. He'd never been there for me. He didn't participate in the relationship. There was nothing, including love, coming back from him. I thought I'd accepted my father's alcoholism and abandonment. The relationship had gone on this way for years. And so had my relationships with alcoholics.

When I was going through my divorce, my father called. It was the first time he'd ever reached out to me. My heart nearly jumped out of my chest. My dad asked how we were—a question he usually avoided. Just as I was wondering if I could tell him about the divorce (I'd always wanted to be comforted by my father), he began whining about how he'd been locked up in a psychiatric ward with no rights, it wasn't fair, and couldn't I do something to help him? I quickly wrapped up the conversation, hung up the phone, sat down on the floor, and bawled.

I remember sitting on the floor screaming, "You've never been there for me. Never! And now I need you. I let myself need you just once, and you weren't there for me. Instead, you wanted *me* to take care of *you*."

When I quit crying, I felt strangely peaceful. I think it was the first time I ever let myself grieve or get angry at my father. Over the next few weeks, I began to understand—really understand. Of course he had never been there for me. He was an alcoholic. He had never been there for anyone, including himself. I also began to realize that while I looked like I had it all together on the surface, I felt deeply unlovable. Somewhere, hidden inside me, I had maintained a fantasy that I had a loving father who was staying away from me—who was rejecting me—because I wasn't good enough. Now I knew the truth. It wasn't me that was unlovable. It wasn't me that was screwed up, although I knew I had problems. It was *him*.

The truth set me free.

I'm not suggesting that all my historical problems were solved by one moment of awareness. I had more grieving to do; I still needed to deal with my codependent characteristics. But what happened helped me move forward and see things clearly.

2. *Nurture and cherish that frightened child inside.* The child may never completely disappear, no matter how self-sufficient you

become. Stress may cause the child to cry out. Unprovoked, the child may come out and demand attention when you least expect it.

I had a dream about this that illustrates the point. In my dream, a girl about nine years old had been left alone, abandoned by her mother for several days and nights. Without supervision, the child ran around the neighborhood late at night. She didn't cause any serious problems. She seemed to be looking for something, trying to fill her empty hours. The child did not want to stay in her house alone when it got dark. The loneliness was too frightening. When the mother finally returned, the neighbors approached her and complained about this child running all over, unsupervised. The mother became angry and started yelling at the child for her misbehavior. "I told you to stay in the house while I was gone. I told you not to cause problems, didn't I?" the mother screamed. The child offered no retort, didn't even cry. She just stood there with downcast eyes and quietly said, "I think I have a stomachache."

Don't pound on the vulnerable child when they don't want to stay in the dark all alone, when they become frightened. We don't have to let the child make our choices for us, but don't ignore the child either. Listen to the child. Let the child cry if needed. Comfort the child. Figure out what they need.

3. *Stop looking for happiness in other people.* Our source of happiness and well-being is not inside others; it's inside us. Learn to center yourself in yourself.

Stop focusing on other people. Settle down with and in yourself. Stop seeking so much approval and validation from others. We don't need the approval of everyone and anyone. We only need our approval. We have all the same sources for happiness and making choices inside us that others do. Make a home for yourself within yourself. Find and develop your own internal supply of peace, well-being, and self-esteem. Relationships help, but they cannot be your source. Taking care of yourself is a huge job. Stop expecting other people to do it.

4. *Learn to depend on yourself.* Maybe other people haven't been there for you, but you can start being there for you.

Let's stop abandoning ourselves, our needs, our wants, our feelings, our lives, and everything that comprises us. Make a commitment to always be there for ourselves. We can trust ourselves. We can handle and cope with the events, problems, and feelings life throws our way. We can trust our feelings and our judgments. We can solve our problems. We can learn to live with our unsolved problems too. We must trust the people we are learning to depend upon—ourselves.

5. *Strive for undependence.* Begin examining the ways you're dependent on the people around you. Start taking care of yourself, whether you're in a relationship that you intend to continue or in a relationship that you're trying to get out of. In *The Cinderella Complex*, Colette Dowling suggests doing this with an attitude of "courageous vulnerability."[7] That means you feel scared, but you do it anyway.

We can feel our feelings, talk about our fears, accept ourselves and our present conditions, and then get started on the journey toward undependence. We *can* do it. We don't have to feel strong all the time to be undependent. We can and probably will have feelings of fear, weakness, and even hopelessness. That's normal and healthy. Real power comes from feeling our feelings, not from ignoring them. Real strength comes from acknowledging our weaknesses, not from pretending to be strong all the time.

Many of us have dark nights. Sometimes the way is foggy and slippery, and we have no hope. All we can feel is fear. All we can see is the dark. I was driving one night in weather like this. I don't like driving, and I particularly don't like driving in bad weather. I was stiff and frightened at the wheel. I could barely see; the headlights were only illuminating a few feet of the road. I started to panic. Anything could happen! Then a calming thought entered my mind. The path was only lit for a few feet, but each time I progressed those few feet, a new section was lit. It didn't matter that I couldn't see far ahead. If I relaxed, I could see as far as I needed for the moment. The situation wasn't ideal, but I could get through it if I stayed calm and worked with what was available.

You can get through dark situations too. You can take care of yourself and trust yourself. Go as far as you can see, and by the time you get there, you'll be able to see farther.

It's called taking things one day at a time.

··· ACTIVITY ···

1. Examine the characteristics listed on the next two pages for dependent (addicted) or healthy (loving) relationships.[8] Use the information to grow in awareness.

GENERAL CHARACTERISTICS

Love (Open System)	Addiction (Closed System)
Offers room to grow, expand—desires for other to grow	Is dependent, based on security and comfort—intensity of need and infatuation used as proof of love (may really be fear, insecurity, loneliness)
Has separate interests—other friends—and maintains other meaningful relationships	Has total involvement—limited social life—neglects old friends, interests
Encourages each other to expand—both partners secure in their own worth	Is preoccupied with other's behavior—dependent on other's approval for personal identity and self-worth
Displays trust—openness	Displays jealousy and possessiveness, fears competition, "protects supply"
Preserves mutual integrity	Suspends one partner's needs for the other's—self-deprivation
Is willing to risk and be real	Searches for perfect invulnerability—eliminates possible risks
Allows room for the exploration of feelings in and out of relationship	Seeks reassurance through repeated, ritualized activity
Is able to enjoy being alone	Is unable to endure separations (even in conflict) and hangs on even tighter; undergoes withdrawal—loss of appetite, restlessness, lethargy, disoriented agony

BREAKUP CHARACTERISTICS

Love (Open System)	*Addiction (Closed System)*
Accepts breakups without feeling a loss of self-adequacy and self-worth	Feels inadequate, worthless after a breakup—often one-sided decision
Wants best for partner, though apart—can become friends	Has violent endings—often feels hate—and tries to inflict pain and manipulate to get partner back

CHARACTERISTICS OF ONE-SIDED ADDICTION

Love (Open System)	*Addiction (Closed System)*
	Denies, fantasizes—overestimates other's commitment
	Seeks solutions outside self—drugs, alcohol, new lover, change of situation

10

Live Your Own Life

Live and let live.

—TWELVE STEP PROGRAM SLOGAN

I f I make one point in this book, I hope it's this: The surest way to make ourselves crazy is to get involved in other people's business, and the quickest way to become sane and happy is to tend to our own affairs.

I have discussed ideas pertaining to that concept. We've examined reactions typical of codependency. We've discussed ways of learning how to react differently using detachment. But, after we've detached and taken our grip off the people around us, each of us is left with ourselves.

I remember the day I faced that truth. For a long time I had blamed my unfortunate circumstances on other people. "You are the reason I am the way I am!" I screeched. "Look what you made me do—with my minutes, my hours, *my life*." After I detached and took responsibility for myself, I wondered if maybe other people weren't the reason I hadn't been living my own life; maybe they were just the excuse I'd needed. My destiny—my todays and tomorrows—looked pretty grim.

Living our lives may not be an exciting prospect to some of you either. Maybe we've been so wrapped up in other people that we've forgotten how to live and enjoy our lives.

We may be in so much emotional distress we think we have no life; all we are is our pain. That's not true. We are more than our problems. We can be more than our problems. We will be more than our problems.[1] Just because life has been this painful so far doesn't mean it has to keep hurting. Life doesn't have to hurt so much, and it won't—if we begin to change. It may not be all roses from here on out, but it doesn't have to be all thorns either. We need to and can develop our own lives.

Some people think a life with no future, no purpose, no great shakes, and no great breaks isn't worth living. That's not true either. I believe there are exciting, interesting things in store for each of us. I believe there is an enjoyable, worthwhile purpose—besides taking care of people and being an appendage to someone—for each of us. I believe we tap into this attitude by taking care of ourselves. We begin to cooperate. We open to the goodness and richness available in us and to us once we find our paths to well-being.[2]

Throughout this book I've used the phrase "taking care of ourselves." I've heard that phrase used and abused. I've heard people use it to control, impose upon, or force their wills on people. ("I dropped in, uninvited, with my five kids and cat. We're going to spend the week. I'm just taking care of myself!") I've heard the phrase used manipulatively to justify persecuting and punishing people instead of dealing appropriately with angry feelings. ("I'm going to holler and scream at you all day because you didn't do what I wanted you to do. Don't get mad at me; I'm just taking care of myself!") I've heard people use these words to avoid responsibility. ("I know my son is up in his bedroom shooting heroin, but that's his problem. I'm not going to worry. I'm going shopping—retail therapy—and I'm not going to worry about how I'll pay that bill either. I'm just taking care of myself!")

Those behaviors are not what I mean by taking care of ourselves. Self-care is an attitude toward ourselves and our lives that says, "I am responsible for myself."

I am responsible for leading my life.

I am responsible for tending to my spiritual, emotional, physical, and financial well-being.

I am responsible for identifying and meeting my needs.

I am responsible for solving my problems or learning to live with those I cannot solve.

I am responsible for my choices.

I am responsible for what I give and receive.

I am responsible for setting and achieving my goals.

I am responsible for how much I enjoy life, for how much pleasure I find in daily activities.

I am responsible for whom I love and how I choose to express this love.

I am responsible for what I do to others and for what I allow others to do to me.

I am responsible for my wants and desires.

All of me, every aspect of my being, is important. I count for something.

I matter.

My feelings can be trusted.

My thinking is appropriate.

I value my wants and needs.

I do not deserve and will not tolerate abuse or constant mistreatment.

I have rights, and it's my responsibility to assert these rights.

The decisions I make and the way I conduct myself will reflect my high self-esteem.

My decisions will take into account my responsibilities to myself.

My decisions will also take into account my responsibilities to other people—my partner, my children, my relatives, my friends.

I will examine and decide exactly what these responsibilities are as I make my decisions.

I will also consider the rights of those around me—the right to live their lives as they see fit.

I do not have the right to impose on others' rights to take care of themselves, and they have no right to impose on my rights.

Self-care is an attitude of mutual respect. It means learning to live our lives responsibly. It means allowing others to live their lives as they choose, as long as they don't interfere with our decision to live as we choose. Taking care of ourselves is not as selfish as some people assume it is, but neither is it as selfless as many believe.

In the chapters that follow, we'll discuss some specific ways of taking care of ourselves: goal setting, dealing with feelings, working a Twelve Step program, and more. I believe taking care of ourselves is an art, and this art involves one fundamental idea that is foreign to many: *giving ourselves what we need.*

This may come as a shock to us and our family systems. Most people with codependency issues don't ask for what we need. Many of us don't know or haven't given much thought to what we want and need.

Maybe we falsely believed that our needs aren't important and we shouldn't mention them. Some of us may even have thought that our needs are bad, wrong, or taboo, so we've learned to repress them and push them out of our awareness. We never learned to identify what we need or listen to what we need because it didn't matter anyway—our needs weren't going to get met. Some of us haven't learned how to get our needs met appropriately.

Giving ourselves what we need isn't difficult. We can learn quickly. The formula is simple: in any given situation, detach and ask, *What do I need to do to take care of myself?* Then listen to your higher self and respect what you hear.

This insane business of punishing ourselves for what we think, feel, and want—this nonsense of not listening to who we are and what our selves are struggling to tell us—must stop. It's a form of self-abandonment. We can be gentle with and accept ourselves. We can be compassionate with ourselves. Then, perhaps, we may develop true compassion for others.[3] Listen to what your precious self is telling you about what you need.

Maybe we need to hurry and get to an appointment. Maybe we need to slow down and take the day off work. Maybe we need exercise or a nap. We might need to be alone. We may want to be around people. Maybe we need a job. Maybe we need to work less. Maybe we need a hug, a kiss, or a back rub.

Sometimes giving ourselves what we need means giving ourselves something fun: a treat, a manicure, a new pair of shoes, an evening at the theater, or a trip to the Bahamas. Sometimes, giving ourselves what we need is work. We need to eliminate or develop a

certain characteristic, work on a relationship, or tend to our responsibilities to other people or to ourselves. Giving ourselves what we
need does not only mean giving presents to ourselves; it means
doing what's necessary to live responsibly—not abide in an excessively responsible or an irresponsible existence.

Our needs are different and vary from moment to moment and
day to day. Are you feeling the crazy anxiety that goes with codependency? Maybe you need to go to an Al-Anon meeting. Are
your thoughts negative and despairing? Maybe you need to meditate. Are you worried about a physical problem? See a doctor. Are
the kids going wild? Establish some ground rules around their behavior. Are people stomping on your rights? Set boundaries. Is your
stomach churning with emotion? Detach, slow down, make
amends, do an intervention, initiate a relationship, file for divorce,
or wait until the path becomes clear. It's up to us. What do we think
we need to do?

Besides giving ourselves what we need, we also begin to ask
people for what we need and want from them because this is part
of taking care of ourselves and being a responsible human being.

Giving ourselves what we need means becoming our own counselors, confidantes, spiritual advisors, partners, best friends, and
caretakers in this exciting, new venture we have undertaken—living
our own lives. We base all our decisions on reality, and we make
them in our best interests. We consider our responsibilities to other
people because that is what responsible people do, but we also
know we count. We try to eliminate "shoulds" from our decisions
and learn to trust ourselves. If we listen to our higher selves, we will
not be misled. Giving ourselves what we need and learning to live
self-directed lives requires faith. We need enough faith to get on

with our lives, and we need to do at least a little something each day to keep moving forward.

As we learn how to care for and meet our own needs, we forgive ourselves when we make mistakes, and we congratulate ourselves when we do well. We also get comfortable doing some things poorly and some things with mediocrity, for that's part of life too. We learn to laugh at ourselves and our humanity, but we don't laugh when we need to cry. We take ourselves seriously but not too seriously.

Ultimately, we may even discover this astounding truth: few situations in life are ever improved by depriving ourselves of what we need. In fact, we may learn most situations are improved when we take care of ourselves and tend to our needs.

I am learning to identify how to take care of myself. I know many people who have either learned or are learning to do this too. All of us can.

•• ACTIVITY ••

1. As you go through the days ahead, stop and ask yourself what you need to do to take care of yourself. Do it as often as you need to but do it at least once daily. If you are going through a crisis, you may need to do it every hour. Then give yourself what you need.

2. What do you need from the people around you? At an appropriate time, sit down with them and discuss what you need from them.

11

Have a Love Affair with Yourself

This above all—to thine own self be true,
And it must follow, as the night the day,
Thou canst not then be false to any man.

—WILLIAM SHAKESPEARE, *Hamlet*

L ove thy neighbor as thyself." For many codependents, we wouldn't dream of treating other people the way we treat ourselves. We wouldn't dare, and others probably wouldn't let us.

Most of us suffer from that vague but penetrating affliction of low self-worth. We don't feel good about ourselves, we don't like ourselves, and we wouldn't consider loving ourselves. For some of us, low self-worth is an understatement. We don't merely dislike ourselves, we hate ourselves.[1]

We don't like the way we look. We can't stand our bodies. We think we're stupid, incompetent, untalented, and, in many cases, unlovable.[2] We think our thoughts are wrong and inappropriate. We think our feelings are wrong and inappropriate. We believe we're not important, and even if our feelings aren't wrong, we think they don't matter. We're convinced our needs aren't important. We think we're inferior to and different from the rest of the world—not unique, but oddly and inappropriately different. We have never made peace with ourselves, and we look at ourselves not through rose-colored glasses but through a dirty, brownish-gray film.

We may have learned to disguise our true feelings about ourselves by managing the way we present to others—our hair, body, clothing, where we live, whom we associate with—it's all about exteriors. We may boast of our accomplishments, but underneath the trappings lies a dungeon where we secretly and incessantly punish and torture ourselves. At times, we may punish ourselves openly before the whole world by saying demeaning things about ourselves. Sometimes, we may allow people to hurt us, but our worst beatings go on privately, inside our minds.

We pick on ourselves endlessly, heaping piles of shoulds on our consciences and creating mounds of worthless, stinking guilt. Don't confuse this with true pangs of conscience, which motivate change, teach valuable lessons, and bring us into a closer relationship with our higher selves. We constantly put ourselves in impossible situations where we have no choice but to feel bad about ourselves. We think negative thoughts, then tell ourselves we shouldn't think that way. We feel negative feelings, then tell ourselves we shouldn't feel that way. We make decisions, act on them, and then tell ourselves we shouldn't have acted that way. There is nothing to correct in these situations, no amends to make; we have done nothing wrong. We are engaged in a form of punishment designed to keep us feeling anxious, upset, and stifled. We're trapping ourselves.

One of my favorite forms of self-torture involves a dilemma between two things to do. I decide to do one of them first. The minute I act on this decision, I say: "I should be doing the other thing." So I switch gears, begin doing the other thing, and I start in on myself again: "I really shouldn't be doing this. I should be doing what I was doing before." Another one of my favorites is this: I fix my hair, put on makeup, look in the mirror, and say, "Gee, I look weird. I shouldn't look this way."

Some of us believe we have made such bad mistakes that we can't reasonably expect forgiveness. Some of us believe our lives are a mistake. Many of us believe everything we've done is a mistake. A few of us believe we can't do anything right, but at the same time, we demand perfection of ourselves. We put ourselves in impossible situations, then wonder why we can't get out.

Then we finish the job by shaming ourselves. We don't like what we do, and we don't like who we are. Fundamentally, we aren't good enough. For some reason, God created in us a person inappropriately equipped for life.

Our low self-worth leads to many problems. We frequently dislike ourselves so much that we believe it's wrong to take ourselves into account—or, in other words, to appear selfish. Putting ourselves first is out of the question. Often, we think we're only worth something if we do things for others or caretake, so we never say no. Anyone as insignificant as us must go an extra mile to be liked. No one in their right mind could like and enjoy being with us. We think we have to do something for people to get and keep their friendships. Much of the defensiveness I've seen in codependents comes not because we think we're above criticism but because we have so little self-worth that any perceived attack threatens to annihilate us. We feel so bad about ourselves and have such a need to be perfect and avoid shame that we cannot allow anyone to tell us about something we've done wrong. One reason some of us nag and criticize other people is because that's what we do to ourselves.

Our low self-worth or self-hatred is tied to all aspects of codependency: martyrdom (refusal to enjoy life), workaholism (staying so busy we can't enjoy life), perfectionism (not allowing ourselves to enjoy or feel good about the things we do and the way things are), and procrastination. It also drives us to avoid intimacy, stay in destructive relationships, initiate relationships with people who are not good for us, and steer clear of people who are good for us.

We can find endless means of torturing ourselves: overeating, starving ourselves, neglecting our needs, comparing ourselves to others, competing with people, obsessing, dwelling on painful memories, or imagining future painful scenes. We think, *What if they drink again? What if they have an affair? What if a tornado hits the house?* This what-if attitude is always good for a strong dose of fear. We scare ourselves, then wonder why we feel so afraid.

We don't like ourselves, and we're not going to let ourselves get any of life's good stuff because we believe we don't deserve it.

As codependents, we tend to enter into totally antagonistic relationships with ourselves.[3] Some of us learned these self-hating behaviors in our families, possibly with the help of a troubled (or codependent) parent. Some of us reinforced our self-disdain by leaving a troubled parent and marrying a troubled person. We may have entered adult relationships with fragile self-worth, then discovered our remaining self-esteem disintegrated. A few of us may have had our self-worth completely intact until we met *them* or until *that problem* came along; then we suddenly or gradually found ourselves hating ourselves. Compulsive disorders destroy self-worth in the afflicted person—and the codependent. Some of us may not even be aware of our low self-esteem and self-hatred because we've been comparing ourselves to the crazy people in our lives; by comparison, we come out on top. Low self-worth can sneak up on us anytime we let it.

It doesn't matter when we began torturing ourselves. We must stop now. We are okay. It's wonderful to be who we are. Our thoughts are okay. Our feelings are appropriate. We're right where we're supposed to be today, in this moment. There is nothing wrong with us. There is nothing fundamentally wrong with us. If we've done wrongs, that's okay; we were doing the best we could.

In all our codependency, with all our controlling, rescuing, and assorted character defects, we're okay. We're exactly as we are meant to be. I've talked a lot about problems, issues, and things to change—these are goals, things we'll do in the future to enhance our lives, but who we are right now is okay. In fact, codependents are some of the most loving, generous, good-hearted, and caring people I know. We've just allowed ourselves to be tricked into doing things that hurt us, and we're going to learn how to stop doing those things. But those tricks are our problems; they aren't us. If we have one character defect that is abhorrent, it's the way we hate and pick on ourselves. That is simply not tolerable or acceptable any longer. And we can stop picking on ourselves for picking on ourselves. This habit isn't our fault either, but it is our responsibility to learn to stop doing it.

We can cherish ourselves and our lives. We can nurture and love ourselves. We can accept our wonderful selves, with all our faults, foibles, strengths, feelings, thoughts, and everything else. *We are the best things we've got going for us.* We are who we are and who we were meant to be. And we are not mistakes. We are the greatest things that will ever happen to us. Believe it. It makes life much easier.

The only difference between codependents and the rest of the world is that most other people don't pick on themselves for being who they are. Most people think similar thoughts and have a range of feelings. All people make mistakes and do a few things right. We can leave ourselves alone.

We aren't second-class citizens. We don't deserve to lead secondhand lives. And we don't deserve second-best relationships! We are lovable, and we are worth getting to know. People who love and like us aren't stupid or inferior for doing that. We have a right to be happy. We deserve good things.

The people who look the most beautiful are the same as us. The only difference is they're telling themselves they look good, and they're letting themselves shine through. The people who say the most profound, intelligent, or witty things are the same as us. They're letting go, being who they are. The people who appear the most confident and relaxed are no different from us. They've pushed themselves through fearful situations and told themselves they could make it. The people who are successful are the same as us. They've gone ahead and developed their gifts and talents and have set goals for themselves. We're even the same as our heroes, our idols. We're all working with approximately the same material—humanity. It's how we feel about ourselves that makes the difference. It's what we tell ourselves that matters.

We are good. We are good enough. We are appropriate to life. Much of our anxiety and fearfulness stems from constantly telling ourselves that we're just not up to facing the world and all its situations. Nathaniel Branden calls this "a nameless sense of being unfit for reality."[4] I'm here to say we are fit for reality. Relax. Wherever we need to go and whatever we need to do, we're appropriate for that situation. We'll do fine. It's okay to be who we are. Who or what else can we be? We just have to do our best at whatever we're called to do. What more can we do? Sometimes, we can't even do our best; that's okay too. We may have feelings, thoughts, fears, and vulnerabilities as we go through life, but all people do. We need to stop telling ourselves we're different for doing and feeling what everyone else does.

We need to be good to ourselves. We need to be compassionate and kind to ourselves. How can we expect to take care of ourselves appropriately if we hate or dislike ourselves?

We need to refuse to enter into an antagonistic relationship with ourselves. Quit blaming ourselves. Put the screws to guilt. Shame and guilt serve no long-term purpose. They are only useful to momentarily indicate when we may have violated our own moral codes. Guilt and shame are not useful as a way of life.

We need to stop the shoulds. Become aware of when we're punishing and torturing ourselves and make a concerted effort to tell ourselves positive messages. If we should be doing something, let's do it. If we're torturing ourselves, let's stop it. It gets easier. We can laugh at ourselves, tell ourselves we won't be tricked, give ourselves a hug, then go about the business of living as we choose.

We don't have to punish ourselves by feeling guilty. If we have real guilt, there are constructive ways to deal with it. First, we need to see and accept the guilt. We need to be clear about whether we violated our own moral code. We need to accept, acknowledge, and then change. Do the work recommended by the Fourth and Fifth Steps (see chapter 18). Making amends can do wonders for relieving and resolving the heavy load of guilt.

Stop shaming yourself. Shame, like guilt, serves absolutely no extended purpose. If people tell us, directly or indirectly, that we ought to be ashamed—don't believe them. Hating or shaming ourselves doesn't help anything. Name one situation that's improved by continuing to feel guilt or shame. Name one time when that's solved a problem. How did it help? Most of the time, guilt and shame keep us so anxious we can't do our best. Guilt makes everything harder.

We need to value ourselves and make decisions and choices that enhance our self-esteem. "Each time you learn to act as if you are valuable, not desperate, it gets easier to repeat that new behavior in the future," Toby Rice Drews advises in *Getting Them Sober*.[5]

We can be gentle, loving, listening, attentive, and kind to ourselves. We can accept ourselves—all of us. Start where we're at, and we will become more. Develop our gifts and talents. Trust ourselves. Honor ourselves. That's where we'll find and make magic. That's our key to the world.

What follows is an excerpt from *Honoring the Self*, an excellent book on self-esteem written by Nathaniel Branden. Read closely:

> Of all the judgments that we pass in life, none is as important as the one we pass on ourselves, for that judgment touches the very center of our existence.
>
> . . . No significant aspect of our thinking, motivation, feelings, or behavior is unaffected by our self-evaluation. . . .
>
> The first act of honoring the self is the assertion of consciousness: the choice to think, to be aware, to send

the searchlight of consciousness outward toward the world and inward toward our own being. To default on this effort is to default on the self at the most basic level.

To honor the self is to be willing to think independently, to live by our own mind, and to have the courage of our own perceptions and judgments.

To honor the self is to be willing to know not only what we think but also what we feel, what we want, need, desire, suffer over, are frightened or angered by—and to accept our right to experience such feelings. The opposite of this attitude is denial, disowning, repression—self-repudiation.

To honor the self is to preserve an attitude of self-acceptance—which means to accept what we are, without self-oppression or self-castigation, without any pretense about the truth of our own being, pretense aimed at deceiving either ourselves or anyone else.

To honor the self is to live authentically, to speak and act from our innermost convictions and feelings.

To honor the self is to refuse to accept unearned guilt and to do our best to correct such guilt as we may have earned.

To honor the self is to be committed to our right to exist, which proceeds from the knowledge that our life does not belong to others and that we are not here on earth to live up to someone else's expectations. To many people, this is a terrifying responsibility.

To honor the self is to be in love with our own life, in love with our possibilities for growth and for experiencing joy, in love with the process of discovering and exploring our distinctively human potentialities.

Thus we can begin to see that to honor the self is to practice *selfishness* in the highest, noblest, and least understood sense of that word. And this, I shall argue, requires enormous independence, courage, and integrity.[6]

We can learn to practice radical self-love. I'm not talking about a half-hearted or wishy-washy commitment to ourselves. I'm also not talking about becoming egocentric or narcissistic. Be humble, be honest, but love yourself. The love we give ourselves will enhance *all* the love we give and receive.

••• ACTIVITY •••

1. How do you feel about yourself? Write about it. Include the things you like or don't like about yourself.

2. Now, write a new script about how you're going to talk to and about yourself.

Learn the Art of Acceptance

I'd like to make a motion that we face reality.

—BOB NEWHART, *The Bob Newhart Show*

A ccepting reality is touted and encouraged by most sane people. It's the goal of many therapies, as it should be. Facing and coming to terms with *what is* can be a beneficial act. Acceptance brings peace. It's frequently the turning point for change. It's also much easier said than done.

People (not just people with codependency) daily face the prospect of either accepting or rejecting the reality of their present circumstances. This includes who we are, where we live, whom we live with or without, where we work, how we get around, how much money we have, what our responsibilities are, what we do for fun, how we address any problems that arise, and the decisions we made that got us here. Some days, accepting these circumstances is a breeze. It comes naturally. Our hair behaves, our kids behave, the boss is reasonable, the money's enough, the house is clean, the car works, and we like our partner. We know what to expect, and what we expect is acceptable. Other days might not go as well. The brakes go out on the car, the roof leaks, the kids sass, we break an arm, we lose our job, or our partner tells us they don't love us anymore.

Something has happened. We have a problem. Things are different. Things are changing. We're *losing* something. Our present circumstances are no longer as comfortable as they once were. We have new situations to accept. We may initially respond by denying or resisting the change, problem, or loss. We want things to be the way they were. We want the problem to be quickly solved. We want to be comfortable again. We want to know what to expect. We aren't at peace with reality. We've temporarily lost our balance.

Codependents never know what to expect, particularly if we're in a close relationship with a person with a serious problem or compulsive disorder. We're bombarded by problems, losses, and change. We endure shattered windows, missed appointments, broken promises, and outright lies. We lose financial security, emotional security, faith in the people we love, faith in religion, and faith in ourselves. We may lose our physical well-being, our material goods, our ability to enjoy intimacy, our reputations, social lives, careers, self-control, self-esteem—ourselves.

Some of us lose respect for and trust in the people we love. This is common. It's a natural, normal consequence of addiction. The booklet *A Guide for the Family of the Alcoholic* discusses this: "Love cannot exist without the dimension of justice. Love must also have compassion which means to bear with or to suffer with a person. Compassion does not mean to suffer because of the injustice of a person. Yet injustice is often suffered repeatedly by families of alcoholics."[1]

Even though this injustice is common, it is no less painful. Betrayal can be overwhelming when someone we love does things that deeply hurt us.

Perhaps the most painful loss many codependents face is the loss of our dreams, the hopeful and sometimes idealistic expectations for the future that most people have. This loss can be the most difficult to accept. As we looked at our children in the hospital nursery, we had certain hopes for them. Those hopes didn't include them having a problem with alcohol or other drugs. Our dreams didn't include this. On our wedding day, we had dreams. The future was full of wonder and promise. This was the start of something great, something loving, something we had long hoped for. The dreams and promises may have been spoken or unspoken, but for most of us, they were there.

Janet Woititz writes:

> For each couple the beginning is different. Even so, the process that occurs in the chemically dependent marital relationship . . . is essentially the same. For the starting point, let's take a look at the marriage vows. Most wedding services include the following statements—for better or worse—for richer or poorer—in sickness and in health—until death do us part. Maybe that's where the trouble began. Did you mean what you said when you said it? If you knew at that time that you were going to have not the better but the worse, not the health but the sickness, not the richer but the poorer . . . would the love that you felt have made it worth it? You may say so, but I wonder. If you were more realistic than romantic, you may have interpreted the

vows to mean through the bad as well as the good, assuming that the bad times would be transitory and the good ones permanent. The contract is one that is entered into in good faith, so there is no benefit of hindsight.[2]

The dreams were there. Many of us held on for so long, clutching those dreams through one loss and disappointment after another. We flew in the face of reality, shaking these dreams at the truth, refusing to believe or accept anything less. But one day the truth caught up to us and refused to be put off any longer. This wasn't what we wanted, planned on, asked for, or hoped for. It never would be. The dream was dead, and it would never breathe again.

Some of us may have had our dreams and hopes crushed. Some of us may be facing the failure of something extremely important such as a marriage or another important relationship. I know there's a lot of pain at the prospect of losing love or losing the dreams we had. There's nothing we can say to make that less painful or to lessen our grief. It hurts deeply to have our dreams destroyed by substance abuse or any other harmful, compulsive behavior.

The disease is deadly. It kills everything in sight, including our noblest dreams.

"Chemical dependency destroys slowly, but thoroughly," Woititz concludes.[3] And nothing dies more slowly or painfully than a dream.

Even recovery brings losses, more changes we struggle to accept.[4] When an addicted spouse gets sober, things change. Patterns of relating change. Although these are good changes, they're still losses—losses of things that may not have been desirable but may have become oddly comfortable. These patterns became a fact of our present circumstances. At least we knew what to expect, even if that meant not expecting anything.

The losses many of us face and accept are enormous, often on-going, and caused by the people we care about. Although the problems are a direct result of an illness, condition, or compulsive disorder, they may feel like deliberate and malicious acts. We are suffering at the hands of those we loved and trusted.

We are continually off balance, struggling to accept changes and problems. We don't know what to expect, nor do we know when to expect it. Our present circumstances are always in a state of flux. We may experience loss or change in many areas. We feel crazy; our kids are upset; our partner is acting crazy; the bills are piling up; nobody has worked for weeks; the house is a mess; and the money has dwindled. The losses may come barreling down all at once, or they may occur gradually. Things then may stabilize briefly, until once more we lose the car, job, home, money, and relationships with the people we care about. We dared to have hope, only to have our dreams smashed again. It doesn't matter that our hopes were based on wishful thinking that the problem would magically go away. Crushed hopes are crushed hopes. Disappointments are disappointments. Lost dreams are dead dreams, and they all bring pain.

Accept reality? Half the time we don't even know what reality is. We're lied to; we lie to ourselves; and our heads are spinning. The rest of the time, facing reality is simply more than we can bear, more than anyone can bear. Why should it be so mysterious that denial is an integral part of addiction or any serious problem that causes ongoing losses? We have too much to accept; our present circumstances are overwhelming. Eventually, though, we must come to terms with *what is* if we ever want things to change. If things are ever to be any different, we must accept reality. If we are ever to replace our lost dreams with new dreams and feel sane and peaceful again, we must accept reality.

Acceptance doesn't mean adaptation. It doesn't mean resignation to the sorry and miserable way things are. It doesn't mean accepting or tolerating any sort of abuse. It means, for the present moment, we acknowledge and accept our circumstances, including ourselves and the people in our lives, as we and they are. It is only from that state that we have the peace and the ability to evaluate these circumstances, make appropriate changes, and solve our problems.

A person who is being abused will not make the decisions necessary to stop that abuse until they acknowledge the abuse. The person must then stop pretending the abuse will somehow magically end and stop making excuses for its existence. In a state of acceptance we are able to respond responsibly to our environment. In this state we receive the power to change the things we can. Alcoholics cannot quit drinking until they accept their powerlessness over alcohol and their alcoholism. Hoarders can't stop hoarding, overeaters can't stop eating, no one with a compulsive disorder can stop doing whatever they feel compelled to do until they accept their powerlessness. Codependents cannot change until we accept our codependent characteristics—our powerlessness over the people and circumstances we have so desperately tried to control. Acceptance is the ultimate paradox: *we cannot change who we are until we accept ourselves the way we are.*

Here's an excerpt from *Honoring the Self* on self-acceptance:

> If I can accept that I am who I am, that I feel what I feel, that I have done what I have done—if I can accept it whether I like all of it or not—then I can accept myself. I

can accept my shortcomings, my self-doubts, my poor self-esteem. And when I can accept all that, I have put myself on the side of reality rather than attempting to fight reality. I am no longer twisting my consciousness in knots to maintain delusions about my present condition. And so I clear the road for the first steps of strengthening my self-esteem. . . .

So long as we cannot accept the fact of what we are at any given moment of our existence, so long as we cannot permit ourselves fully to be aware of the nature of our choices and actions, cannot admit the truth into our consciousness, we cannot change.[5]

Acceptance isn't forever. It's for the present moment. But it must be sincere and gut level.

How do we achieve this peaceful state? How do we stare at reality without blinking or covering our eyes? How do we accept all the losses, changes, and problems that life and people hurl at us?

Not without a little kicking and screaming. We accept things through a five-step process. Elisabeth Kübler-Ross first identified the stages and this process as the way dying people accept the ultimate loss of their lives.[6] She called it the grief process. Since then, mental health professionals have observed people go through these stages whenever they face any loss. The loss could be minor—a five-dollar bill, not receiving an expected letter—or it could be significant, such as the loss of a loved one or the loss of a job. Even positive change brings loss (e.g., when we buy a new house and leave the old one) and requires a progression through the following Five Stages of Grief™.[7]

1. DENIAL

The first stage is a state of shock, numbness, panic, and general refusal to accept or acknowledge reality. We do everything and anything to put things back in place or pretend the situation isn't happening. There is much anxiety and fear in this stage. Reactions typical of denial include: refusing to believe reality ("No, this can't be!"); denying or minimizing the importance of the loss ("It's no big deal"); denying any feelings about the loss ("I don't care"); or mental avoidance (sleeping, obsessing, compulsive behaviors, and keeping busy).[8] We may feel somewhat detached from ourselves, and our emotional responses may be flat, nonexistent, or inappropriate (laughing when we should be crying; crying when we should be happy).

I'm convinced we do most of our codependent behaviors in this denial stage—obsessing, controlling, repressing feelings. Many of our feelings of "craziness" are connected to this state. We feel crazy because we're lying to ourselves. We feel crazy because we are believing other people's lies. Nothing will help us feel crazy faster than being lied to. Believing lies disrupts the core of our being. The deep, instinctive part of us knows the truth, but we're pushing that part away and telling it, "You're wrong. Shut up." According to counselor Scott Egleston, we then decide there's something fundamentally wrong with us for being suspicious, and we label ourselves and our innermost, intuitive beings as untrustworthy.

We're not denying whatever we're denying because we're stupid, stubborn, or deficient. We're not even consciously lying to ourselves. "Denial isn't lying," Noel Larsen, a licensed consulting psychologist, explained. "It's not letting yourself know what reality is."

Denial is the bugaboo of life. We aren't aware that we're in denial until we come out of it. It's like sleeping; we're not aware that we were sleeping until we wake up. On some level, we really believe the lies we tell ourselves. There is a reason for that too.

"Denial is the earliest psychological defense to develop," Claudia Jewett Jarratt explains in *Helping Children Cope with Separation and Loss*. "Conscious or unconscious, it is a mechanism that helps us prevent, avoid, or reduce anxiety when we feel threatened. Much the same way we may feel little pain after a severe physical injury, in times of great stress, this built-in mechanism may allow us to shut down our emotional awareness and screen out potentially overwhelming or devastating information."[9]

Denial is the shock absorber for the soul. It's an instinctive and natural reaction to pain, loss, and change. It protects us. It wards off the blows of life until we can gather our other coping resources.

2. ANGER

When we're done denying our losses, we move into the next stage: anger. Our anger may be reasonable or unreasonable. We may be justified in venting our wrath, or we may irrationally vent our fury on anything and anyone. We may blame ourselves, the universe, and everyone around us for what we have lost. Depending on the nature of the loss, we may be a little peeved, somewhat angry, downright furious, or caught in the grips of a soul-shaking rage.

This is why setting someone straight, showing someone the light, or confronting a serious problem often doesn't turn out the way we expect. If someone is in denial, they won't move directly into acceptance of reality—chances are good they'll move into anger. That's why we need to be careful about major confrontations.

"The vocation of putting people straight, of tearing off their masks, of forcing them to face the repressed truth, is a highly dangerous and destructive calling," John Powell writes in *Why Am I Afraid to Tell You Who I Am?*[10] "He cannot live with some realization. In one way or another, he keeps his psychological pieces intact by some form of self-deception.... If the psychological pieces come unglued, who will pick them up and put poor Humpty Dumpty Human Being together again?"[11]

I've witnessed frightening and violent acts when people finally face a long-denied truth. If we are planning an intervention, seek professional help.

3. BARGAINING

After we've calmed down, we attempt to strike a bargain with life, ourselves, other people, or the universe. If we do such and such or if someone else does this or that, then we won't have to suffer the loss. We're not attempting to postpone the inevitable; we're attempting to prevent it. Sometimes the deals we negotiate are reasonable and productive: "If my spouse and I get counseling, then we won't have to lose our relationship." Sometimes our bargains are absurd: "I used to think if I just worked harder, did everything better, then my husband wouldn't drink anymore," the wife of an alcoholic recalled.

4. DEPRESSION

When we see that our bargains didn't work, when we finally become exhausted from our struggle to ward off reality, and when we decide to acknowledge what life has thrown at us, we become sad, sometimes terribly depressed. This is the essence of grief—mourning at its fullest. This is what we've been attempting at all costs to avoid. This is the time to cry, and it hurts.

5. ACCEPTANCE

This is it. After we've closed our eyes, kicked, screamed, negotiated, and finally felt the pain, we arrive at a state of acceptance.
Elisabeth Kübler-Ross writes:

> It is not a resigned and hopeless "giving up," a sense of "what's the use" or "I just cannot fight it any longer," though we hear such statements too. (They also indicate the beginning of the end of the struggle, but the latter are not indications of acceptance.)
>
> Acceptance should not be mistaken for a happy stage. It is almost void of feelings. It is as if the pain had gone, the struggle is over.[12]

We are at peace with what is. We're free to stay; free to go on; free to make whatever decisions we need to make. Free! We've accepted our loss, however minor or significant. It has become an acceptable part of our present circumstances. We're comfortable with it and with our lives. We've adjusted and reorganized. Once more, we are comfortable with our present circumstances and ourselves.

What's more, we're not only comfortable with our circumstances and the changes we have endured, but also assured that we have in some way benefited from the loss or change, even if we can't fully understand how or why. We have faith that all is well, and we have grown from our experience. We deeply believe our present circumstances—every detail of them—are exactly as they ought to be for the moment. Despite our fears, feelings, struggles, and confusion, we understand everything is okay even if we lack insight. We accept what is. We settle down. We stop running, ducking, controlling, and hiding. And we know it is only from this point that we can move forward.

This is how people accept things. Counselor Esther Olson, besides calling it the grief process, calls it the forgiveness process, the healing process. It isn't particularly comfortable. In fact, it's awkward and often painful. We may feel like we're falling apart. When the process begins, we usually feel shock and panic. As we go through the stages, we often feel confused, vulnerable, lonely, and isolated.

We will probably go through this process for anything that is a fact in our lives that we have not accepted. A codependent person or a chemically dependent person may be in many stages of the grief process for several losses, all during the same time. Denial, depression, bargaining, and anger may all come rushing in. We may not know what we're trying to accept. We may not even know we're struggling to accept a situation. We may simply feel like we've gone crazy. We haven't.

Grief isn't a tidy process. The five stages are fluid and don't unfold precisely as outlined. They may take place in thirty seconds for a minor loss; the process may last years or a lifetime when the loss is significant. We may travel back and forth: from anger to denial, from denial to bargaining, from bargaining back to denial. Regardless of the speed and route we travel through these stages, we must travel through them. It's not only a normal process but also a necessary process, and each stage is necessary too: We ward off the blows of life with denial until we're better prepared to deal with them. We feel anger and blame until we've gotten that out of our system. We try to negotiate; we cry. Each of us will spend as much time as we need in each stage. To quote a popular paraphrase of Robert Frost's poem "A Servant to Servants," the only way out is through.

We are sturdy beings. But in many ways, we are fragile. We can accept change and loss, but this comes at our own pace and in our own way. And only we and our souls can determine that timing.

"Healthy are those who mourn," Donald L. Anderson, a minister and psychologist, explains in *Better than Blessed*. He writes:

> Only very recently have we begun to realize that to deny grief is to deny a natural human function and that such denial sometimes produces dire consequences. Grief, like any genuine emotion, is accompanied by certain physical changes and the release of a form of psychic energy. If that energy is not expended in the normal process of grieving, it becomes destructive within the person. . . . Even physical illness can be a penalty for unresolved grief. . . . Any event, any awareness that contains a sense of loss for you can, and should, be mourned. This doesn't mean a life of incessant sadness. It means being willing to admit to an honest feeling rather than always having to laugh

off the pain. It's not only permissible to admit the sadness that accompanies any loss—it's the healthy option.[13]

It can be a draining, exhausting process. Be gentle with yourself. It can deplete your energy and throw you off balance. Watch how you pass through the stages and feel what you need to feel. Talk to people who are safe and will provide the comfort, support, and understanding you need. Talk it out; talk it through. One thing that helps me is being grateful for my present circumstances—regardless of how I feel or what I think about them. Another thing that helps many people is the Serenity Prayer. Understanding the way we deal with loss helps us be more supportive to other people, and it gives us the power to decide how we will behave and take care of ourselves when we go through it.

Make friends with the grief process. Give yourself and others the space to go through messy feelings for all losses, large or small. Learn the art of acceptance.

··· ACTIVITY ···

1. Are you or is someone in your life grieving a major loss? Which stage do you think you or that person is in?

2. Review your life and consider the major losses and changes you have gone through. Recall your experiences with the grief process. Write about your feelings as you remember them.

3. Observe yourself and others when going through even a minor loss. Watch how you, your loved ones, friends, and even co-workers accept losses and sudden changes in their lives.

13

Feel Your Own Feelings

So I keep it inside myself, and each time . . . my stomach keeps score.

—JOHN POWELL, *Why Am I Afraid to Tell You Who I Am?*

I used to facilitate groups to help people deal with their feelings," the wife of an alcoholic said. "I used to openly express my emotions. Now, after eight years in this relationship, I couldn't tell you what I was feeling if my life depended on it."

As codependents, we frequently lose touch with the emotional part of ourselves. Sometimes we withdraw emotionally to avoid being crushed. Being emotionally vulnerable is dangerous when hurt becomes piled on hurt and no one seems to care or notice. It becomes safer to go away. We become overloaded with pain, so we short-circuit to protect ourselves.

We may withdraw emotionally from certain people—people we think may hurt us. We don't trust them, so we hide the emotional part of us when we're around them.

Sometimes we feel forced to withdraw our emotions. Deeply dysfunctional family systems reject emotional honesty and even, at times, seem to demand dishonesty. Consider our attempts to tell a drunk how we *felt* about them smashing up the car, ruining the birthday party, or throwing up in the bed. Our feelings may provoke unpleasant reactions in others, such as anger. Expressing our feelings may even be dangerous to our physical well-being because they rock the family boat.

Even families that have no history of substance abuse reject feelings. "Don't feel that way. That feeling is inappropriate. In fact, don't even feel," may be the message we hear. We quickly learn the lie that our feelings don't count, that our feelings are somehow wrong. Our feelings are not listened to, so *we* quit listening to them too.

It may appear easier, at times, not to feel. We have taken on so much responsibility for the people around us. Why take the time to feel? What would it change?

Sometimes we try to make our feelings disappear because we're afraid of them. To acknowledge how we really feel would demand a decision—action or change—on our part.[1] It would bring us face-to-face with reality. We would become aware of what we're thinking, what we want, and what we need to do. And we're not ready to do that yet.

Codependents are often oppressed, depressed, and repressed. Many of us can quickly tell what someone else is feeling, why that person is feeling that way, how long they've felt that way, and what that person is probably going to do because of that feeling. Many of us spend our lives fussing about other people's feelings. We try to fix people's feelings. We try to control other people's feelings. We don't want to hurt people, we don't want to upset them, and we don't want to offend them. We feel so responsible for other people's feelings, yet we don't know what we ourselves are feeling. If we do, we don't know what to do to fix ourselves. Many of us have abandoned or never taken responsibility for our emotional selves.

Just how important are feelings, anyway? Before I answer that question, let me tell you about when I was in treatment for chemical dependency at Willmar State Hospital in Minnesota. The year was 1973. I was twenty-three then, faced with kicking a ten-year habit of alcohol, heroin, Dilaudid, morphine, methadone, cocaine, barbiturates, amphetamines, marijuana, and any other substance that even remotely promised to change the way I felt. When I asked my counselor, Ruth Anderson, and other counselors how to do this, they replied: "Deal with your feelings." (They also suggested I attend Alcoholics Anonymous. More on that later.) I did start "dealing" with my feelings, even though I wasn't entirely sure what that meant. All I knew was that it felt terrible. I had emotional explosions that I thought would rip the top of my head off. Once I began allowing my feelings to bubble up, they weren't all that polite about making an appearance. My only visitor during my eight-month treatment stay was my mother. Although I was under court order to successfully complete treatment or go to prison, she demanded that I come home with her. She wouldn't stop; she kept insisting with a vengeance. Spontaneously, without any thought involved, I blew up like a volcano. I told her she had to leave and not to come back. Twenty-three years of abuse and not being allowed to feel erupted, and the rage shook the walls of the building. It scared my mom, the counselors, and even Father Garvey, the priest on duty. It scared me.

But it worked. I experienced my first days and months of sobriety. "Dealing with feelings" felt forced, methodical, didactic, but I began to understand that *allowing* my feelings was a more harmonious, natural approach for me. It reminded me of the way that waves hit the shore. They rise, they crest, they recede. Allowing your feelings takes practice and mindfulness.

Then it came time to leave treatment. I was faced with the unlikely prospect of trying to fit myself into society. I had no résumé; it can be difficult for an addict to find and maintain gainful employment. I had to discontinue my relationships with everyone I knew who used chemicals, which was everyone I knew. My family was skeptical about my recovery and still understandably peeved about some of the things I had done. Generally, I had left a trail of destruction and chaos behind me, and I didn't think there was any place in society for me. My life stretched ahead of me, and it held little promise. At the same time, my counselor was telling me to go ahead and start living. Again, I asked her exactly how I should do that. Again, she and others replied: "Keep dealing with your feelings. Go to AA, and everything will be okay."

Almost fifty years later, allowing my feelings is still a daily practice. It's worked for me so far.

• • •

After a bit of time in the world, though, another problem reared up. Untreated codependency caught up with me. I was stunned. I'd naively thought that facing my addiction was the only problem of that magnitude I'd have to deal with in this lifetime. I had formed good substance abuse recovery habits. I had my meetings, my sponsor, and my Steps. But codependency took hold. Two years after I finished treatment, in 1975, I unknowingly married an alcoholic. New, unfelt feelings began accumulating. I began ignoring my feelings because they overwhelmed and confused me. I was about to learn once more how important unfelt feelings are. As I allowed and made friends with the emotional part of myself, I began my codependency recovery, my path to well-being.

Feelings shouldn't dictate or control our behaviors, but we can't ignore them either. They won't be ignored.

Our feelings count. They matter. The emotional part of us is special. If we make feelings go away, if we push them away, we lose an important part of us and our lives. Feelings are our source of joy as well as sadness, fear, and anger. The emotional part of us is the part that laughs as well as cries. The emotional part of us is the center for giving and receiving the warm glow of love. That part of us lets us feel close to people. That part of us lets us enjoy touch and other sensual feelings. It's not all pain.

Our feelings are also indicators. When we feel happy, comfortable, warm, and content, we usually know all is well in our world, for the present moment. When we feel uncomfortable with anger, fear, or sadness, our feelings are telling us there's a problem. The problem may be inside us—something we're doing or thinking—or it may be external. Those annoying feelings are indicators that we need to pay attention to something.

Feelings can be positive motivators too. Anger can motivate us to solve a bothersome problem. Fear encourages us to run from danger. Repeated hurt and emotional pain tell us to stay away.

Our feelings can also provide us with clues to ourselves: our desires, needs, and ambitions—the things that keep us moving forward in life. They help us discover ourselves, what we're *really* thinking, what we feel passionately about. Our emotions also tap into that deep part of us that seeks and knows truth and desires self-preservation, self-enhancement, safety, and goodness. Our emotions are connected to our conscious, cognitive thought process and to that mysterious gift called instinct or intuition.

There is, however, a darker side to emotions. Emotional pain hurts. It can hurt so badly that we think all we are or ever will be is our pain. Fear can stop us cold; it can prevent us from doing the things we want and need to do to live our lives fully.

Sometimes we can get stuck in emotions—trapped in a well of a certain dark feeling—and think we'll never get out. Anger can fester into resentment and bitterness and threaten to linger indefinitely. Sadness can turn into depression, smothering us. Some of us live with fear for long periods of time.

Our feelings can trick us too. Our emotions can lead us into situations where our heads tell us not to go. Sometimes feelings are like cotton candy; they appear to be more than they actually are.

In spite of the darker side of emotions—the painful ones, the ones that linger, and the tricky ones—there is an even bleaker picture if we choose to become unemotional. Not feeling our feelings, withdrawing emotionally, and pushing that part of us away can be unpleasant, unhealthy, and self-destructive.

Repressing or denying feelings can lead to headaches, stomach disorders, backaches, and generally weakened physical conditions, which can open the door to many illnesses. Repressing feelings—particularly if we're doing it during the denial stage of the grief process—can lead us into trouble with eating disorders, substance abuse, sexual behaviors, out-of-control spending, sleeping disorders, obsessing, controlling, and other compulsive behaviors.

Feelings are energy. Repressed feelings block energy. We don't do our best when we're blocked.

Another problem with repressed feelings is they don't go away. They linger, sometimes growing stronger and causing us to do many peculiar things. We have to stay one step ahead of the feelings, we have to stay busy, we have to do *something*. We don't dare get quiet and peaceful because we might then feel these emotions. And the feelings might squeak out anyway, causing us to do things we never intended to do: scream at the kids, kick the cat, make a mess, or cry in public. We get stuck in feelings because we're trying to repress them, and like a persistent neighbor, they don't go away until we acknowledge their presence.

A compelling reason for not repressing feelings is that emotional withdrawal causes us to lose the ability to feel. Sometimes, this may be a welcome relief if the pain becomes too great or too constant, but this is not a good plan for living. And in extreme cases can lead to disassociation, another handy survival tool. We may shut down our deep needs—our need to love and be loved—when we shut down our emotions. We may lose our ability to enjoy human touch. We lose the ability to feel close to people—intimacy. We lose our capacity to enjoy the pleasant things in life.

No longer in touch with our instincts, we lose touch with ourselves and our environment. We become unaware of what our feelings are telling us and fail to detect problems in our environment. We lose the motivating power of feelings. If we aren't feeling, we're probably not examining the thinking that goes with those feelings, and we don't know what our bodies are trying to tell us. And if we don't *allow* our feelings we don't change, we don't grow. We stay stuck.

Feelings might not always be a barrel of endless joy, but repressing them can be downright miserable. So what's the solution? What do we do with these pesky feelings that seem to be both a burden and a delight?

We feel them. We *can* allow our emotions—all of them. Feelings aren't wrong. They're not inappropriate. We don't need to feel guilty about feelings. Feelings aren't actions; feeling homicidal rage is entirely different from committing homicide. Feelings shouldn't be judged as either good or bad. Feelings are emotional energy, not personality traits. (But they can become personality traits if we keep denying them.)

People say there are hundreds of different feelings, ranging from peeved to miffed to exuberant to delighted and so on. Some therapists have cut the list to four: anger, sadness, joy, and fear. These are the four primary feeling groups, and all the rest are shades and variations. For instance, lonely and depressed would fall in the sadness category; anxiety and nervousness would be variations of fear; love, closeness, and happiness qualify as joy. You can call them whatever you want; the important idea is to feel them.

That doesn't mean we have to always be on guard for a feeling. It doesn't mean we have to devote an extraordinary amount of our lives to wallowing in emotional muck. In fact, dealing with our feelings will move us out of the muck. Feeling our feelings simply means if a feeling—emotional energy—comes our way, we feel it. We take a few moments, acknowledge the sensation, and move on to the next step. We don't censor. We don't block. We don't run from. We don't tell ourselves, *Don't feel that. Something must be wrong with me.* We don't pass judgment on ourselves for our feelings. We experience them mindfully, consciously. We allow the energy to pass through our bodies, and we accept it as being our emotional energy, our feelings. We say, "Okay."

Next, we do that mystical thing so many people refer to as "dealing with our feelings." We appropriately respond to our emotions. We examine the thoughts that go with them, and we accept them without repression or censorship.[2]

Then, we decide whether there's a next step. This is where we do our judging. This is where our moral code comes into play. We still don't judge ourselves for having feelings. We decide what, if anything, we want to do about them. We evaluate a situation, then choose a behavior in line with our moral code and our new ideal of self-care. Is there a problem we need to solve? Is our thinking off base? Many therapies acknowledge a direct correlation between what we think and what we feel. Sometimes inaccurate, overreactive, or inappropriate thought patterns trigger our emotions or cause them to persist longer than necessary. Is the problem something we can solve? Does it concern another person? Is it necessary or appropriate to discuss the feeling with that person? Perhaps it's sufficient to merely feel the emotion and acknowledge the thought. If you're in doubt about what action to take, if the feeling is particularly strong, or if the action you decide to take is radical, pause until you're peaceful. Let the path ahead become clear. In other words: detach.

Our feelings don't need to control us. Just because we're angry, we don't have to scream and hit. Just because we're sad or depressed, we don't have to lie in bed all day. Feeling scared doesn't mean we don't apply for that job. I'm not in any way implying or suggesting that we allow emotions to control our behaviors. In fact, what I'm saying is the opposite: if we don't feel our feelings and deal with them responsibly, they *will* control us. If we're dealing with our emotions responsibly, we submit them to intellect, reason, and a moral and behavioral code of ethics.[3]

Responding appropriately to our feelings also means we're liable for our feelings. Each person's feelings are their own. Nobody makes anyone feel; no one is ultimately responsible for our feelings except us, *no matter how much we insist they are.* People might help us feel—or trigger feelings in us—but they don't *make* us feel. People also cannot change the way we feel. Only we can do that. Furthermore, we are not responsible for anyone else's feelings, although we are responsible for choosing to be considerate of people's feelings. Responsible people choose to do that. However, many of us choose to overdo that. We need to consider our own feelings too.

There are times when we may need to discuss our feelings and thoughts with other people. It's not healthy to live in isolation. Sharing the emotional part of us with others creates genuine closeness and intimacy (as opposed to the superficial intimacy and false sense of friendship often on display in social media). Also, being accepted by someone else for being who we are helps us accept ourselves. This is always a marvelous experience. Sometimes, we may want to discuss things with a friend who'll just listen while we try to figure ourselves out. Things we lock inside can get too big and powerful. Letting them out in the air makes them smaller. We gain perspective. It's always fun to share the pleasant feelings too: the joys, the successes, the gladness. And if we want an intimate relationship, we need to discuss any persistent feelings with that person. It's called emotional honesty.

Caution: intense happy feelings can be as distracting and scary as intense sad feelings, especially to people unused to experiencing happiness. Any extreme emotion can pull us off-center, whether it's joy, excitement, or profound sadness. Let the emotional energy pass through, and strive for the middle road of peace and balance.

There are times when we may need professional help to deal with our emotions. If we're stuck in any particular feeling, we should give ourselves what we need. Seek out a counselor, a therapist, or a helping professional, one that feels right to you. (It helps if you get references.)

Sometimes, awakening the emotional part of us just takes a little practice and awareness. The following activities help me get in touch with my feelings: physical exercise, writing in a journal, talking to people I feel safe with, and meditation. We need to make self-awareness and mindfulness a habit. We need to pay attention to the "shouldn't feel that way" attitudes we tell ourselves; we need to listen to what we're thinking and saying and the tone of voice we use; we need to keep an eye on what we're doing. We will find our way to and through our emotions, a way that works for us.

Invite emotions into your life. Then make a commitment to take gentle, loving care of them. Feel your feelings. Trust your feelings; trust yourself. You are wiser than you think.

··· ACTIVITY ···

1. Read through your writings from activities in previous chapters. What emotions were squeaking or pouring out as you wrote?

2. Read through some of your posts on social media. What emotions do you think were driving those posts? Did the posts reflect what you were really feeling—your higher self?

3. Let's play a what-if game. What if you could be feeling anything you wanted right now. How do you want to feel? Happy? At peace? Trusting the flow of life? Or anxious, worried, and trying to control everything? Getting what we want isn't going to magically change our feelings. It's our job to change how we feel. So let's imagine what we might be feeling when we have our life put back together and try to incorporate some of those feelings into our lives right now. Write about how you imagine you're going to feel when you get what you want. Lean into that feeling now.

4. Find someone who is safe, a good listener, nonjudgmental, and nonrescuing, and begin honestly and openly discussing your feelings with them. Listen to their feelings without judgment or the impulse to caretake. It's nice, isn't it? If you don't know anybody you feel safe doing that with, join a support group specific to your current challenge or call 1-800-950-NAMI (6264). An Al-Anon meeting can also provide a safe space to express yourself. A list of additional resources is available in the back of this book.

14

Anger

"What is it about me that you hate so much?" a man asked his wife six months into his sobriety. "Everything," she replied.

—ANONYMOUS

For many years I rarely felt anger. I cried. I felt hurt. But anger? No, not me.

After I began my recovery from codependency, I wondered if I would ever *not* be angry.

Janet Woititz describes what I was feeling in this passage from *Marriage on the Rocks*: "You become rigid and distrustful. Rage consumes you without a satisfying outlet. Anyone who walks into your house can feel the angry vibrations. There is no escape from it. Whoever thought you would turn into such a self-righteous witch?"[1]

Angry feelings are part of almost everyone's life. Children feel anger; teenagers feel anger; adults feel anger. For some, anger plays a relatively small part in our lives and presents no particular problem. We blow off steam, and we're done with it. Maybe the problem gets resolved and we go on with the business of living.

That's usually not the case with codependents. Anger can become a large part of our story. It can *become* our story. The person we're involved with is mad, we're mad, the kids are mad, and so is the dog. Everyone is mad all the time. Nobody ever seems to blow off enough steam. Even if we aren't shouting, even if we're trying to pretend we're not angry, we are. Hostility lurks just below the surface, waiting for a chance to come out in the open. The anger sometimes explodes like a bomb, but it's not over. The other person says, "How dare you become angry with me? I'll get angry with you, but not the other way around." The codependent says, "After all I've done for you, I'll get angry whenever I please." But silently, we wonder: *Maybe they're right. How dare I get angry. There must be something wrong with me for feeling this way.* We deal another blow to our self-worth with a little guilt tacked on. Plus, the anger is still there. The problems don't get resolved; the anger festers and boils.

Even with the gift of recovery, the anger may linger—and usually does.[2] It may have reached its peak by the time the troubled person gets help. Nobody, including this person, can stand the insanity any longer. But once we're out of survival mode, we realize how angry we are. We may even feel new anger for having believed for so long that this mess was our fault! It may be the first time we have felt safe expressing anger. This can cause more conflicts. The person recovering from addiction may expect and want to start fresh—minus the dirty laundry from the past—now that they have begun a new life.

So they say, "How dare you get angry now? We're starting over." And we reply, "That's what *you* think. I'm just getting started."

Then we may add to our low self-worth and guilt another silent, torturing thought: *They're right. I should be ecstatic. I should be grateful.* But the resentment doesn't just disappear.

Then everyone feels guilty because everyone feels angry. Then everyone feels cheated and mad because sobriety didn't bring the happiness it promised. It wasn't the turning point for living happily ever after—nothing is. Don't misunderstand. It's definitely better. It's a lot better when people become sober. But sobriety isn't a magical cure for all the codependency that preceded it. The old anger burns away. New anger fuels the fire. The addict can no longer medicate their anger. Codependents can no longer get the sympathy and nurturing we need from friends. After all, it's wonderful that the alcoholic has quit drinking and the problem has been "solved." *What's wrong with us?* we ask. *Can't we forgive and forget?*

Anger may be a commonplace emotion, but it's tough to deal with. Most of us haven't been taught how to deal with anger because people show—rather than teach—us how they deal with anger. And most people show us inappropriate ways to deal with anger because they're not sure either.

People may give good advice. "Don't go to bed angry."[3] "Don't seek revenge." "Don't harbor resentments." Many of us can't adhere to these mandates. Some of us think they mean "Don't feel anger." Many of us aren't sure what we believe about anger. Some of us believe lies.

Frequently, we believe the following myths about anger:

- It's not okay to feel angry.

- Anger is a waste of time and energy.

- Nice people don't get angry.

- If we allow ourselves to feel our anger, we'll lose control of ourselves.

- People will leave if we get angry with them.

- People will leave if they get angry with us.

- If people get angry with us, we must have done something wrong.

- If people are angry with us, we made them feel that way, and we're responsible for fixing their feelings.

- If someone made us angry, they're responsible for fixing our feelings.

- If we feel angry with someone, the relationship is over, and that person has to leave.

- If we feel angry with someone, we should punish them for making us feel angry.

- If we feel angry with someone, they have to change what they're doing so we don't feel angry anymore.

- If we feel angry, we have to hit someone or break something.

- If we feel angry, we have to shout and holler.

- If we feel angry with someone, it means we don't love them anymore.

- If someone feels angry with us, it means they don't love us anymore.

- Anger is a sinful emotion.

- It's okay to feel anger (or any other emotion) only when we can *justify* our feelings.[4]

Many people in recovery programs such as AA believe they should never feel angry in recovery because one of the goals of recovery is to avoid walking around filled with resentment. The idea is to learn to deal with anger appropriately and immediately *before* it turns into hardened resentment.

As codependents, we may be frightened of our anger and other people's anger. Maybe we believe one or more of the myths just listed. Or maybe we're frightened of anger for other reasons. Someone may have abused us when they were angry. Some of us may have abused someone else when we felt angry. Sometimes the raw level of energy that accompanies someone's anger can be frightening, particularly if that person is intoxicated or bigger than we are.

We react to anger, both ours and other people's. Anger proliferates on social media. It's a provocative emotion. It can be contagious. And many of us have a lot of it to react to. We have collective anger on many issues. We have anger that accompanies grief. We have anger that comes from rescuing or caretaking. (Many of us are stuck on that corner of the triangle.) We have anger that may be caused by reactive, disastrous thinking: the shoulds, nevers, and alwayses. We have justifiable anger—the things anyone would feel if someone did that to them. And most of it is repressed, just waiting to burst forth.

We may turn fear and hurt into anger to feel less vulnerable and more powerful. We may puff ourselves up with anger to feel stronger or bluff our way out of a tense or scary situation, but we can't run away from our truth forever. We need to set clear boundaries, but we can't fake our way into a boundary; threats and coercions aren't setting boundaries.

Guilt, both earned and unearned, easily converts into anger.[5] Codependents have a lot of both. So do addicts. They're just more adept at converting guilt into anger.

We have reactive anger. We get angry because the other person is angry. Then they get angrier, and we get angrier because they got angrier. Soon everybody is really angry, and no one's sure why. (This is a common feature of both social media and severely dysfunctional families.)

Sometimes, we prefer to stay angry. It helps us feel less vulnerable and more powerful. It's a protective shield. If we're angry, we won't feel hurt or scared, at least not noticeably so.

Many of us have been in a quagmire with our anger, especially if we're living in a family system that says, "Don't feel; especially don't feel angry." The substance abuser certainly doesn't want to hear about how angry we feel. They probably think our anger is unreasonable anyway, and it may bother them when we discuss it. Our anger may push the substance abuser's guilt buttons. They may even overpower us with their anger just to keep us off balance— and then we feel guilty when we react.

Sadly, many of us have had no place to go with all that anger. We swallow it, bite our tongues, stiffen our shoulders, push it into our stomachs, let it rattle around in our heads, run from it, medicate it, or give it a cookie. We become passive aggressive. When people ask us what's wrong, we tighten our jaws and say, "Nothing. I'm fine, thank you." We blame ourselves, turn anger into depression, put ourselves to bed, hope to die, and get sick because of it.

Unpleasant feelings are like weeds. They don't go away when we ignore them; they grow wild and take over. Our angry feelings may one day come roaring out. We may say things we don't mean. Or, as usually happens, we may say what we really mean. We may lose control and unleash ourselves in a fighting, spitting, screeching, hair-pulling, dish-breaking rage. Or the anger may harden into bitterness, hatred, contempt, revulsion, or resentment. We may develop a repertoire of self-harming behaviors to give us a sense of control over our uncontrollable feelings.

Like the book title says, *Of Course You're Angry!*[6] We're that angry because anybody in their right mind would be that angry.

An excellent quote from *Marriage on the Rocks* follows:

> You cannot live with active alcoholism without being profoundly affected. Any human being who is bombarded with what you've been bombarded with is to be commended for sheer survival. You deserve a medal for the mere fact that you're around to tell the story.[7]

Anger is one profound effect of alcoholism. It is also an effect of many of the other compulsive disorders or problems codependents find themselves living with. Even if we're not living with a serious problem or a seriously ill person, it's still okay to feel angry when that's how we feel.

"I don't trust people who never get mad. People either get mad or get even," my friend Sharon George, who is a professional in the mental health field, said.

We have every right to feel anger. We have every right to feel as angry as we feel. So do other people. But we also have a responsibility—primarily to ourselves—to deal with our anger appropriately.

We're back to our original advice: deal with our feelings. Allow our feelings.

How do we allow an emotion as potent as anger? How do we quit feeling that angry? When does it happen? Where does it go? Who can we talk to? Who would want to listen to all that? We probably don't even want to hear our anger expressed. After all, the person we're mad at has a disease. So shouldn't we be feeling compassion? Is it really okay to be this mad at a sick person?

Yes, we have the right to be mad at a sick person. Although compassion is the ideal, we probably won't arrive at compassion until we deal with our anger. Somewhere between homicidal rage and biting our tongues lies a way to get past our angry feelings— the old ones and the new ones. But dealing with repressed emotions won't happen overnight. It may not happen in a month or even a year. How long did it take us to get this angry? Dealing with a significant amount of repressed anger may take time and effort. Dealing with new anger takes practice.

Here are some suggestions for dealing with anger:

- *Address any myths you have subscribed to about anger.* Give yourself permission to feel angry when you need to. Give other people permission to feel angry too.

- *Feel the emotion.* Even though it's anger, it's only emotional energy. It's not right or wrong; it calls for no judgment. Anger doesn't have to be justified or rationalized. If the energy is there, feel it. Feel any underlying emotions too, such as hurt or fear.

- *Acknowledge the thoughts that accompany the feeling.* Preferably, say these thoughts aloud.

- *Examine the thinking that goes with the feeling.* Hold it up to the light. See if there are any flaws in it. Watch for patterns and repetitive situations. You'll learn much about yourself and your environment.

- *Make a responsible decision about what, if any, action you need to take.* Figure out what your anger is telling you. Is your anger indicating a problem in you or in your environment that needs attention? Do you need change? Do you need something from somebody else? Much anger comes from unmet needs. One quick way to resolve anger is to stop screaming at the person you're angry with, figure out what you need from them, and simply ask for that. If they won't or can't give it to you, figure out what you need to do next to take care of yourself.

- *Don't let anger control you.* If you find yourself being controlled by angry feelings, you can stop yourself. You don't have to continue screaming. Listen, sometimes screaming helps; sometimes, however, it doesn't. It's better if you decide instead of letting your anger decide for you. We don't have to lose control of ourselves. It's just energy, not a magical curse over us. Detach. Go to another room. Go to another house. Get peaceful. Then figure out what you need to do. You don't have to let other people's anger control you. I frequently hear codependents say, "I can't do this or that because they will get angry." Don't jeopardize your safety, but strive to be free from anger's control—your anger or anyone else's.

- *Openly and honestly discuss your anger when it's appropriate.* But don't talk to someone when they're drunk or high. You can make good decisions about expressing your anger openly and appropriately. Beware of how you approach people, though. Anger frequently begets anger. Instead of venting your rage on someone, you can feel your feelings, think your thoughts, figure out what you need from that person, and then go back to them and express that need.

- *Take responsibility for your anger.* We can say: "I feel angry when you do this because ..." not, "You made me mad." Or we can explain what action triggered us. Just understand that we are responsible for our angry feelings—even if they're an appropriate reaction to someone else's inappropriate behavior.

- *Talk to people you trust.* Talking about anger and being listened to and accepted really helps clear the air. It helps us accept ourselves. Remember, we can't move forward until we accept where we are. And yes, people care. We may have to reach out to find them, but they are out there. If you have angry feelings that have hardened into resentments, seek out someone to talk to—a helping professional or a support group. Resentments may be hurting you a lot more than they're helping.

- *Burn off the angry energy.* Walk. Run. Dance. Go to the gym. Do yoga. Shovel snow. Rake the yard. Walk the dog. Anger is extremely stressful, and it helps to physically discharge that energy.

- *Don't abuse others or let anyone abuse you.* Seek professional help if abuse has occurred.

- *Write letters you don't intend to send.* If you're feeling guilty about anger, this really helps. Start the letter with: "This is what I'm really angry about ..." Once your anger is out on paper, you can figure out how to deal with it.

- *Deal with guilt.* Get rid of the unearned guilt. Get rid of all of it. Guilt doesn't help. If you've done something inappropriate, address the guilt that's legitimately there, figure out what you did that you don't approve of, make any necessary amends, and move forward from there. Strive for progress.

Once you begin dealing with anger, you may notice that you feel angry much of the time. That's common. Be patient. You aren't going to deal with it perfectly. No one does. You'll make mistakes, but you'll also learn from them.

We need to be gentle with ourselves if we've been repressing loads of angry feelings. Things take time. We may need to be that angry for now. When we don't need to be angry anymore, we'll quit feeling angry. If you think you might be stuck in anger, seek professional help.

Some people believe if we control our thinking and are appropriately detached, we will never react with or wallow in anger. That's probably true; however, I prefer to relax and see what happens rather than guard myself rigidly. And like my friend, I'm leery of people who smile and tell me they never get mad. Don't misunderstand—I'm not advising us to hang on to anger or resentments, teach people lessons, or get even. I don't believe anger should become our focus in life, nor should we look for reasons to become angry to test ourselves. "It's not good to be angry all the time," counselor Esther Olson says. It's not healthy to act hostile.

But it's okay to feel anger when we need to.

··· ACTIVITY ···

1. What do you think would happen if you started allowing your anger? Imagine worst-case scenarios if you started expressing your anger. Imagine best-case scenarios. Then find the middle ground.

2. How have people dealt with their anger or taken their anger out on you? How did you handle that? What did it teach you about anger—and is that something you need to unlearn?

3. How does your family deal with anger? How did your mother, father, brothers, and sisters deal with their anger? Are you repeating family patterns? Write your answers in your journal.

4. If you have repressed anger, write about it in your journal. You may want to dedicate a notebook exclusively to anger.

5. If anger is a troublesome emotion for you, keep a pencil and paper handy and start writing about your anger as it occurs throughout the day. If social media is an anger trigger for you, pay attention and include it in your journal.

15

Yes, You Can Think

For God hath not given us the spirit of fear; but of
power, and of love, and of a sound mind.

—2 TIMOTHY 1:7, KING JAMES VERSION

W hat do *you* think I should do?" a client, who was in the
throes of codependency, once asked me. The woman
was facing a significant decision regarding her husband and children.

"What do *you* think?" I asked.

"You're asking *me*?" she asked. "It takes me fifteen minutes at the
grocery store to decide if I want to buy the $1.59 or the $1.63 bottle of bleach. I can't make the tiniest decision. How do you expect
me to make a big, important one like this?"

As codependents, many of us don't trust our minds. We understand the horror of indecision. The smallest choices, such as what
to order at the restaurant or which bottle of bleach to purchase, can
paralyze us. The significant decisions we face, such as how to solve
our problems, what to do with our lives, and who to live with, can

overwhelm us. Many of us simply give up and refuse to think about these things. Some of us allow other people or circumstances to make these choices for us.

This is a short chapter, but it's an important one. Throughout the book, I've been encouraging you to think about things, figure things out, decide what you need, decide what you want, and decide how to solve your problems. Some of you may be wondering if any of that's possible. The purpose of this chapter is to tell you that you can think, you can figure things out, and you can make good, healthy decisions.

For a variety of reasons, we may have lost faith in our ability to think and reason things out. Believing lies, lying to ourselves (denial), chaos, stress, low self-esteem, and a stomach full of repressed emotions may cloud our ability to think. We become confused. That doesn't mean we *can't* think.

Impulsively overreacting may impair our mental functioning. Decisiveness is hindered by worrying about what other people think, telling ourselves we have to be perfect, and telling ourselves to hurry. We falsely believe we can't afford to make the "wrong" choice, we'll never have another chance, and the whole world waits and rises on this particular decision. We don't have to do these things to ourselves.

Hating ourselves, telling ourselves we won't make good decisions, and then throwing in a batch of shoulds every time we try to make decisions doesn't help our thinking process either.

Not listening to our needs and wants cheats us out of the information we need to make good choices. Second-guessing and what-ifs certainly don't help. We're learning to love, trust, and listen to ourselves.

Maybe we've been using our minds inappropriately, to worry and obsess, and we're tired, abused, and filled with anxiety. We're also learning to stop these patterns.

Perhaps we lost faith in our ability to think because people have told us we can't think and make good decisions. Our parents may have directly or indirectly done this when we were children. They may have told us we were stupid. Or they may have made every decision for us. Maybe they criticized our choices. Or they could have confused us by denying or by refusing to acknowledge our ability to think when we pointed out problems in the home.

Maybe we had difficulties with subjects in school when we were young; instead of doing what we needed to do to solve the problem, we gave up and told ourselves we couldn't think and figure things out.

We may be living with people now who are telling us directly or indirectly that we can't think. Some of them may even be telling us we're crazy, but addicts do that to people they live with.

We *can* think. Our minds work well. We can figure things out. We can make decisions. We can figure out what we want and need to do and when it is time to act. And we can make choices that enhance our self-esteem.

We're even entitled to opinions. We can think appropriately and rationally. We have the power to evaluate ourselves and our thoughts, so we can correct our thinking when it becomes disastrous or irrational.

We can evaluate our behaviors. We can make decisions about what we need and want and when it's time to change course. We can figure out what our problems are and what we need to do to solve them. We can make little decisions and big decisions. We may feel frustrated when we try to make decisions or solve problems, but that's normal. Sometimes we need to become frustrated to make a breakthrough in our thinking. It's all part of the process; trust it.

Remember, decisions don't have to be made perfectly. We don't have to be perfect. We don't even have to be nearly perfect. We can just be who we are. We're not so fragile that we can't handle making mistakes.

We can even change our minds. Then change them again. Then again. People vacillate.[1] We're often in the midst of upsetting situations. We may go back and forth a lot; we may throw the other person out, then take them back. We may leave, then come back, then leave again. This is how we get to where we're going. It's okay. Let's take it one step further—it's normal and often necessary.

"But," some of you may object, "you don't know my mind. Sometimes I think terrible thoughts. Sometimes I have unspeakable fantasies." Many of us do, and it's normal, especially if we're living close to addiction. We may have attended the substance abuser's funeral one hundred times in our minds. Our thoughts are keys to our feelings. Our feelings are keys to our thoughts. We don't have to repress. We need to let the thoughts and feelings pass through, then figure out what we need to do to take care of ourselves.

The following suggestions may help you gain confidence in your power to think and reason:

- *Treat your mind to some peace.* Detach. Get calm. If you're facing a decision, big or small, get peaceful first, then decide. If you absolutely can't make a decision on a particular day, then it's obviously not time to make that decision. When it is time, you'll be able to do it. And do it well.

- *Ask your Higher Power to help you think.* Every morning, I ask for the right thought, word, or action. I ask my Higher Power to send inspiration and guidance. I ask for help in solving problems. I believe my Higher Power does help but also expects me to do my part and think. Some days go better than others.

- *Quit abusing your mind.* Worry and obsession constitute mental abuse. Stop doing those things.

- *Feed your mind.* Get the information you need about problems and decisions. Give your mind a reasonable amount of data, then let it sort through things. You will come up with good answers and solutions.

- *Feed your mind healthy thoughts.* Indulge in activities that uplift your thoughts and give you a positive charge. Listen to a guided meditation every morning. Read from an inspirational book. Find something that leaves you saying, "I can," instead of "I can't."

- *Stretch your mind.* Many of us become so concerned with our problems and other people's problems that we stop following the news, watching documentaries, reading books, and learning new things. Get interested in the world around you. Feed your curiosity. Take an online class in a subject that interests you. Learn something new.

- *Quit saying bad things about your mind.* Stop telling yourself things like, "I'm so stupid," "I can't make good decisions," or "I've never been good at figuring things out." It's just as easy to say good things about yourself as it is to say negative things. You'll probably start believing the positive things and, over time, find out they're true. Isn't that exciting?

- *Use your mind.* Make decisions. Formulate opinions. Express them. Create! Think things through, but don't worry and obsess. We don't have to let anyone make our decisions for us, unless we're wards of the state. And even if we are, we can still think and make some of our choices. Letting people make our decisions for us means we're getting rescued, which means we're feeling like victims. We're not victims. Furthermore, it's not our business to make decisions for other adults. We can take possession of our power to think. And we can let others be responsible for their thinking. We will gain more confidence in ourselves as we start feeling better and begin to make decisions, big and small. The people around us will grow as they are allowed to make choices and mistakes.

Trust your mind and your ability to think. Become comfortable with your mind.

••• ACTIVITY •••

1. Does someone make decisions for you? How do you feel about that?

2. Did someone important in your life tell you that you couldn't think and make good decisions? Do some writing about what they told you and how that affected you. Did you begin to discount your own ability to think, decide, and choose?

3. Begin doing one thing every day to feed your mind: memorize (or write) a poem, play Wordle, read one chapter in a book.

16

Set Your Intention

Be not afraid of life. Believe that life is worth living,
and your belief will help create the fact.

—WILLIAM JAMES, "IS LIFE WORTH LIVING?"

The most exciting idea I have discovered in my sobriety
and codependency recovery is the magic in setting
goals—becoming clear in our desires and intentions.
Things happen. Things change. *I* change. I accomplish important
projects. I meet new people. I find myself in interesting places. I
make it through difficult times with a minimum of chaos. Problems
get solved. My needs and wants get met. Dreams come true. Maybe
not every day, but on many days.

I am ecstatic about goal setting, and I hope I can transmit my
enthusiasm to you. There's nothing in the world like going where
we want to go, getting what we want, solving a problem, or doing
something we always wanted to do.

Many of us don't know this joy. It was new to me too. I spent
years of my life not thinking about what I wanted and needed,

where I wanted to go, and what I wanted to do. Life was to be endured. I didn't think I deserved good things. I didn't think most good things were within my reach. I wasn't that interested in my life, except as an appendage to other people. I didn't think about living my life; I was too focused on others. I was too busy reacting rather than acting.

I'm not suggesting that we can control all the events in our lives. We can't. We don't have the final say on much of anything. But I believe we can cooperate with goodness, our highest destiny. I believe we can plan, make requests, and start a process in motion.

"Desire, when harnessed, is *power*," David Schwartz writes in his bestseller *The Magic of Thinking Big*. Failure to follow desire, to do what you want to do most, paves the way to mediocrity. "Success requires heart and soul effort, and you can only put your heart and soul into something you really desire."[1]

Goals also give us direction and purpose. I don't get into my car, turn on the ignition, start driving, and hope I get someplace. I decide where I want to go or approximately where I would like to end up, then I steer the car in that direction. That's how I try to live my life too. Sometimes things happen, and for a variety of reasons I may not end up where I wanted to go. If I change my mind or problems beyond my control interfere, I find myself doing something other than what I had planned. Timing and exact circumstances may vary. That's okay. I usually end up someplace that's better for me. That's where acceptance, trust, faith, and letting go come in. But at least I'm not driving aimlessly through life. More of the things I want come to pass. I'm less worried about solving my problems because I've turned my problems into goals. And I'm starting to think about and consider what *I* want and need.

Goals are fun. They generate interest and enthusiasm in life. They make life interesting and, sometimes, exciting.

"Surrender to desire and gain energy, enthusiasm, mental zip, and even better health," Schwartz writes. "Energy increases, multiplies, when you set a desired goal and resolve to work toward that goal. Many people, millions of them, can find new energy by selecting a goal and giving all they've got to accomplish that goal. Goals cure boredom. Goals even cure many chronic ailments."[2]

There is magic in setting and writing down our intentions. It sets into motion powerful psychological, spiritual, and emotional forces. We become aware of and do the things we need to do to achieve and accomplish. Things come to us. Things begin to happen! The following is another excerpt from *The Magic of Thinking Big*:

> Let's probe a little deeper into the power of goals. When you surrender yourself to your desires, when you let yourself become obsessed with a goal, you receive the physical power, energy, and enthusiasm needed to accomplish your goal. But you receive something else, something equally valuable. You receive the "automatic instrumentation" needed to keep you going straight to your objective.
>
> The most amazing thing about a deeply entrenched goal is that it keeps you on course to reach your target. This isn't double-talk. What happens is this. When you surrender to your goal, the goal works itself into your subconscious mind. Your subconscious mind is always in balance. Your conscious mind is not, unless it is in tune with what your subconscious mind is thinking. Without full cooperation from the subconscious mind, a person is

hesitant, confused, indecisive. Now, with your goal absorbed into your subconscious mind you react the right
way automatically. The conscious mind is free for clear,
straight thinking.[3]

What are your goals? What do you want to happen in your life—
this week, this month, this year, for the next five years? What problems do you want solved? What material things would you like to
possess? What changes do you want to make in yourself? What
would you love to do for a career? What do you want to accomplish?

And—why do you want all these things? Consider the subconscious motivation for the goal. Make sure your intentions align
with your values when you set goals because your intentions will
manifest, too, as part of the vision. Also, beware: perfectionism,
negativity, or a desire to control may sabotage you. You may not
recognize the "dream" when it arrives because it doesn't perfectly
match the vision you had in your head.

Review the following important ideas around setting goals and
find a way that works for you:

- *Turn everything into a goal/intention.* If you have a problem,
  you can make its solution your goal. You don't have to know
  the solution. Your goal is solving the problem—finding the
  solution.

  - Do you want something? A new sweater, a new car, longer
    hair, tickets to a show?

  - Do you want to go someplace—Europe, South America,
    Asia?

  - Do you want a loving, healthy relationship?

- Is there something you've always wanted to do—go back to school, start running, work for a particular company?

- Do you want to change something about yourself—learn to say no, make a particular decision, resolve some anger?

- Do you want to improve your relationships with your children, certain friends, or relatives?

- Do you want to form new relationships, make a new friend, start dating again? Is it time to let go of old relationships that no longer serve us?

- Do you want to achieve acceptance of some particular person or incident, forgive someone? Do you want to quit worrying, stop contolling, heal from your codependency issues?

- We can successfully turn almost every aspect of our lives into a goal/intention. If it bothers you, make it a goal.

- *Increase awareness of what you want, need, and desire.* If you haven't allowed yourself to become aware of what you want, you may not recognize it when it comes along. This is an ongoing process that depends on your curiosity, your unique self, your emotions, your path through life, and your self-awareness. Learn to recognize and become comfortable with who you are and what drives you.

- *Omit the shoulds.* We have enough shoulds controlling our lives; we don't need them in our goals. Make it a goal to get rid of 75 percent of your shoulds.

- *Don't limit yourself.* Go for all of it: everything you want and need, all the problems you want solved, all your desires, and even some of your whims.

- *Write down your goals.* There is extraordinary power in committing your goals to paper rather than storing them loosely in your mind. It gives focus and organization to your goals. It makes them concrete, tangible.

- *Surrender your goals to a Higher Power.* Keep your goals close, but don't obsess about how, when, if, and what if. Once your goals are on paper, try to not control or force. Let go.

- *Do what you can, one day at a time.* Within the framework of each twenty-four-hour day, do what seems fitting and appropriate. Do what you're inspired to do. What your intuition suggests you do. Do what comes your way that needs to be done. Do it in peace; trust the process. If it's time to do something, you'll know. If it's time for something to happen, it will.

- *Set goals/intentions regularly and as needed.* I like to set intentions for each year at the beginning of that year. I also write down goals as they occur to me throughout the year. I use goals to get me through crisis times when I'm feeling shaky. Then, I write down all the things I want and need to accomplish on a daily, weekly, or monthly basis.

- *Check off the goals you reach.* Yes, you will start reaching your goals. You will achieve certain things that are important to you. When this happens, you can cross off that goal, congratulate yourself, and thank your Higher Power. You will gain confidence in yourself, in goal setting, and in the rhythm of life. You will see for yourself that good things do happen. You can trust the process in your life.

- *Strike a balance between achieving goals and identifying new ones.* We may never be without a list of problems that we need to turn into goals. We will probably never be without wants and needs. But this process of goal setting needs to include periods of rest in between so we don't become goal-oriented workaholics, enslaved to achievement. Develop faith in the ebb and flow and general goodness of life. Problems arise. Problems get solved. Wants and needs come into awareness. Wants and needs get met. Dreams are born. Dreams are reached. Things happen. Good things happen. Then, more problems arise. But it's all okay.

- *Be patient.* Trust in the universe's timing. Don't take an item off the list if it's still important to you just because you didn't achieve or receive something you thought you'd have by now. Sometimes my goals carry over for years. When I do my annual intention setting, I sometimes look at my list and think, *Oh, this problem will never get solved. It's been on my list for years.* Or, *This dream will never come true. It's the fourth year in a row I've written it down.* Or, *I'll never be able to change this character defect.* Not true. It just hasn't happened yet. Here's one of the best thoughts I've ever encountered on patience. It's an excerpt from Dennis Wholey's book on alcoholism, *The Courage to Change*: "I've started to realize that waiting is an art, that waiting achieves things. Waiting can be very, very powerful. Time is a valuable thing. If you can wait two years, you can sometimes achieve something that you could not achieve today, however hard you worked, however much money you threw up in the air, however many times you banged your head against the wall."[4]

Things happen when the time is right—when we're ready, when the universe is ready. Give up. Let go.

Set a goal now, today—in the activity section below. If you don't have any goals, make your first goal "getting some goals."

··· ACTIVITY ···

1. Write your intentions/goals on a sheet of paper. Try to think of at least ten items such as wants, problems to be solved, and changes in yourself. Write as many as come to mind.

2. Review the checklist of "codependency characteristics" in chapter 4. Make it a goal to change any of those characteristics that are problematic for you (especially those you scored with a number 2).

3. Remember, it's our business to set goals only for ourselves. Review your list and make sure there aren't goals on it that are meant for other people.

17

Communication

When you're doing what's right for you, it's okay to
say it once, simply, and then refuse to discuss anything
further.

—TOBY RICE DREWS, *Getting Them Sober*

Read through the following conversations. You may identify
with the dialogue, which appears in bold type, and the
italicized interpretations, which explain the codependents'
intentions and thought patterns.

• • •

Danielle is about to call Stacy on the phone. Danielle wants Stacy
to babysit Danielle's three children over the weekend, but she
doesn't intend to ask Stacy outright; she intends to manipulate her
into doing it. Pay attention to her techniques.

STACY: **Hello.**

DANIELLE *(mumbling)*: **Hi.** *(Sighs.) The sigh means, "Poor me. I'm just
so helpless. Ask me what's wrong. Rescue me."*

STACY *(pausing for a moment)*: **Oh, hi, Danielle. Glad you called. How're you doing?** *During the pause, Stacy thought, "Oh, no. Not her. God, what does she want this time?"*

DANIELLE *(sighing again)*: **I'm doing about the same as always. Problems, you know.** *What Danielle is really saying is: "C'mon. Ask me what's wrong."*

STACY *(pausing again)*: **What's the matter? You sound terrible.** *During the pause this time, Stacy thought, "I'm not going to ask her what's wrong. I won't get trapped. I refuse to ask her what's wrong." Upon thinking this, Stacy felt angry, then guilty (the rescue feelings), then went on to rescue Danielle by asking her what was wrong.*

DANIELLE: **Well, my husband just found out he's got to go out of town this weekend for work, and he's asked me to come. I would love to go with him. You know I never get to go anywhere. But I don't know who I'd get to watch the kids. I hated to say no, but I had to turn him down. He feels so bad. I hope he's not too upset with me.** *(Sighs.)* **Oh, well, that's just the way things go I guess.** *(Sighs again.) Danielle is laying it on thick. She wants Stacy to feel sorry for her, guilty, and sorry for her husband. Her words have been carefully chosen. Danielle, of course, told her husband she could go. She told her husband she was going to get Stacy to babysit.*

STACY *(pausing yet again)*: **Well, I suppose I could see if I could maybe help you out.** *During the pause this time, Stacy thought, "Oh, no. No, no, no. I hate watching her kids. She never watches mine. I don't want to. I won't. To hell with her for putting me in this spot all the time. But how could I say no? I should help people. Do unto others. And she needs me so much. God, I don't want her to get angry at me. Besides, if I don't help her out, who will? She leads such a pathetic life. But this is the last time. The last time ever." She felt anger, pity, guilt, saintliness, and then* *returned back to anger. Notice how Stacy demeaned Danielle by labeling her helpless; notice her grandiose feelings of responsibility (i.e., "I'm the only person in the world who can help her.") Also, notice how she worded her response. She was hoping Danielle would notice Stacy's lack of enthusiasm and rescue her by telling her to forget it.*

DANIELLE: **Would you really babysit? Thanks so much. You're the greatest. I never dreamed you'd actually do this for me.** *Danielle is thinking, "Aha! Got what I wanted."*

STACY: **No problem. Glad to help.** *Stacy is thinking, "I don't want to do this. Why does this always happen to me?"*

· · ·

In the next conversation Robert wants his wife, Sally, to text his boss and tell him Robert is too sick to work, too sick even to text. (Robert was out drinking until three o'clock the night before.) His alcoholism is causing increasing problems at home and on the job. During the conversation he feels sick, angry, guilty, and desperate. Sally feels the same way.

ROBERT: **Good morning, honey. How's my sweetie pie today?** *Robert is thinking, "Damn, I feel awful. I can't go to work. I can't face the boss. She's mad. Better shower her with attention, get her to text him for me, and then I'll go back to bed. Better yet, I need another drink. Quick."*

SALLY *(responding in a clipped, martyred voice after a long silence)*: **I'm fine.** *(Stares at him coldly.) What Sally really means is: "I feel hurt. I feel angry. How could you do this to me? You were out again drinking last night. You promised not to do it anymore. Our lives are falling apart, and you don't care. Look at you—you're a mess. I can't stand this!"*

ROBERT: **Honey, I feel so sick today. I think I'm getting the flu. I can't even eat breakfast. Text my boss, okay? Tell him I'm in bed and I can't even lift my head off the pillow to text. I'll be in tomorrow if I'm better. Could you do that for me? C'mon. Be my little sweetheart. I'm so sick.** *What Robert really means is: "I'm helpless, and I need you. Take care of me and do it right now. I know you're angry at me, so I'll try to get you to feel sorry for me."*

SALLY: **I really don't think I should be the one texting your boss. What if he has questions that I can't answer? It would be better if you did it. You know what you want to say.** *Sally is thinking, "I hate lying for him. But if I say no, he'll get angry. I'll try to act more helpless than he is."*

ROBERT: **What's with you, anyway? Can't you just do this one thing for me? Are you that selfish? I know you're mad at me. You're always mad at me. Fine. Don't do it.**

SALLY: **Fine. I'll do it. But don't ever ask me to do it again.** *(Feeling trapped, Sally texts Robert's boss.) Robert made his points well. He hit Sally on all her weak spots. She's afraid of being called selfish because she thinks it would be terrible if she was selfish; she feels guilty because he's right—she* is *mad all the time; she feels responsible for Robert's drinking; and she's afraid he'll lose his job because it's happened before. And the next time Robert asks her, she will surely text his boss again.*

After Sally sends the text she flies into a rage at Robert, persecuting him. She then ends up feeling sorry for herself and victimized. She also continues to feel extremely guilty, harboring the thought that there's something wrong with her for all her feelings and reactions because Robert appears so powerful while she feels so weak and insecure.

. . .

In this conversation, a counselor is talking to an alcoholic husband and his wife in a family therapy group. They appear to be the perfect couple. This is not their first time attending this group, but it is the first time the counselor focuses on them.

COUNSELOR: **Steven and Joanne, I'm glad you're both here tonight. How are you doing?**

STEVEN: **We're good. Everything's great. Wouldn't you say, hon?**

JOANNE *(smiling)*: **Yes. Everything's fine.** *(Laughs nervously.)*

COUNSELOR: **Joanne, you're laughing, but I sense something is wrong. It's okay to talk in here. It's okay to talk about your feelings, and it's okay to talk about your problems. That's what this group is for. What's going on underneath your smile?**

JOANNE *(starting to cry)*: **I'm so sick of this. I'm sick of the lies. I'm sick of the promises that are never kept. I'm so sick of being scared of him. I'm sick of all of it.**

. . .

Now that we've "listened" to some codependents talk, let's consider the dialogue we use. Many of us have poor communication skills. We carefully choose our words to manipulate, people please, control, cover up, and alleviate guilt. Our communication reeks of repressed feelings, repressed thoughts, ulterior motives, low self-worth, and shame. We laugh when we want to cry, we say we're fine when we're not. We allow ourselves to be bullied and buried. We sometimes react inappropriately. We justify, rationalize, compensate, and take others all around the block. We are nonassertive.

We badger and threaten, then back down. Sometimes we lie. Frequently, we're hostile. We apologize a lot and hint at what we want and need.

Codependents are indirect. We don't say what we mean, we don't mean what we say.[1]

We don't do it on purpose. We do it because we've learned to communicate this way to survive. At some point, either in our childhood or adult family, we learned not to talk about problems, express feelings, and express opinions. We've learned not to say what we want and need. To never say no or stand up for ourselves. An alcoholic parent or spouse will be glad to teach these rules that are still controlling our lives.

Why are we afraid to let people know who we are? Each of us must answer that question. John Powell says it's because who we are is all we've got, and we're afraid of being rejected.[2] Some of us may be afraid because we're not sure who we are and what we want to say. Many of us have been inhibited and controlled by family rules that told us not to think, feel, or rock the boat. Some of us have had to follow these rules to protect ourselves, to survive the emotional and sometimes physical wrath of our families. However, I believe most of us are afraid to tell people who we are because we don't believe it's okay to be who we are.

Many of us don't like and don't trust ourselves. We don't trust our thinking. We don't trust our feelings. We may think our opinions don't matter. We don't think we have the right to say no. We're not sure what we want and need; if we do know, we feel guilty about having wants and needs, and we're surely not going to be upfront about them. We may feel ashamed for having problems. Many of us don't even trust our ability to accurately identify problems, and we're more than willing to back down if somebody else insists the problem isn't there.

Communication isn't mystical. The words we speak reflect who we are: what we think, judge, feel, value, honor, love, hate, fear, desire, hope for, believe in, and commit to.[3] If we think we're not up to the task of living our lives, our communication will reflect this. We will judge others as having all the answers; feel angry, hurt, scared, guilty, needy, and controlled by other people. We will desire to control others, value pleasing others at any cost, and fear disapproval and abandonment. We will hope for everything but believe we deserve and will get nothing unless we force things to happen and remain committed to being responsible for other people's feelings and behaviors. We're congested with negative feelings and thoughts.

No wonder we don't communicate clearly.

Talking clearly and openly isn't difficult. In fact, it's easy. And fun. Start by knowing that who you are is okay. Your feelings and thoughts are okay. It's okay to talk about your problems. And it's okay to say no.

We *can* say no—whenever we want to. It's easy. Say it right now. Ten times. See how easy that was? By the way, other people can say no too. It makes it easier if we've got equal rights. We're not one down from anyone. Whenever our answer is no, we should start our response with the word *no* instead of saying "I don't think so" or "Maybe" or some other waffling phrase.

Say what you mean and mean what you say (but don't be mean). If you don't know what you mean, be quiet and think about it. If your answer is "I don't know," say "I don't know." Learn to be concise. Stop taking people all around the block. Get to the point and stop when you make it.

Talk about your problems. We're not being disloyal to anyone by revealing who we are and what kinds of problems we're working on. All we're doing is pretending by not being who we are. Share secrets with trusted friends who won't use them against you. You can make appropriate decisions about who to talk to, how much to tell them, and when is the best time to talk.

Express your feelings openly, honestly, appropriately, and responsibly. Let others do the same. Learn the words: *I feel.* Let others say those words and learn to listen—not fix—when they do.

We can say what we think. Learn to say: "This is what I think." Your opinions can be different from other people's opinions; that doesn't mean you're wrong.

But we can even be wrong.

We can say what we expect, without demanding that other people change to suit our needs. Other people can say what they expect, and we don't have to change to suit them either—if we don't want to.

We can express our wants and needs. Learn the words: "This is what I need from you. This is what I want from you."

We can tell the truth. Lying about what we think, how we feel, and what we want isn't being polite—it's lying.

We don't have to be controlled by what other people say; we don't have to try to control them with our words and special effects. We don't have to be manipulated, guilted, coerced, or forced into anything. We can open our mouths and take care of ourselves! Learn to say: "I love you, and I love me too."

We can refuse to talk to someone's illness. Or their crazy. If it doesn't make sense, it doesn't make sense. We don't have to waste time trying to convince the other person that what they said makes no sense. Learn to say, "I don't want to discuss this."

We can set and hold boundaries in conversation and stand up for ourselves without being abrasive or aggressive. Learn to say: "This is as far as I go. This is my limit. I will not tolerate this." And mean those words.

We can show compassion and concern without rescuing. Learn to say, "Sounds like you're having a problem. What do you need from me?" Or learn to say, "I'm sorry you're having that problem." Then, let it go. *You don't have to fix it.*

We can discuss our feelings and problems without expecting people to rescue us too. We can settle for being heard. That's probably all we ever wanted anyway.

One common complaint I hear is, "Nobody takes me seriously!" Take yourself seriously. Balance that with an appropriate sense of humor and you won't have to worry about what anyone else is or isn't doing.

Learn to listen to what people are saying and not saying.

Learn to listen to yourself, the tone of voice you use when you talk to others, the words you choose, the way you express yourself, *what* you're saying, and how it's being received.

Learn to align with and tune into yourself too. We can't be intimate and honest with others if we're not intimate and honest with ourselves. Are your words congruent with who you really are—your higher self?

We talk to express ourselves. We talk to be listened to. We talk to understand ourselves and others. Talking helps us get messages to people. Sometimes we talk to achieve closeness and intimacy. Maybe we don't always have something earth shattering to say, but we want human contact. We want to bridge the gap between self and others. We want to share and be close. Sometimes we talk to have fun—to play, enjoy, banter, and entertain. There are times when we talk to stand up for ourselves—to make it clear that we won't be bullied or abused, that we love ourselves, and that we have made decisions in our best interests. And sometimes we just talk.

We need to take responsibility for the way we communicate. We need to set boundaries with ourselves. Let our words reflect high self-esteem and esteem for others. Be honest, direct, open. Be gentle and loving when that's appropriate. Be firm when the situation requires firmness. Above all else, be who we are and say what we need to say.

In love and dignity, speak the truth—as we think, feel, and know it—and it shall set us free.

··· ACTIVITY ···

1. Slowly become conscious of the way you speak and the way others to speak to you. You may want to get a small notebook or use a notes app on your phone to record these exchanges as they happen. Doing so will help you become mindful of how you communicate. Become aware of:

   - your tone of voice (Are you snapping back at or retorting angrily to someone consistently because you have unresolved emotions with that person?)

   - the other person's tone of voice

   - your words (Are you saying what you want to say?)

   - your feelings (When a conversation ends, do you feel fear? Anger? Do you feel like you've been manipulated? Do you feel anxious?)

2. After troubling conversations (including via text), shine a light on the exchange. Why do you suppose this conversation went so poorly?

3. Make a practice of pausing before you speak, text, send an email, or post something online. Are you reacting? Is it necessary to say what you're about to say? Is it necessary to say it now? Is there a kinder or more tender way you can express yourself?

4. We can't do anything about whether people make amends to us, but we can control when we make amends. An "I'm sorry" can go a long way. Practice saying this when it's appropriate.

18

Work a Twelve Step Program

"How do the Twelve Steps work?"
"They work just fine, thank you."

—ANONYMOUS

I detest the disease of alcoholism. Substance abuse and other compulsive disorders destroy people—beautiful, intelligent, sensitive, creative, loving, caring people who do not deserve to be destroyed. The illness kills love and dreams, hurts children, and tears apart families. Substance abuse leaves in its wake shattered, fragmented, bewildered victims. Sometimes the early death it brings to the addict causes far less pain than the wretched illness caused during their lifetime. It is a horrid, cunning, baffling, powerful, and deadly disease.

I unabashedly love the Twelve Steps. I have great respect for all the Twelve Step programs: Alcoholics Anonymous, for people with a desire to stop drinking; Al-Anon, for people affected by someone else's drinking; Alateen, for teenagers affected by someone's drinking; Al-Atots, for children affected by someone's drinking; and

Narcotics Anonymous, for people addicted to drugs. (Some of these programs are open to people with general substance abuse problems, not just alcoholism.)

Other Twelve Step programs that I highly respect include Nar-Anon, for people affected by another's chemical addiction; Overeaters Anonymous, for people with eating disorders; O-Anon, for people affected by others' eating disorders; Families Anonymous, for people concerned about the use of chemicals and/or related behavioral problems in a relative or friend; Adult Children of Alcoholics; and Emotions Anonymous, for people with a desire to become well emotionally.

And there are even more good Twelve Step programs, including Sex Addicts Anonymous, for people with compulsive sexual behavior; COSA, for people affected by another person's sexual addiction; Gamblers Anonymous, for people with a desire to stop gambling; Gam-Anon, for people affected by another person's gambling; Parents Anonymous, for parents who are abusive, neglectful, or afraid of becoming so, or for adolescents who are encountering problems due to past or current abuse; and Sexaholics Anonymous. There may also be other programs that I have either overlooked or that were founded since the writing of this book. A list of resources is available in the back of the book.

Twelve Step programs are not merely self-help groups that help people with compulsive disorders stop doing whatever it is they feel compelled to do (drinking, helping the drinker, etc.). The programs teach people how to live—peacefully, happily, successfully. They promote healing. They give life to their members—frequently a richer, healthier life than those they knew before they developed whatever problem they developed. The Twelve Steps are a way of life.

In this chapter I'm going to focus on the programs for people who have been affected by another person's compulsive disorder because this is a book on codependency and that's what codependency is about. I'm going to refer specifically to the Al-Anon program because that's one program I "work." (I will discuss that little piece of jargon, "working a program," later in this chapter.) However, with a bit of creativity on your part, the information I present can be applied to any of the Twelve Step programs.

THE TWELVE STEPS

The Twelve Steps are at the heart of the Twelve Step programs. The Steps, in their basic forms, belong to various programs. But all the programs adapted their Steps from those of Alcoholics Anonymous.

The interpretations following the Steps are my personal opinions and are not related to, endorsed by, or affiliated with any Twelve Step program. The programs also have Traditions, which guard the purity of the programs to ensure that they continue to operate effectively. The Eleventh Tradition in the Al-Anon program says, "Our public relations policy is based on attraction rather than promotion."[1] Please understand that I'm not promoting this program or any program. I'm just saying what I think, and I happen to think highly of the Twelve Steps.

1. *"We admitted we were powerless over alcohol—that our lives had become unmanageable."* This is an important Step. It must be taken first. That's why it's the First Step. Much of our struggle to accept whatever it is we must accept—a loved one's alcoholism or eating

disorder, for example—brings us to this door. My denial, my bargains, my efforts to control, my rescuing, my anger, my hurt, my grief propelled me to this place. Not once but twice in my lifetime, I had tried to do the impossible. I'd tried to control alcohol. I'd battled with alcohol in my own drinking and using days; I went to war again with alcohol when people I loved were using and abusing it. Both times, I lost. When will I learn to quit fighting lions? Both times, alcohol gained control of me. It didn't matter, though, how it had gained control. It had. My thoughts, emotions, behaviors— my life—were regulated and directed by alcohol and its effects on another person's life. People were controlling me, but those people were being controlled by alcohol. Once the light was turned on, it wasn't difficult to see who was boss. The bottle was. Once I saw that, I could easily see how my life had become unmanageable. Spiritually, emotionally, mentally, behaviorally, I was out of control. My relationships with people were unmanageable. My career was unmanageable. I couldn't even keep my house clean.

If this Step sounds like giving up, that's because it is. It's where we surrender to the truth. We are powerless over alcohol. We are powerless over the disease of alcoholism. We are powerless over other people's drinking and the effects of alcoholism in their lives. We are powerless over people—what they do, say, think, feel, or don't do, say, think, or feel. We have been trying to do the impossible. At this point we understand this and make a rational decision to quit trying to do what we cannot ever do, no matter how hard we try. We turn our eyes on ourselves—to the ways we have been affected, to our characteristics, to our pain. It sounds hopeless and defeatist, but it isn't. It's acceptance of what is. We can't change things we can't control, and trying to do that will make us crazy.

This Step is appropriately humbling. It is also the bridge to the Second Step. For with our surrender to powerlessness, we receive the power which is appropriately ours—our own power to change ourselves and live our lives. When we quit trying to do the impossible, we're allowed to do the possible.

2. *"Came to believe that a Power greater than ourselves could restore us to sanity."* If the First Step left us despairing, this Step will bring hope. I didn't doubt for a minute that I was crazy once I stopped comparing myself to the crazy people around me. The way I had been living was insane; the way I had not been living my life was insane. I needed to believe I could become sane. I needed to believe the pain I felt could somehow be lessened. Listening to, talking with, and actually seeing people at meetings who had been as upset as I was, and seeing they had found peace in circumstances sometimes far worse than mine, helped me *come to believe.* There is no substitute for visualization. As someone once said, seeing is believing.

And, yes, this is a spiritual program. We are spiritual beings. This program meets our spiritual needs. We aren't talking about religion here; the word I use is *spiritual.* We select and come to terms with a power greater than ourselves.

3. *"Made a decision to turn our will and our lives over to the care of God as we understood Him."* I had turned my will and my life over to the care of alcohol and other drugs; I had turned my will and my life over to the care of other human beings; I had spent many years trying to impose my own plan onto the scheme of things. It was time to remove myself from anyone's or anything's control (including my own) and place myself in the hands of an extraordinarily

loving Creator. "Take it," I said. "All of it—who I am, what's happened to me, where I shall go, and how I'll get there." I said it once. I say it every day. Sometimes, I say it every half hour. This Step does not mean we resign ourselves to a bunch of shoulds and ought tos and don our sackcloth. It in no way implies a continuation of martyrdom. The exciting thing about this Step is it means there is a purpose and a plan—a great, perfectly wonderful, usually enjoyable, and worthwhile plan that takes into account our unique needs, desires, abilities, talents, and feelings. This was good news to me. I thought I was a mistake. I didn't think there was anything significant planned for my life. I was just stumbling around, trying to make the best out of being here, when I learned this: *we are here to live as long as we are alive, and there is a life for each of us to live.*

4. *"Made a searching and fearless moral inventory of ourselves."* We take our eyes off other people and look at ourselves. We see just what we're working with, how we've been affected, what we're doing, and what our characteristics are, and we write on a piece of paper what we see. We look fearlessly—not in self-hate and self-castigation but in an attitude of love, honesty, and self-care. We may even discover that hating ourselves, not loving ourselves enough, has been a real moral problem. We root out any other problems, including guilt. We also look at our good qualities. We examine our anger and hurt. We examine ourselves and the role we and our decisions have played in our lives. This Step also gives us an opportunity to examine the standards we judge ourselves by, choose those we believe to be appropriate, and disregard the rest. We are now on our way to dumping our earned guilt (the guilt that comes when we violate our own moral code), getting rid of

unearned guilt (the anxiety and fear that comes when we allow other people's moral codes to dictate our behavior and induce guilt in us), accepting the package we call ourselves, and starting on the path to growth and change.

5. *"Admitted to God, to ourselves, and to another human being the exact nature of our wrongs."* They say confession is good for the soul. There's nothing like it. We don't have to hide any longer. We tell our worst, most shameful secrets to a trusted person skilled in listening at the Fifth Step. We tell someone how hurt and angry we are. Someone listens. Someone cares. We are forgiven. Wounds begin to heal. We forgive. This Step is liberating.

6. *"Were entirely ready to have God remove all these defects of character."* We realize some of the things we've been doing to protect ourselves have been hurting us and possibly others. We decide we're ready to take a risk and let go of these outdated survival behaviors and attitudes. We become willing to be changed and to cooperate in the process of change. I use this and the next Step as daily tools to rid myself of any defects that come to my attention. I consider my low self-worth a defect and I use this Step on it too.

7. *"Humbly asked Him to remove our shortcomings."* From my experience, *humbly* seems to be the key here.

8. *"Made a list of all persons we had harmed, and became willing to make amends to them all."* Willingness is the important qualifier here, although I suspect it's directly connected to humility. Don't forget to put yourself on this list. Note that, as Jael Greenleaf writes,

"The Eighth Step does not read 'Made a list of all persons we had harmed and became willing to feel guilty about it.'"[2] This is our chance to take care of our earned guilt. This is an important Step in a tool that will be available to us all our lives so we can clear guilt whenever it raises its ugly head.

9. *"Made direct amends to such people wherever possible, except when to do so would injure them or others."* This is a simple Step in a simple program. Sometimes the simplest things help us feel happy.

10. *"Continued to take personal inventory and when we were wrong promptly admitted it."* We keep our eyes on ourselves. We continually and regularly evaluate our behavior. We figure out what we like about ourselves and what we've done right. Then we either congratulate ourselves, feel good about it, feel grateful, or do all three. We figure out what we don't like that we've been doing, then we figure out how to accept and take care of that without hating ourselves for it. Here's the difficult part: if we're wrong, we say so. If we have worked Steps Eight and Nine and dumped all our guilty feelings, we will know when we need to say "I'm wrong" and "I'm sorry." If we feel guilt, we will be able to notice it. If, however, we are still feeling guilty all the time, it may be difficult to distinguish when we do something wrong because we're consumed by guilty feelings and we don't feel changed. It's just one more shovel of guilt thrown onto an already heaping pile. The moral of that story is: dump guilt. If guilt creeps back in, take care of it immediately.

11. *"Sought through prayer and meditation to improve our conscious contact with God as we understood Him, praying only for knowledge*

of His will for us and the power to carry that out." This Step, used daily and as needed, will successfully take us through our entire lives. This Step requires learning the difference between rumination and meditation. It also requires us to decide whether we believe our Higher Power/Creator is benevolent and "knows where we live," as a friend of mine says. Get quiet. Detach. Pray. Meditate. Ask for guidance. Ask for the power to do what you need to do. Then let go and watch what happens. Sometimes, you'll get surprises. Learn how to go with the flow, learn to trust yourself. And again, learn to trust the process.

12. *"Having had a spiritual awakening as the result of these Steps, we tried to carry this message to others, and to practice these principles in all our affairs."* We will awaken spiritually. We will learn to take care of ourselves spiritually. This program will enable us to love ourselves and other people instead of rescuing and being rescued. Carrying the message does not mean we become evangelists; it means our lives become a light. We will learn to shine. If we apply this program to all areas of our lives, it will work in all areas of our lives.

WORKING THE PROGRAM

Now that we are familiar with the Steps, let's discuss what "working the program" and "working the Steps" mean. All over the world, "anonymous" people meet at various locations—churches, homes, community centers, etc.—or virtually. They might meet once a day, twice a week, or seven nights a week. No registration necessary. They simply find out where a particular group meets that focuses on the problem troubling them. At the meeting, they don't have to give their last names or any other identifying fact about themselves; they don't have to say anything if they don't want to. They don't have to pay, although they can make a donation of any amount to help cover the cost of coffee and meeting room expenses if they want to. They don't have to sign up. They don't have to fill out a card. They don't have to answer any questions. They just walk in and sit down. This is called going to a meeting. It is an essential part of working the program.

One nice thing about meetings is that people can be who they are. They don't have to pretend they don't have a particular problem because everybody there has the same problem.

Meeting formats vary with each group. Some groups sit around a table and the people who want to talk, discuss feelings or problems. Some meetings are speaker meetings, where one person gets up in front of everyone and talks about a Step or an experience. At some groups, the Steps are the theme, and the people just put their chairs in a circle, and each person gets a chance to say something about whatever Step is the theme that day. There are many meeting variations. People learn about the Steps at the meetings, and they learn what the Steps mean to other people. They also hear slogans. Al-Anon and AA slogans include such catchy little sayings as "Let go and let God," "Easy does it," and "One day at a time." These sayings have become slogans because they are true. And even if people get sick of saying and hearing these slogans, they keep repeating and listening to them because they are true. And the slogans help people feel better. After the meeting is over, people usually stay and chat or go out to a restaurant and have a soda or coffee. Learning the Steps and slogans, listening to other people's experiences, sharing personal experiences, and fellowship, are all parts of working the program.

At the meetings, books, pamphlets, and literature are sold at cost. These books contain information on the problems common to that group. Some groups sell meditation books, which contain suggestions for approaching each day. Reading the literature and reading the daily meditation books are also parts of working the program.

During their daily routines, the people who go to these meetings think about the Steps and slogans. They try to figure out how the Steps and slogans apply to them, what they're feeling, what they're doing, and what's going on in their lives at that time. They do this regularly and when a problem arises. Sometimes, they call a friend they met at the meeting and discuss a problem with that person. This can be a formally arranged relationship between them and "a sponsor"—someone whose recovery they appreciate and respect. Sometimes, they do the things a Step suggests they do, such as write out an inventory, make a list of people they have harmed, or make appropriate amends. If these people think about and work these Steps enough, eventually the Twelve Steps may become habits—habitual ways of thinking, behaving, and handling situations—much the same as codependent characteristics become habits. When they become habits, the program becomes a way of life. This is called working the Steps and working the program.

That's all there is to working a program. People don't graduate and go on to more complicated things—they stick with the basics. Twelve Step programs work because they are simple and basic.

I get excited about such simple things as going to meetings and working the Steps. I can try to explain, but words only convey a

little bit of the important idea here. Something happens if we go to
these meetings and work a program. A peace and a healing set in.
We start to change and feel better. The Steps are something we
work on, but they also work on us. There is magic at these meetings.

We never have to do anything we are unable to do, find offen-
sive, or don't want to do. When it's time to do or change a certain
thing, we'll know it's time, and we'll want to do so. There will be a
rightness and an appropriateness to our actions. Our lives begin to
work this way too. Healing—growth—becomes a natural process.
The Twelve Steps capture and are a formula for our natural healing
process.[3] Upon reading them, we may not think the Steps look like
much, but when we work them something happens. Their power
appears. We may not understand it until it happens to us.

The best description of the Twelve Steps I've heard is the "invisible boat" story, told by a man at a meeting I attended. He was
talking about AA, but his story applies to Al-Anon and other
groups. I have changed some of his words so his idea fits Al-Anon,
but here is the essence of his analogy:

> Picture ourselves standing on the shore. Way across the
> water is an island called Serenity, where peace, happiness,
> and freedom exist from the despair of alcoholism and
> other problems. We really want to get to that island, but
> we've got to find a way to get across the water—that huge
> void that stands between us and where we want to be.
>
> We have two choices. In the water is an ocean liner, a
> cruise ship that looks very posh and cozy. It's called
> *Treatment*, therapy. Next to it, on the beach, sits a group
> of odd-looking people. They appear to be rowing a boat,

but we can't see the boat, and we can't see the oars. We only see these happy people sitting on the beach, rowing an invisible boat with invisible oars. The invisible boat is called Al-Anon (or AA or any other Twelve Step program). The ocean liner honks, summoning us aboard the treatment and therapy cruise. We can see the people onboard: they're happy and waving to us. Then there's these goofy people hollering at us to join them in their invisible boat. Would we choose the liner or the invisible boat? Of course, we'll get on the ocean liner, the luxury cruise. The next thing we know, we're heading toward Serenity Island.

The problem is about midway across the water, the ocean liner stops, turns around, and heads back to the shore where we started from. Then the captain orders everyone off the ship. When we ask why, he says, "Our cruise only goes so far. The only way you can ever get to Serenity Island is by getting in the invisible boat (called Al-Anon)."

So we shrug our shoulders and walk over to the people in the boat. "Get in!" they holler.

"We can't see any boat to get into!" we holler back.

"Get in anyway," they say. So we get in, and pretty soon they say, "Pick up an oar and start rowing (working the Steps)."

"Can't see any oars," we holler back.

"Pick 'em up and start rowing, anyway!" they say. So we pick up invisible oars and start rowing, and pretty soon we

see the boat. Before we know it, we see the oars too. Next
thing we know, we're so happy rowing the boat with the
goofy people that we don't care if we ever get to the other
side.[4]

That is the magic of the Twelve Step programs—they work. I'm
not saying, implying, or suggesting treatment and therapy are not
helpful. They are. For many of us, treatment or a little therapy is
just what we need to get *started* on our journeys. But that ride ends,
and if we have a compulsive disorder or love someone with a compulsive disorder, we may discover we need to get on the invisible
boat with those happy people.

At the end of this chapter, I have included tests we can take to
help determine if we are candidates for Al-Anon or Alateen. I have
also included further questions from Adult Children of Alcoholics
(ACOA). Please understand that the "anon" and ACOA groups are
not for people with the drinking problem; they are for people who
have been affected by someone else's problem. People frequently
misunderstand this. Also, many chemically dependent people who
attend AA find they also need to go to Al-Anon or ACOA to deal
with their codependent characteristics. If you believe you might be
a candidate for any of the Twelve Step programs—if you even suspect you have a problem common to one of the groups discussed at
the beginning of this chapter—find a group and start going to
meetings. It will help you feel better.

I know it's difficult to go to meetings. I know it's difficult to
present ourselves to a group of strangers and hold up our problems
for the world to see. I know many of us probably don't understand

how going to meetings could help anything—especially if it's not us but someone else who has the problem. But it will help. I was so angry when I started attending Al-Anon meetings. I was already working a program for my alcoholism. I didn't want or need another program or another problem in my life to work on. Besides, I felt I had already done enough to help the alcoholics in my life. Why should I have to go to meetings? The alcoholics were the ones who needed help. At my first meeting, a cheery woman walked up to me, talked to me for a few minutes, smiled, and said, "Aren't you lucky? You're a double winner. You get to work both programs!" I wanted to choke her. Now, I agree. I am lucky; I am a double winner.

Some of us may be reluctant to go to meetings because we feel we've already done enough for the *other people* in our lives. Well, we're right. We probably have. That's why it's important to go to our meetings. We're going for ourselves.

Others of us may want to go only to help the *other people* and may feel disappointed that the meetings expect us to work on ourselves. That's okay too. Health begets health. If we start working on ourselves, our good health may rub off on the other people, in the same fashion that their illnesses rubbed off on us.

Some of us may be embarrassed to go. All I could do at the first meetings I attended was sit and cry, and I felt terribly awkward. But for once, it was a good cry: my tears were tears of healing. I needed to sit and cry. When I stopped crying and looked around, I saw other people crying too. Al-Anon is a safe place to go and be who we are. The people there understand. So will you.

I've addressed most of the common objections I've heard to attending meetings. There may be other objections, but if you qualify for membership in a program, go anyway. The Twelve Steps are a gift to people with compulsive disorders and to people who love people with compulsive disorders. If you're feeling crazy and reacting to people and things, go. If you don't like the first group you attend, find another meeting and go there. Each group has its own personality. Continue going to different groups until you find one that feels comfortable.

How often do we need to go? We need to answer that for ourselves. A rule of thumb for substance disorders is that you're likely going to need to attend Twelve Step groups for most/all of your life. For "codependency meetings," go as often as needed. Our codependent tendencies may follow us around for the rest of our lives. Go whenever they become a problem. Go whether the other people in your life get better or not.

Go until you feel grateful that you can go.

Go until you see the boat and the oars and you get happy. Go until the magic works on you. And don't worry—if you go long enough, the magic will work.

··· ACTIVITY ···

1. Complete the tests or read over the list of characteristics on the following pages.

2. If you are a candidate for any of the Twelve Step programs discussed in this chapter, do an online search for meetings. Find out where and when meetings are being held, then go. If you qualify for more than one program, choose the one that appeals to you most and go.

Al-Anon: Is it for You?

Millions of people are affected by the excessive drinking or substance abuse of someone close to them. The following twenty questions are designed to help you decide whether Al-Anon might benefit you:

1. Do you worry about how much someone else drinks?	Yes	No
2. Do you have money problems because of someone else's drinking?	Yes	No
3. Do you tell lies to cover up for someone else's drinking?	Yes	No
4. Do you feel that drinking is more important to your loved one than you are?	Yes	No
5. Do you think that the drinker's behavior is caused by his or her companions?	Yes	No
6. Are mealtimes frequently delayed because of the drinker?	Yes	No
7. Do you make threats such as, "If you don't stop drinking, I'll leave you"?	Yes	No
8. When you kiss the drinker hello, do you secretly try to smell his or her breath?	Yes	No
9. Are you afraid to upset someone for fear it will set off a drinking bout?	Yes	No
10. Have you been hurt or embarrassed by a drinker's behavior?	Yes	No
11. Does it seem as if every holiday is spoiled because of drinking?	Yes	No
12. Have you considered calling the police because of drinking behavior?	Yes	No

13. Do you find yourself searching for hidden liquor?	Yes	No
14. Do you feel that if the drinker loved you, he or she would stop drinking to please you?	Yes	No
15. Have you refused social invitations out of fear or anxiety?	Yes	No
16. Do you sometimes feel guilty when you think of the lengths you have gone to control the drinker?	Yes	No
17. Do you think that if the drinker stopped drinking, your other problems would be solved?	Yes	No
18. Do you ever threaten to hurt yourself to scare the drinker into saying, "I'm sorry" or "I love you"?	Yes	No
19. Do you ever treat people (children, employees, parents, coworkers, etc.) unjustly because you are angry at someone else for drinking too much?	Yes	No
20. Do you feel there is no one who understands your problems?	Yes	No

If you answered yes to three or more of these questions, Al-Anon or Alateen may help.[5] You can contact Al-Anon or Alateen online at https://al-anon.org/.

Adult Children of Alcoholics: Is It for You?
Are you an adult child of an alcoholic?

1. Do you recall anyone drinking or taking drugs or being involved in some other behavior that you now believe could be dysfunctional?

2. Did you avoid bringing friends to your home because of drinking or some other dysfunctional behavior in the home?

3. Did one of your parents make excuses for the other parent's drinking or other behaviors?

4. Did your parents focus on each other so much that they seemed to ignore you?

5. Did your parents or relatives argue constantly?

6. Were you drawn into arguments or disagreements and asked to choose sides with one relative against another?

7. Did you try to protect your brothers or sisters against drinking or other behavior in the family?

8. As an adult, do you feel immature? Do you feel like you are a child inside?

9. As an adult, do you believe you are treated like a child when you interact with your parents? Are you continuing to live out a childhood role with your parents?

10. Do you believe that it is your responsibility to take care of your parents' feelings or worries? Do other relatives look to you to solve their problems?

11. Do you fear authority figures and angry people?

12. Do you constantly seek approval or praise but have difficulty accepting a compliment when one comes your way?

13. Do you see most forms of criticism as a personal attack?

14. Do you overcommit yourself and then feel angry when others do not appreciate what you do?

15. Do you think you are responsible for the way another person feels or behaves?

16. Do you have difficulty identifying feelings?

17. Do you focus outside yourself for love or security?

18. Do you involve yourself in the problems of others? Do you feel more alive when there is a crisis?

19. Do you equate sex with intimacy?

20. Do you confuse love and pity?

21. Have you found yourself in a relationship with a compulsive or dangerous person and wonder how you got there?

22. Do you judge yourself without mercy and guess at what is normal?

23. Do you behave one way in public and another way at home?

24. Do you think your parents had a problem with drinking or taking drugs?

25. Do you think you were affected by the drinking or other dysfunctional behavior of your parents or family?

If you answered "yes" to three or more of these questions, you may be suffering from the effects of growing up in an alcoholic or other dysfunctional family.[6] We welcome you to attend an ACA meeting in your area to learn more.

The Twelve Steps of AA

1. We admitted we were powerless over alcohol—that our lives had become unmanageable.

2. Came to believe that a Power greater than ourselves could restore us to sanity.

3. Made a decision to turn our will and our lives over to the care of God *as we understood Him.*

4. Made a searching and fearless moral inventory of ourselves.

5. Admitted to God, to ourselves, and to another human being the exact nature of our wrongs.

6. Were entirely ready to have God remove all these defects of character.

7. Humbly asked Him to remove our shortcomings.

8. Made a list of all persons we had harmed, and became willing to make amends to them all.

9. Made direct amends to such people wherever possible, except when to do so would injure them or others.

10. Continued to take personal inventory and when we were wrong promptly admitted it.

11. Sought through prayer and meditation to improve our conscious contact with God *as we understood Him*, praying only for knowledge of His will for us and the power to carry that out.

12. Having had a spiritual awakening as the result of these Steps, we tried to carry this message to alcoholics, and to practice these principles in all our affairs.[7]

19

Pieces and Bits

Taking care of myself is a big job.
No wonder I avoided it for so long.

—ANONYMOUS

This chapter contains miscellaneous tidbits about codependency and self-care.

DRAMA ADDICTS

Strangely enough, problems can become addicting, and many codependents become drama addicts. If we live with misery, crises, and turmoil long enough, the fear and stimulation caused by problems can become a comfortable emotional experience. In the second volume of *Getting Them Sober*, Toby Rice Drews refers to this feeling as "excited misery."[1] After a while, we can become so used to involving our emotions with problems and crises that we get and stay involved with problems that aren't our concern. We may even start creating drama or making troubles greater than they are to stimulate ourselves. This is especially true if we have neglected our own lives and feelings. When we're involved with a problem, we know we're alive. When the problem is solved, we may feel empty and lifeless. Being in crisis becomes a comfortable place, and it saves us from our humdrum existence. It's like getting addicted to soap operas, except the daily crises occur in our lives and the lives of our friends and family. "Will Ginny leave John?" "Can we save Michael's job?" "What will Jennifer do?"

After we have detached and begun minding our own business and our lives finally become serene, we may occasionally crave a little of the old excitement. We are used to so much turmoil and excitement that peace can seem bland at first. We'll get used to it. As we develop our lives, set our goals, and find things to do that interest us, peace will become comfortable—more comfortable than chaos. We will no longer need nor desire excited misery.

We need to learn to recognize when we're seeking out excited misery. Understand that you don't have to make problems or get involved with others' problems. Find creative ways to fill the need for drama—in hobbies, recreation, work. Go to a movie, or write one. Take up a sport. In midlife, I took up skydiving, mountain climbing, and aikido, a soft form of martial arts. Have fun with drama, make money from drama, but keep the excited misery out of your life.

EXPECTATIONS

Expectations can be a confusing topic. Most of us have expectations. We entertain certain notions, on some level of consciousness, about how we hope things will turn out or how we want people to behave. But it's better to relinquish expectations. It's better to refrain from forcing our expectations on others or from trying to control the outcome of events since doing so causes problems and is usually impossible, anyway. So where do we go with our expectations?

Some people strive to relinquish all expectations and live moment to moment. That's admirable. But I think the important idea here is to take responsibility for our expectations. Get them out into the light. Examine them. Talk about them. If they involve other people, talk to the people involved. Find out if they have similar expectations. See if they're realistic. For example, expecting healthy behavior from unhealthy people is futile. Then let go. See how things turn out. Let things happen—without forcing. If we are constantly disappointed, we may have a problem to solve—either with ourselves, another person, or a situation.

It's okay to have expectations. At times, they are real clues to what we want, need, hope for, and fear. We have a right to expect good things and appropriate behavior. We will probably get more of these things (the good stuff and the appropriate behavior) if we consistently expect these things. If we have expectations, we will also realize when they aren't being met. But we need to realize these are only expectations; they belong to us, and we're not always boss. Like an Al-Anon member said, "Expectations are resentments waiting to happen." Make sure our expectations are realistic. Don't let them interfere with reality or spoil the good things that are happening.

FEAR OF INTIMACY

Most people want and need love. Most people want and need to be close to people. But fear is an equally strong force, and it competes with our need for love. More specifically, this force is fear of intimacy.

For some of us, the fear of intimacy overpowers the desire for it. It feels safer to be alone or in relationships where we are "unemotionally involved" than it does to be emotionally vulnerable, close, and loving. I understand that. In spite of the range of needs and wants that go unmet when we don't love, it may feel safer to not love. We don't risk the uncertainty and vulnerability of closeness. We don't risk the pain of loving, and for many of us love has caused a great deal of pain. We don't risk being trapped in relationships that don't work. We don't risk being emotionally honest and the possible rejections that come with sharing feelings. We don't risk people abandoning us. We don't risk. And we don't put ourselves through the awkwardness of initiating relationships. When we don't get close to people, at least we know what to expect: nothing. Denial of love feelings protects us from the anxiety caused by loving. Love and closeness often bring a sense of loss of control. Love and closeness challenge our deepest fears about who we are and whether it's okay to be ourselves and about who others are and whether that is okay. Love and closeness—involvement with people—are the greatest risks a person can take. Relationships require honesty, spontaneity, vulnerability, trust, responsibility, self-acceptance, and acceptance of others—a lot of work. Love brings joy and warmth, but it also requires us to be willing to occasionally feel hurt and rejection.

Many of us have learned to run from closeness rather than take the risks involved. We run from love or prevent closeness in many ways. We push people away or do hurtful things to them so they won't want to be close to us. We do ridiculous things in our minds to talk ourselves out of wanting to be close. We find fault with everyone we meet; we reject people before they have a chance to reject us. We wear masks and pretend to be something other than who we are. We scatter our energies and emotions among so many relationships that we don't get too close to or vulnerable with anyone. We settle for artificial relationships, where we will not be expected nor asked to be close. We play roles instead of being real. We withdraw emotionally in our existing relationships. As a friend says, "We all have a pair of running shoes in our closet."

We run from intimacy for many reasons. Some of us may never have learned how to initiate relationships and how to be close once a relationship begins. Closeness wasn't safe, taught, or allowed in our families. For many people, caretaking and chemical use became substitutes for intimacy.

Some of us learned to run from relationships that aren't good for us. But for others, running from or avoiding closeness and intimacy may have become a destructive habit that has prevented us from getting the love and closeness we really want and need.

It's okay to feel afraid of intimacy, but it's also okay to allow ourselves to love and feel close to people. We can make good decisions about who to love and when to do that. It's okay for us to be who we are around people. Take the risk of doing that. We can trust ourselves. We can go through the awkwardness and uncertainty of initiating relationships. We can find people who are safe to trust. We can open up, become honest, and be who we are. We can even handle feeling hurt or rejected from time to time. We can love without losing ourselves or giving up our boundaries. We can love and think at the same time because we're learning to trust ourselves. We can learn when it's safe to trust other people. We can take off our running shoes.

FINANCIAL RESPONSIBILITY

Some of us become financially dependent on others. Sometimes this is by agreement; for example, one partner is a stay-at-home parent while the other works and provides the money. Sometimes this is not by agreement. Some of us become so victimized that we believe we cannot take care of ourselves financially. Many of us were, at one time, financially responsible, but as alcoholism or other compulsive disorders progressed in a loved one, we gave up.

Sometimes, codependents become financially responsible for other adults. I have frequently seen a codependent work two or even three jobs while their partner brought home not one penny.

Neither way is preferable. Each person is financially responsible for themselves as well as in all other ways. Assuming financial responsibility for oneself is an attitude. It means figuring out exactly what our responsibilities are, then taking care of those responsibilities. It also means we allow—even insist that—other people be financially responsible for themselves. That includes becoming familiar with all areas of one's finances and deciding which tasks belong to which person. Which bills need to be paid? When? When are taxes due? How much money has to last for how long? Are we doing less or more than our appropriate share? Do we feel financially responsible for ourselves? Are the people around us assuming appropriate financial responsibility for themselves, or are we doing it for them?

Taking care of money is part of life. Earning money, paying bills, and feeling financially responsible is part of taking care of ourselves.

Being financially dependent on a person can trigger emotional dependency. Emotional dependency on a person can trigger financial dependency.[2] Becoming financially responsible for ourselves—however we accomplish that—can help trigger undependence.

FORGIVENESS

Compulsive disorders twist and distort many good things, including the principle of forgiveness. We repeatedly forgive the same people. For the same things. We hear promises, we believe lies, and we try to forgive some more. Some of us may have reached a point where we cannot forgive. Some of us may not want to because forgiveness would leave us vulnerable to further hurt, and we cannot endure more pain. Forgiveness turns on us and becomes a painful experience.

Some of us may be truly trying to forgive; some of us may think we have forgiven, but the hurt and anger won't go away.

Some of us can't keep up with the things we need to forgive; the problems are happening so fast we barely know what's going on. Before we can register the hurt and say, "I forgive," another nasty thing has been dumped on us.

Then we feel guilty because someone asks, "Why can't you just forgive and forget?" People uninformed about the world of compulsive disorders frequently ask that. For many of us, the problem is not forgetting. Forgiving and forgetting feed our denial system.

We need to think about, remember, understand, and make good decisions about what we are forgiving, what can be forgotten, and what is still a problem. And forgiving someone doesn't mean we have to let that person keep hurting us. An alcoholic doesn't need forgiveness; they need treatment. We don't need to forgive the alcoholic, at least not initially. We need to step back so they can't keep stomping on our toes.

I'm not suggesting we adopt an unforgiving attitude. We all need forgiveness. Grudges and anger hurt us; they don't help the other person much either. Forgiveness is wonderful. It wipes the slate clean. It clears up guilt. It brings peace and harmony. It acknowledges and accepts the humanity we all share, and it says, "That's okay. I love you anyway." We need to be gentle, loving, and forgiving with ourselves before we can expect to forgive others. We need to think about how, why, and when we dole out forgiveness.

Forgiveness is closely tied to the acceptance or grief process. We cannot forgive someone for doing something if we haven't fully accepted what this person has done. It does little good to forgive an alcoholic for going on a binge if we haven't yet accepted that they have the disease of alcoholism. Ironically, the kind of forgiveness we often give to soothe an alcoholic's "morning after" remorse may help them continue drinking.

Forgiveness comes in time—its own time—if we're striving to take care of ourselves. Don't let other people use this principle against us. Don't let other people badger us into forgiving. We can dole out forgiveness based on good decisions, high self-esteem, and mindfulness. If we're taking care of us, we will understand whom to forgive and when it's time to do that.

While we're at it, don't forget to forgive ourselves.

THE FROG SYNDROME

There is an anecdote circulating through codependency groups. It goes like this: "Did you hear about the woman who kissed a frog? She was hoping it would turn into a prince. It didn't. She turned into a frog too."

Many codependents like to kiss frogs, no matter our gender or sexual preference. We see so much good in them. Some of us even become chronically attracted to frogs after kissing enough of them. Alcoholics and people with other compulsive disorders are attractive people. They radiate power, energy, and charm. They promise the world. Never mind that they deliver pain, suffering, and anguish. The words they say sound so good.

If we don't deal with our codependent characteristics, probabilities dictate we will continue to be attracted to and kiss frogs. Even if we deal with our characteristics, we may still lean toward frogs, but we can learn not to jump into the pond with them.

FUN

Fun does not go hand in hand with codependency. It's difficult to have fun when we hate ourselves. It's difficult to enjoy life when there is no money for food because the alcoholic has drunk it all up. It's almost impossible to have fun when we're bottled up with repressed emotions, worried sick about someone, saturated with guilt and despair, rigidly controlling ourselves or someone else, or worried about what other people are thinking about us. However, most people aren't thinking about us; they're worried about themselves and what we think of them.

As codependents, we need to learn to play and to enjoy ourselves. Arranging for and allowing ourselves to have fun is an important part of taking care of ourselves. It helps us stay healthy. It helps us work better. It balances life. We deserve to have fun. Fun is a normal part of being alive. Fun is taking time to celebrate being alive.

Schedule fun into your routine. Learn to recognize when you need to play and what kinds of things you enjoy doing. If needed, you can make "learning to have fun" an immediate goal. Start doing things just for yourself, just because you want to. It might feel uncomfortable at first, but after a while it'll feel better. It'll become fun.

Let go and enjoy life. We can find things we enjoy doing, then let ourselves enjoy doing them. We can learn to relax and enjoy the things we do daily, not just the recreational activities. Martyrdom can interfere with our ability to feel good long after the substance abusers are gone from our lives. Suffering can become habitual, but so can enjoying life and being good to ourselves. Try it.

LIMITS/BOUNDARIES

Codependents, it has been said, have boundary problems. I agree. Most of us don't have boundaries.

Boundaries are limits that say: "This is how far I'll go. This is what I will or won't do for you. This is what I won't tolerate from you."

Most of us began relationships with boundaries. We had certain expectations, and we entertained certain ideas about what we would or wouldn't tolerate from people. Substance abuse and other compulsive disorders laugh in the face of limits. The diseases not only push on our boundaries but also step boldly across them. Each time a disease pushes or steps across our limits, we give in. We move our boundaries back, giving the disease more room to work. As the disease pushes more, we give in more until we're tolerating things we said we would never tolerate and doing things we said we would never do.[3] Later, this process of "increased tolerance" of inappropriate behaviors may reverse. Suddenly, we may become totally intolerant of even the most human behaviors. In the beginning, we make excuses for a person's inappropriate behavior; toward the end, there is no excuse.

Not only do many of us begin tolerating abnormal, unhealthy, and inappropriate behaviors, we take it one step further: we convince ourselves these behaviors are normal and what we deserve. We may become so familiar with verbal abuse and disrespectful treatment that we don't even recognize when these things are happening. But deep inside, an important part of us knows. Our selves know and will tell us if we listen. Sometimes living with subtle problems, such as a nondrinking alcoholic who is not in any recovery program, can be harder on us than the more blatant problems. We sense something is wrong. We start feeling crazy, but we can't understand why because we can't identify the problem.

We need boundaries. We need to set limits on what we do to and for people. We need to set limits on what we will allow people to do to and for us. The people we relate to need to know we have boundaries. It will help them and us. I am not suggesting we become tyrants. I also advise against absolute inflexibility, but we can understand our limits. As we grow and change, we may want to change our boundaries too. Here are some examples of boundaries common to recovering codependents:

- I will not allow anyone to physically or verbally abuse me.

- I will not knowingly believe or support lies.

- I will not allow chemical abuse in my home.

- I will not allow criminal behavior in my home.

- I will not rescue people from the consequences of their substance abuse or other irresponsible behaviors.

- I will not finance a person's substance abuse or other irresponsible behaviors.

- I will not lie to protect you or me from your addiction.

- If you want to act crazy, that's your business, but you can't do it in front of me. Either you leave or I'll walk away.

- You can spoil your fun, your day, your life—that's your business—but I won't let you spoil my fun, my day, or my life.

Sometimes it's necessary to set a boundary that applies to a particular relationship, such as, "I won't babysit Alana's children anymore because she takes advantage of me."

Set boundaries, but make sure they're *your* boundaries. The things you're sick of, can't stand, and make threats about may be clues to some boundaries you need to set. They may also be clues to changes you need to make within yourself. Remember, mean what you say, say what you mean, but don't be mean.

People may get angry at us for setting boundaries; they can't use us anymore. They may try to help us feel guilty so we will remove our boundary and return to the old system of letting them use or abuse us. Don't feel guilty, and don't back down. We can stick to our boundaries and enforce them. Be consistent. We will probably be tested more than once on every boundary we set. People do that to see if we're serious, especially if we weren't in the past. As codependents, we have made many empty threats. We lose our credibility, then wonder why people don't take us seriously. Tell people what your boundaries are—once, quietly, in peace. Watch your level of tolerance so the pendulum doesn't swing too far to either extreme.

Some codependents, particularly those of us in the latter stages of a relationship with an addict, may find we have a difficult time setting and enforcing boundaries. Setting limits takes time and thought; enforcing limits takes even more energy and consistency.

We don't set boundaries to control other people. Boundaries are about taking responsibility for ourselves. We often need to set limits on our own behaviors, not just on other people's behaviors. Self-love, like love for others, including our children, includes discipline. Do we have any areas of our lives, any behaviors, that we need to accept, address, and set limits on?

Boundaries are *a lot* of work, but they're essential and worth every bit of time, energy, and thought required to set and enforce them. Ultimately, they will provide us with more time and energy.

What are our limits? What boundaries do we need to establish?

PHYSICAL CARE

Sometimes in the stressful stages of codependency, we neglect our health and grooming. Look in the mirror; if you don't like what you see, fix it. If you can't fix it, you can stop hating yourself and accept it.

Self-care is important. Exercise is essential to feelings of well-being. If you're sick, go to a doctor. If you need to lose weight—or change any of your other behaviors—figure out what you need to do to take better, more loving care of yourself. The less we care for our bodies, the worse we will feel about ourselves.

Taking care of our emotional selves is also connected to our bodies. If we refuse long enough to take care of ourselves, our bodies will rebel and become sick, forcing us and the people around us to caretake in the way we need. It's easier to take care of ourselves before we get sick.

PROFESSIONAL HELP

We need to seek professional help if:

- We are depressed and thinking about suicide.

- We want to do an intervention and confront an alcoholic or other troubled person.

- We have been the victim of physical or sexual abuse.

- We have been physically or sexually abusing somebody else.

- We are experiencing problems with alcohol or other drugs.

- We can't seem to solve our problems or get "unstuck" by ourselves.

- We believe, for any other reason, we might benefit from professional help.

Remember to trust ourselves when we go to professionals. Pay attention to our feelings. If we aren't comfortable with the agency or person we're working with, if we don't agree with the direction the counseling is taking, or if we in any way don't trust the help we're receiving (or not receiving), find another professional. We may be experiencing a normal resistance to change, but it could be the person we're working with isn't right for us. Not all professionals are able to work well with every human.

If you seek help and it doesn't seem right for you, seek different help. You don't have to give up your power to think, feel, and make good decisions to anyone—including someone with a PhD after their name. A list of resources is available at the back of this book.

We can get ourselves the best care possible.

TRUST

People with codependency issues frequently aren't certain whom or when to trust. "Heather's been in treatment for alcoholism two weeks. She's lied to me 129 times. Now she's mad at me because I say I don't trust her. What should I do?"

I've repeatedly heard variations of this. My answer is usually the same: there's a difference between trust and stupidity. Of course you don't trust Heather. Quit trying to make yourself trust someone you don't trust.

Throughout the book I have repeated this phrase, and I will say it again: *we can trust ourselves.* We can trust ourselves to make good decisions about whom to trust. Many of us have been making inappropriate decisions about trust. It is not wise to trust an alcoholic to never drink again if that alcoholic has not received treatment for the disease of alcoholism. It is not even wise to trust an alcoholic never to drink again if they *have* received treatment—there are no guarantees on human behavior. But we can trust people to be who they are. We can learn to see people clearly.

Figure out if people's words match their behaviors. Is what they say the same as what they *do*? As one woman put it, "He's looking real good, but he's not acting any better."

If we pay attention to ourselves and the messages we receive from the world, we will know whom to trust, when to trust, and why to trust a particular person. We may discover we've always known whom to trust—we just weren't listening to ourselves.

SEX

In one breath, a codependent will tell me her marriage is falling apart. In the next breath, she will ask if it's normal to have sexual problems when things get that bad.

Yes, it's normal to have sexual problems. Many people have problems with sex. Many codependents experience sexual problems. Addiction and the whole range of compulsive disorders attack all areas of intimacy.[4] Sometimes, the physical expression of love is the last and final loss we suffer—the blow that tells us the problem won't go away, no matter how long we close our eyes.

Sometimes the substance abuser has the problem. They become impotent or lose sexual desire. This can happen both before and after recovery. Frequently, it's the codependent who has problems with sex. There is a range of difficulties that can be encountered in the bedroom. We may be unable to achieve orgasm, fear loss of control, or lack trust in our partners. We may withdraw emotionally, be unwilling to be vulnerable with, or lack desire for our partners. We may feel revulsion toward our partners, or we may not be getting our needs met because we're not asking to get these needs met. The relationship probably isn't going to be much better in bed than it is outside the bedroom. If we're caretaking in the kitchen, we'll probably be caretaking in the bedroom. If we're angry and hurt before we make love, we'll probably feel angry and hurt after we make love. If we don't want to be in the relationship, we won't want to have sex with that person. The sexual relationship will echo and reflect the overall tone of the relationship.

Sexual problems can sneak up on people. For a while, sex can be the salvation of a troubled relationship. It can be a way of making up after an argument. Talking seems to clear the air, and physical intimacy makes it all better. After a certain point, though, talking may no longer clear the air. Talking just fogs it up more, and sex stops making it better. Instead, sex can make things worse.

For some, sex may become a purely clinical act that provides approximately the same emotional satisfaction as brushing one's teeth. For others, it can become a time of humiliation and degradation: another chore, another duty, something else we should but don't want to do. It becomes one more area that isn't working, that we feel guilty and ashamed about, that we try to lie to ourselves about. We have one more area in our lives that causes us to wonder, *What's wrong with me?*

I'm not a sex therapist. I have no cures or technical advice—just some common sense. I believe taking care of ourselves means we apply the same principles in the bedroom as we do in any other area of our lives. First, we stop blaming and hating ourselves. Then we get honest with ourselves. We stop running, hiding, and denying. We gently ask ourselves what we're feeling and thinking, then we trust our answers. We respectfully listen to ourselves. We don't abuse and punish ourselves. We understand the problem we're experiencing is a normal response to the system we've been living in.

Of course we're having that problem—it's a normal part of the process. It would be abnormal not to feel revulsion, withdrawal, lack of trust, or other negative feelings. There's nothing wrong with us.

After we've sorted things out and gotten honest with ourselves, it's time to get honest with our partner. We need to tell them what we're thinking and feeling, and what we need from them. We can explore possibilities, negotiating and compromising when appropriate. If we can't solve our problems by ourselves, we can seek professional help.

Some of us may have sought comfort in affairs. We need to forgive ourselves and figure out what we need to do to take care of ourselves. Take the Fourth and Fifth Steps; talk to a counselor. We can try to understand that our actions were common reactions to the problems we've been living with.

Some of us may be trying to run from our problems by having a series of unsatisfactory sexual relationships. That frequently occurs during the denial stage, when compulsive behaviors tend to set in. We don't have to continue doing that. We can face and solve our problems in other ways. We can forgive ourselves and quit hurting ourselves.

Some of us may be looking for love and coming up with sex instead. If that's you, figure out what you need and how to best meet your needs.

Some of us may need to start asking for what we need. Others may need to learn to say no. Some of us may be trying to force love back into a dead relationship by trying to feign sexual enjoyment. That technique may not work. Sex isn't love; it's sex. It doesn't make love exist if the love wasn't there to start with. Sex is a way to express the love that already exists.

Some of us may have given up and decided that sex isn't all that important. I happen to believe sex is important. It's not the most important thing in life, but it's an important part of my life.

Sex is a powerful force, a source of intimacy and pleasure. We can take care of ourselves if our sex lives aren't working the way we'd like them to. We are responsible for our sexual behavior—for our enjoyment or lack of pleasure in bed. We can ask ourselves, What are our sex lives telling us about our relationships?

20

Soothe Yourself

Happiness is not something ready-made. It comes
from your own actions.

—HIS HOLINESS THE 14TH DALAI LAMA

It's Christmas week, 1990, and my daughter's friend, Joey,
brings us a family gift.

During the gift exchange, Joey's present for us—a snow
globe containing a mom and her little girl and boy—crashes to the
floor, shattering into shards. It felt awkward, slightly ominous, the
way accidents do.

None of us could know the tragedy foreshadowed by this meta-
phorical gift until a month later, when my son Shane died on his
twelfth birthday in an accident on the ski slopes at Afton Alps, ten
minutes from our home in Minnesota. His sister and Joey were at his
side. Our family shattered into pieces as surely as that snow globe.

Irreparably.

Many of us have had our worlds shattered. The shattering may
not be as instantly noticeable as when a loved one dies, but the

trauma lines—the cracks and psychological fault lines—are still there.

In *Lead Me Home*, a Netflix documentary about homelessness on the West Coast, people serving those without shelter responded to the plight of a mother living in a tent encampment with her two young children.

"This is an extreme situation," a helper said. "We gotta get you guys into housing."

"You know, this is funny," the mother said to the people wanting to help her. "You gradually get into an extreme situation, and it doesn't seem as . . . *extreme*."[1]

This minimization can occur when a situation overpowers and sweeps us along. For instance, we discover that the person of our dreams is an alcoholic. Or we're born into a family with existing alcoholism, addiction, or abuse. We may not consciously register that our lives are traumatic or psychologically devastating when we live with the same behaviors and trauma every day. To cope, to keep the balance, we often internalize, normalize, deny, ignore. We go on to develop our own repertoires of psychological tics, self-harming behaviors, and other addictive or self-hating patterns, including the beliefs that we're not lovable, that we're not enough, and that for some reason, somehow, we deserve this mess. Meanwhile, our fear, anxiety, and trauma bubble away under the surface, eroding our foundation and possibly leading to illness—headache, tummy ache, or worse. Even when the conscious mind forgets (or denies), "the body keeps the score," as Bessel van der Kolk's bestselling book on trauma declares.[2]

Panic/panic attacks, anxiety attacks, trauma, post-traumatic stress disorder (PTSD), complex PTSD (c-PTSD), social anxiety disorder, phobias, obsessive-compulsive disorder (OCD), separation anxiety, attachment disorder, disassociation—all are spin-offs and first cousins of anxiety and trauma that have been categorized, identified, and labelled since 1621 when Robert Burton first penned *The Anatomy of Melancholy*.

According to the National Institute of Mental Health, anxiety disorders are currently the most prominent mental health issue in the US (though human responses to anxiety and trauma are universal),[3] yet only about one-third of those suffering are seeking and finding solutions.[4] Fear, anxiety, panic, and trauma have worked their way into the hearts, minds, souls, and bodies of the people, the culture, the consciousness until becoming part of—a dominant part of—many of our stories.

I'm not referring to an occasional sleepless night, everyday worries, or occasionally overthinking big decisions. This chapter is about the kind of anxiety and trauma that cripples and how to break free from its grip.

"I didn't know I was wounded," said one sufferer. "I just limped when I walked."

. . .

"Anxiety? I've had it as long as I can remember, even before I knew what it was," Leah, a nineteen-year-old college freshman, said. "It's crippling. Paralyzing."

Born into a loving, supportive family, this smart, creative young woman has so much anxiety that it makes her family chronically anxious, though like many of us, she hides it from all but her most trusted.

"I think a lot of it comes from FOMO [fear of missing out]. I get triggered by relationships, social settings, friends. And social media, though I don't use it much anymore," Leah said. "I go to therapy; I tried meditation; and occasionally, I use medication. The school I attend is surrounded by nature. Getting out in it—going for walks—helps. So does working out, even if it's just a little."

The biggest relief, Leah said, happens when she can completely immerse herself in an art project and she transcends her anxiety. Leah loves to draw.

"It bugs me when I have a long day of classes and I'm feeling anxious, depressed—which goes to hopeless—because I feel incapable of completing my day. But when I don't have school or plans, it doesn't bother me as much because I use art and homework as an outlet."

Without these positive outlets, she can't do much. "I—and most of my classmates—aren't that interested in getting married, having families," she said. "We're trying to figure out how to make the world a better, safer place."

Some days, similar to others with anxiety or trauma disorders, she's immersed in anxiety. *Anxiety-ing.* Paralyzed—frozen in place with a windmill of fearful thoughts and emotions whirring inside and around her at high speed.

"If I pick up my phone and start scrolling—looking outside myself for a distraction—it worsens," Leah said. "And when I have a good day, I instantly think, *Oh, this won't last.* Then I get more anxious."

"Anxiety's real," American singer/songwriter Adam Lambert said. "It's a beast."[5]

• • •

So are trauma and PTSD, although they can manifest differently from their cousins, anxiety and panic.

Geoff, now in his midforties, described his family and childhood as idyllic.

"My parents loved—adored—each other and us."

Geoff has two siblings; he's the youngest. "I'd just hit puberty; I was pretty sure I was gay," Geoff said. "I'd started to talk to my mom about it when she got sick, was misdiagnosed, and suddenly died from colon cancer."

Geoff's snow globe shattered.

"I felt like I lost control," Geoff said. And gradually, he did lose control (as many of us do because control is an illusion).

Geoff began pouring all his energy into controlling what he could. In school in New York, he became the perfect student, an overachiever. College was pre-alcoholism time, as Geoff divided his energy between studying hard all week and partying hard on the weekends. "I was a binge drinker, but until age thirty my favorite drink with dinner was milk."

On September 11, 2001, Geoff lost friends and, like many people, got swept up in a wave of cultural trauma that triggered fault lines in many psyches. He volunteered on weekends, feeding workers at Ground Zero and visiting firemen and others who were hospitalized. Unable to sleep, he went to a doctor who prescribed Xanax, a benzodiazepine used to treat panic and anxiety, and Ambien for sleep. He was just twenty-two. Geoff took a Xanax. For the first time in as long as he could remember, he felt relaxed. Calm. "I could think one thought at a time," Geoff said. "I was unflappable."

He took an Ambien, and finally he could sleep.

For the next ten years, he maintained his routine of weekend binge drinking and medicating nightly with Xanax and Ambien. He worked two summers as an intern in Mayor Giuliani's office ("Something I used to be proud of," he said) and then was offered a job connected to the New York State division of tourism, tasked with helping to make New York a tourist destination once again.

After a few years, it was time for a change. Geoff decided to move to Los Angeles and pursue a career in the entertainment business. But on the night of the first big premier for a film he'd worked on, he received an emergency phone call. His brother, Frankie, had been discovered lying on the floor of his home alone— bleeding out. He had stabbed himself five times in a deliberate act of self-harm.

"He's my brother, and I love him," Geoff said. "I flew to the East Coast, got him into a hospital, made sure he was okay."

"After Mom died, Frankie had started eating. A lot," Geoff explained. "When he began cutting himself, he was topping the scales at four hundred pounds and telling himself he could be happy only when he lost the weight. In retrospect, he was also an alcoholic. So was my sister—though our parents weren't. They were old-school normies when it came to drinking. Occasionally Mom and Dad had a cocktail or glass of wine while we all watched Dan Rather on the news. On special occasions—like their anniversary—they'd go out and come home a little buzzed. That was it! But since Mom's death, my two older siblings had become roaring alcoholics."

Frankie returned to drinking as soon as he was released. Geoff was on his way too.

Around this time, Geoff's dad, concerned about the mental health of his two older children, named Geoff his medical proxy.

As his siblings continued to drink themselves into oblivion, Geoff returned to Los Angeles and his routine of weekend binge drinking and nightly doses of Xanax and Ambien.

Then in 2010 Geoff's dad was diagnosed with terminal lung cancer. In his role as medical proxy, it fell to Geoff to tell him. Geoff stopped drinking and flew to the East Coast to care for his dad. "I hadn't visited him in a while," Geoff said. "He was so happy, so excited to see me. He didn't know why I was there, no idea at all ... until I told him."

His dad didn't have much time left, but he wanted one last Christmas with his children. "It was our family's—and his— favorite holiday," Geoff said. "We did our traditional holiday routines. Two days after Christmas, the family drove into the city for a musical and a fabulous dinner—one of our favorite holiday traditions. On the way home, I saw—I watched—my dad make the decision: he was ready to go now."

Three weeks later, Geoff's father passed.

After the funeral, Geoff stayed to pack up his dad's house, overwhelmed by the memories. When he left, he also took the remaining hospice medications (but not the Fentanyl patches). "Thank God I never got into opiates," he said. The following spring, 2011, Geoff went on a two-month binge. For the first time, he realized the depth of his problem and admitted himself to a well-known hospital claiming a nervous breakdown. Hospital staff, reassured that he wasn't self-harming, let him rest—then prescribed more Xanax and sleeping pills to treat his anxiety and grief.

After his release, he resumed his old habits. In time, Geoff was drinking a handle of vodka (1.75 liters) daily. He drank to wash down his daily prescribed medications, which now included:

Xanax, Klonopin (another benzodiazepine for anxiety), Ativan (a benzodiazepine for anxiety), Ambien (for sleep), and Lunesta (a sedative for insomnia). At the tail end of an eight-week binge, at an art event gathering, Geoff had an awakening: *I've ingested enough alcohol and antianxiety medication to kill, or at least tranquilize, a horse, and I'm still standing—and still anxious. Whatever I'm doing isn't working.*

It was 2015, four years since he had presented at the hospital with a nervous breakdown and was sent home with more prescriptions for antianxiety drugs. Unsure what to do next but knowing something needed to be done, Geoff turned to his brother for help.

Frankie was still struggling with weight loss. "And was and is a total narcissist," Geoff said. "We'd never been close. He resented me because I'm buff and he's not. And because I was *out* and he wasn't." But his brother had accomplished one major feat: he'd stopped drinking the year before. Geoff explained as best he could what he was going through, and on the anniversary of 9/11, Frankie flew to LA in response to his brother's call for help.

Sometimes traumatic events can go the other way; they can be the catalyst for healing. This time, that's what happened.

Frankie took Geoff back to the hospital that had failed him in 2011, one of the best in LA, because of its many resources. The brothers waited while the doctors reviewed Geoff's case and the medications he was taking. And then the doctors suggested some additional anxiety and sleep medications.

"My brother was here four years ago, and the medications you prescribed then didn't help him," Frankie said. "If you do not take helpful action now and do something truly of benefit to him, *I. Will. Sue. You.*"

"I love my brother, but he'd never been a big brother, a protec-tor," Geoff said. "Until that moment. I'd never even seen him stand up for himself."

They left the hospital and found a treatment center in Pasa-dena. After eight days in detox and twenty-eight days in inpatient treatment, Geoff stopped drinking and taking pills. Besides spending time in nature, walking, and working out, Geoff now uses the Twelve Steps, talk therapy, and Calm, a meditation app, to soothe his anxiety and trauma. He's been free from alcohol for seven years, living his life, managing his anxiety, and addressing his codependency.

"What happened with my brother, and then treatment, really opened my heart," Geoff said. "It opened my relationship with Frankie. We started talking about stuff that matters." They'd built enough trust that Frankie had come out to him.

Geoff is also dealing with codependency and setting boundaries with his sister, who finally entered treatment herself. "I can let go of her now," Geoff said. "No matter what happens, I did my best."

He is learning that he can't control anything but himself and his responses to life. "If I'm hollering at two people in one day, it isn't them," he said. "It's me."

"Open to people. If you need help, ask. People will open to you; they'll help when they can," he said. "My heart is open; I have compassion and empathy now for others and myself. And I'm learning to set boundaries."

His journey and experiences have helped him create a better life. He understands that tending to his trauma, anxiety, alcoholism, and codependency will be part of his future, but he doesn't mind. "I like me now and the people I meet in recovery and life. They've expanded and helped change my world."

Geoff also has a new appreciation for his past. "I'm seeing what a blessed and fairly unusual childhood I had, to be born to such loving, great parents. To be loved that much. Many people I meet have had horrid, traumatic childhoods. In some ways, having such an idyllic childhood made losing Mom—and later Dad—so much more devastating," Geoff said. "Yet the blessing was all the gifts they gave me: a solid belief in myself, the belief that I'm lovable, the importance of being kind and living by values. I'm seeing how rare that is. Having my parents was such a gift, though it ripped out my heart when I lost them."

. . .

Isabella (Izzy), age fifty-two, has been married twenty-two years. She and her husband have two daughters, both in college. Izzy's codependency is centered around her daughter, Leah, who, as described in a previous story, suffers from extreme anxiety. On top of that, Izzy's introduction to trauma came seven years ago, when the doctors told her she had breast cancer. Izzy's illness may likely have been the trigger for Leah's anxiety too. "My older daughter lets things out dramatically, then gets over them and gets on with her life," Izzy said. "Leah bottles everything inside. You never know what's going on with her."

When Izzy got her diagnosis, she was scared to death. "It was high anxiety. I learned I'd be going through a double mastectomy, chemo, radiation, and then reconstructive surgery," she said. "I have a lot of friends who are breast cancer survivors; many of them had been diagnosed before me. Seeing that they were fine and getting on with their lives reassured me that I'd be okay."

Izzy began researching what she could do to help herself get through this time. "The first thing I did was switch to a plant-based diet. Then I started meditating daily, began walking two to three miles every morning, did restorative yoga, and started weekly acupuncture. All of this helped," Izzy said. Being self-aware and taking good care of herself also helps her codependency with Leah.

Izzy works as the manager of the business that she and her husband are part owners of. "The pandemic didn't give me anxiety," she said. "Reopening understaffed—and all the crazies I deal with on the job—did."

A now healthy, vital Izzy observed, "I remind myself that everything will be okay, and I have to just think about the present and not the future. And—meditation still helps!"

. . .

Whether we're born into trauma or trauma and anxiety find us later in life (or both)—or whether we're born or come into idyllic circumstances that later become shattered—the common denominator is a loss of control. We can't control a situation that's already hurt or threatening to harm us. We're overwhelmed. And oftentimes stuck—feeling controlled by forces we cannot control and not knowing how to free ourselves.

Grief isn't trauma; grief isn't codependency. But trauma and grief can exacerbate and trigger codependency, other addictions, and a multitude of dysfunctions. Grief—mixed with trauma, anxiety, and PTSD—can create an emotional, spiritual, and sometimes physical mess. No matter who or what contributed or contributes to this, it's unfailingly and relentlessly *our job and responsibility* to sort this mess along our path to well-being.

"I've learned that my life is a journey through increasingly challenging events, all of which I need to surrender to," Joseph Teralis Arison said. Born in 1952, Teralis comes from a unique background in Eastern philosophy, yoga, and metaphysics. First licensed as an acupuncturist and bodyworker in 1982, and having enriched his education with years of study abroad, he now combines the art and practice of healing with mysticism.

Although they never met in person, Teralis credits Paramahansa Yogananda with being his first guru and the man who set him on his spiritual path.

"He began coming to me in my dreams," Teralis said. "In each dream encounter, he'd first comfort me, then tell me—pointing toward an indistinct but welcoming place—that I needed to visit it often to find the direction, healing, and comfort I so needed. And would need throughout my life."

After repeated dreams in which the yogi Paramahansa delivered the same message, the light came on for Teralis. "I realized he wasn't talking about me visiting a physical location," Teralis explained. "He was talking about regular visits to that sacred space—*inside myself*—to reset, heal, and find guidance."

The yogi was telling him to meditate.

Like Xanax, meditation can help us feel calm, unflappable, and think one thought at a time. Unlike Xanax, there are no untoward or cumulative negative side effects. If there was a gift I could give every child, every incarcerated adult, every veteran, every human—it would be the gift of learning to meditate and visit this place. Imagine living in a world with calm, peace-loving, unflappable people.

Many different meditation techniques exist. I'm not writing about reading a meditation daily, although that can help ground and settle us. I'm suggesting a serious, committed meditation practice that daily realigns our minds, bodies, souls, and emotions; a practice that stabilizes us and resets our internal clocks, especially for those of us held hostage by panic, anxiety, trauma, or PTSD.

We can't think our way out of panic, trauma, PTSD, and extreme anxiety attacks. We cannot criticize, badger, or bully ourselves out of these states. But meditation flicks the Off switch. There are many types of meditation and many ways to meditate and many apps and books to help guide us. Geoff started meditating one minute a day (using an app), then increased it to two minutes, then three, and so on. There are many good YouTube videos on meditation as well.

Some gurus and Eastern teachers suggest staring at a flower or a beautiful scene in nature until we go into a heightened state and become peaceful. Unfortunately, I've had too much trauma for that. While immersing myself in nature helps me maintain calm, when I'm in a heightened state of anxiety, staring at a rose and waiting to become peaceful just annoys me.

It wasn't until I took classes in Transcendental Meditation (TM) that I discovered a meditation technique that quelled my trauma and took me to that sacred space. Every time. In TM, I received a mantra. The mantra is in Aramaic; it makes no sense to my monkey mind. Thinking this mantra repeatedly while in a meditative pose allows me to relax and reset. I began meditating twice daily for twenty minutes each time, and before long, I knew when the twenty minutes had passed as I could feel—*I knew*—that I had reset and realigned.

Meditating has calmed my PTSD; it doesn't irritate me, and it facilitates a continual sense of calm that allows me to become truly unflappable. If or when I start flapping anyway, a meditation session brings me home—into my body and to my soul.

What works for me may not work for you. The point is, we can each find a meditation technique that works for us. Anxiety and trauma take us out of our bodies; meditation brings us back home—to our highest selves.

• • •

Anxiety, trauma, and PTSD are counterintuitive. They may scream at us (or strongly suggest) that we do something, anything—even if it's wrong—just to relieve the pressure. Often the action is an impulsive behavior that serves only to wreak more havoc in our lives.

What follows are some ideas and tools that won't bring harmful negative consequences (and more trauma) upon us. Lean into the ideas; investigate and play with the ones that appeal to you. Discover what soothes, comforts, and helps you come back to and stay in that sacred space, no matter what's going on around you. Fortunately, the most helpful approach to trauma, anxiety, and PTSD is similar to that for treating codependent behaviors: extreme doses of self-love administered daily and as needed.

1. *Get comfortable with saying, "I don't know."* Living with uncertainty can cause pressure and tension—if we let it. So can living in

resistance. Much personal power comes when we surrender to uncertainty. None of us *knows*—not really. We may have inklings from time to time, but we'll know when we know, won't we? A perk of allowing ourselves to live in the unknown is that, often, life becomes more magical and spontaneous because we're not trying to control everything to get it to conform to what we've already decided it should be. We become more open to the daily smaller miracles. Becoming comfortable with not knowing helps us discover, trust, and believe in life.

2. *Slow down; don't skip steps.* Anxiety uninterrupted can cause us to take untimely, rushed, or hurried steps. When we're overwhelmed, we can attempt to do everything at once, then get paralyzed. Or we can attempt to "push through" the anxiety and force ourselves to the finish line with whatever we're not doing well because we're not acting from a place of peace. Forced action usually breaks something—often that something is us. If we're vibrating with anxiety and fear, treat the anxiety first. Then move forward. It works better.

3. *Learn to pause before speaking or acting. Or deciding.* Knee-jerk reactions and responses usually don't work; they create more tension and trauma drama. Our best responses and reactions don't come from trauma. Strive to speak and act from a place of peace.

4. *Let your yes mean yes and your no mean no.* Doing so decreases our anxiety and simplifies life. It also connects us to power and our highest selves. When Teralis was an adolescent, his mom used to strike him—often on the face. One day, as her hand reached out to

hit him, he blocked her attack. "Don't do that anymore," he said. "I don't like it." She never struck him again. Not having boundaries creates more stress and anxiety. Clear boundaries help. Pay attention to yourself—what you like and what you don't. It's how we discover what really matters, who we're becoming, and what we want to create in our lives.

5. *Make destiny-friendly decisions.* Make choices that won't create more problems—and more anxiety and stress—in the future. Watch for red flags. If we're doing something that could or will hurt us but we can't stop, we should ask for help and practice harm reduction until we can cease the behavior.

6. *Try not to use denial more than is necessary.* Denial creates anxiety even though it may bring temporary relief. When I know I'm running from something, I attempt to slow down and then consciously become open to seeing and facing the truth.

7. *Ground yourself—in your body, your life.* So much of trauma, panic, and anxiety is about these frenzied fight-or-flight attempts triggering us to escape our bodies, our lives, our emotions. If we can't escape, disassociation is our next tactic. Living life from disconnection to our souls/emotions/bodies—our interior worlds—creates unaligned lives, unaligned behaviors, and potential future drama. We can go a bit "off." Easy-to-do grounding behaviors include belly breathing and the rule of three for anxiety, recommended by the East Central Minnesota Adult Mental Health Initiative: (1) name three things you can see, (2) name three things you can hear, and (3) move three body parts until you can feel them

(hand, arm, foot, leg—any body part will do). We're right where we need to be, each moment in time. We're not missing out.

8. *Feel your feelings.* "I ran from my feelings like they were this big slobbering monster chasing me," a woman once said to me. They're not. And we can't run from them; they're inside us, part of us, until we feel them. After experiencing deep loss or trauma, we may think any additional pain or loss will completely devastate us, or we may feel like we're invincible when it comes to emotional pain and don't need to acknowledge "the small stuff." Neither attitude is helpful. The middle road is acknowledging and accepting what we feel; no need for a big production. Then we can comfort ourselves if need be. Once we're at peace, we'll know if we need to take action and what that should be (but remember, not all emotions require follow-up). We don't need to fear our feelings; that reflex may be a response to the survival device we learned during childhood: *don't feel.* All we need to do is acknowledge our feelings and allow ourselves to feel them.

9. *Support yourself with helpful, kind self-talk.* Often the voice in our heads that narrates as we go through our days is the voice of the most hypercritical, negative, judging, scolding, and mean person involved with our formative years. Become aware of self-talk; make it loving and kind while holding yourself accountable. Once every so often, a "poor baby" said lovingly to console ourselves doesn't hurt either.

10. *Unless it's a true emergency, learn to extend beginnings and endings.* Anxiety wants to know *now*, wants it done *now*, wants it

over—whatever it is we've decided we might need to do. Sometimes that's initiating a relationship, sometimes it's ending one. Don't be in such a rush to cram your life together—or break it apart. Sudden, abrupt endings—with a friend, partner, lover, or job—create trauma. (The exception: if you're being abused, you need to act quickly, but acting quickly *and calmly* is key.)

11. *Stop playing to the cameras.* I'm talking about social media here. When we know we're being watched, when we seek being watched, it changes everything. Seek calmness and integrity with yourself instead. See yourself.

12. *Build a life in the real world; it can be much more rewarding than one built in the ethers.* Make a friend in the "real world," not online. Go outside—for walks, for runs, even just to sit and observe sometimes. Nature can do miracles for calming and healing a raw nervous system. There's a palpable difference between watching a screensaver of a magnificent nature scene and being in nature. Soak up as much sunshine and fresh air as you can. If possible, get a plant and a pet. Service animals have enormously benefitted those with PTSD. Watch and engage with how living creatures in the real world live and respond; watch how life continually changes— usually slowly and incrementally. Phones and computers are tools; we're not meant to live in them.

13. *Move your body as much as possible.* Exercise works. It helps discharge pent-up energy; it releases stress. This is something we may have to lean into, depending on our age, health, and physical condition. We don't have to torture ourselves with working out either.

Choose something you enjoy. Go for a walk (outdoors is best, but a treadmill can work too). Strength training, cardio, yoga (hot and regular)—there's a large menu of physical activities available. My favorite and daily workout is the Five Tibetan Rites, five yoga moves done in a particular order, starting with one to three repetitions and working up to twenty-one—at your own pace. Most of my friends are walkers; a few ride bicycles. My neighbor in her early sixties (and living with multiple sclerosis for more than thirty years) manages an AirBnB, walks, rides a bike, scuba dives, cooks, builds things, and does many repairs herself. She inspires me to move my body. Recently she broke her ankle, requiring two surgeries and a month confined to bed in her garage apartment. "Gotta be grateful," she said. "At least they can fix this!"

14. *Clean house—often.* We need to clean both our living environment and our emotional interior. Too much clutter, whether it's outdated stuff we need to sort or emotions of resentment, anger, or unforgiveness we're holding on to, blocks us.

15. *Ensure you feel as safe as possible.* When trauma, anxiety, PTSD, and stress hijack the brain—with the fight-or-flight mechanism wailing like a siren only we can hear—it can be challenging to distinguish whether the threat is real or a response to the past. As children, we may have been forced to live with unsafe people. As adults, we may have encountered them at home or in the workplace. We don't have to start reacting to every microexpression of the people around us; that's not helpful to anyone. Who do you like being around? (And remember, just because we like someone or

something doesn't mean they're good for us.) Who's safe? Who do you want to let in? You get to choose now.

16. *Be of service. Deliberately.* Be of service when you choose to and when it feels right. Use your intuition; follow your spirit. Acts of service, love, and kindness aren't codependent. They benefit others and help heal our souls.

17. *Be flexible and willing to start over as often as needed.* GOGI— Getting Out by Going In—refers to getting out of any prison we find ourselves in by going within. The GOGI nonprofit was founded by volunteer Coach Mara Taylor to help the incarcerated create a sense of internal freedom, regardless of their surroundings or circumstance. The tools she and the incarcerated population developed include: Tools of the Body (Boss of My Brain, Belly Breathing, and Five Second Lightswitch—which involves finding five reasons to make the best, most destiny-friendly decision possible in various circumstances); Tools of Choice (Positive Thoughts, Positive Words, Positive Actions); Tools of Moving Forward (Claim Responsibility, Let Go, For-Give); and Tools of Creation (What If, Reality Check, Ultimate Freedom)—a helpful blend of easy, practical wisdom for anyone starting over. You can learn more at https://www.gettingoutbygoingin.org.

18. *Don't gaslight yourself.* Although gaslighting has left the realm of jargon and entered the vernacular, this term refers to what most of us who've loved an alcoholic or addict have experienced and confronted when realizing we're not crazy; we have codependency

issues and are responding to a dysfunctional situation. Don't buy in. We can't control whether someone attempts to gaslight us. But we can choose whether or not we accept, agree with, take in, and absorb the negative talk aimed at us. If you have bought into some gaslighting (which creates anxiety and usually anger), detach, feel your feelings, and realign with yourself. We tend to be most vulnerable to gaslighting when there's a power imbalance or the person gaslighting us has something we want (or something we don't want to lose). It's not helpful to berate and discredit ourselves or willingly step into or stay in a one-down position; it doesn't work to love someone else more than we love ourselves.

19. *Don't drink the Kool-Aid.* Don't believe the hype from anyone, including yourself. It leaves a bad taste in the mouth (and soul) after the sugar rush subsides, and it creates anxiety. Take time. Investigate the person or organization. Don't think something just because the other person says it's real and true; you decide. When we're feeling disconnected, frustrated, and anxious, we're most likely to fall prey—and it doesn't have to be because the other person/organization is attempting to manipulate us (though sometimes they are). Anyone can become disconnected from themselves. People may be trying to sell us on something. We don't have to become defensive; just mindful.

20. *No, the ends* don't *justify the means.* We are each responsible for our own behaviors and choices; sometimes we may delude ourselves or abandon our own values. Do you know what you value? Honesty, peace, kindness? Integrity? Or lots of "likes"? What's most important at the end of each day is that we like ourselves and

enjoy our lives. I was talking to a neighbor recently; he'd just returned from visiting his wife and child in Nepal. "Such a completely different world. Even when they're working, the Nepalese are at peace, enjoying themselves. Not working like crazed animals," he said. "Even the words we use are anxiety-producing. Like *deadline*." I've also discovered that the word *intention* is more helpful than *goal*, though we can use both. *Intention* allows more room for freedom of spirit, creativity, and everyday miracles. *Intention* puts *control* into the back seat (or trunk)—where it belongs.

21. *Loving and accepting yourself unconditionally is paramount and key to daily recovery for anxiety and codependency.* When I was in chemical dependency treatment back in 1973, one of the orientation lectures was about work and love. The lecturer used to drill into us once a week (which, because I was there eight months, I heard approximately thirty-three times) that work and love are ultimately the same, but it may take us a while to discover what this means. He was correct. Don't ever abandon your soul and self-love for any relationship or job. Bring your beautiful self to each thing you do and each human and creature you interact with. When we do this, we create a beautiful life.

22. *Understand that you are a human being—not a brand.* We may have brands, but we're not one. We're people. Subjects, not objects—subjects with souls.

23. *Remember that every moment, action, and interaction doesn't need to be (and usually isn't) a make-or-break, end-of-the-world, life-changing, and defining moment.* Every moment matters; so does

each stage of our growth. Immerse yourself in nature; see what a brilliant job it does—one moment at a time—slowly, incrementally, in season. We can allow and appreciate our own growth that way too. Holistically. Unpanicked. Patiently, in love.

24. *Laugh at least once a day.* Preferably more.

25. *Have your own back.* Don't turn on yourself. When you most need comfort, love, forgiveness, acceptance, or a listening ear, don't start judging and accusing yourself. Don't grow cold toward yourself; don't call yourself names. Comfort yourself the way you would a young child—tenderly, lovingly, with kindness. Don't scold; that's not comforting. Nobody's perfect, and what's "perfect" anyway? People do wonderful things and sometimes awful things, then more wonderful things because of the lessons learned from the awful things they did. We lose touch with ourselves and go off course at times. Then we learn, get back on track, and move forward. Let yourself have all your lessons and experiences. Stop with the hypervigilance. It isn't our job to be a human lie detector and ensure everyone is telling us the whole truth each time they speak. Our job is to not deceive ourselves or others. Take the superpowers you learned from the hard stuff; enjoy the love you give and receive along the way. Create the most fulfilling life you can—little by slowly—one day, moment, intention, feeling, new belief at a time. Don't lock yourself into the worst moment of your life and then remind yourself of it daily, keeping your self-contempt attached to that vision. It's also not helpful to judge others based on the worst moments of their lives. What we can do is hold them and ourselves

accountable. People change every moment. Life changes every moment (though it may seem entirely tedious at times). Grow more compassion for others. But get a big bunch for yourself too, then generously apply as needed. Our mistakes help create our challenges and often our greatest lessons. Life shapes us the way the winds shape a tree. Of all the damage trauma does, of all the things it can and does take from us—an inherent sense of safety, a trusting spirit, a receptive heart—possibly the most damage is what it does internally to our confidence in life and ourselves. We may come through the traumatic event convinced we're not lovable, that something is fundamentally wrong with us, that we deserved to have our world shattered. No matter what trauma tells you, you can tell yourself you're enough. You're up to the task at hand; you can face your life every day. You're lovable—completely capable of giving love and open to receiving it as well. Maybe perfection is being who we are—not when we get to that one moment in time when we arbitrarily decide we've made it, but in all the moments along the way.

．．．

Whether the globe of your life shatters in one moment or develops fault lines and cracks slowly, trauma is about more than endings; it's the beginning of transformation. The purpose of the shattering isn't to stay broken; we can allow ourselves to be transformed and even take an active role in that transformation.

It begins by making our personal world—our own life and environment—better and safer. We are the carers, caregivers, empaths, and nurturers, right? It's not like we don't know how to do it, we just have to learn to care for ourselves. So go ahead: make yourself feel warm and cozy.

Then let your light shine.

1. Many codependent behaviors have their roots in anxiety/trauma. Get acquainted with your trauma, anxiety, panic, or PTSD. Keep a journal, a dedicated trauma notebook. Plan on writing in it over an extended period. Keep a gentle watch on yourself. This anxiety beast, when it has a hold on us, will drive us to do things that won't help, such as doomscrolling on our phones or worse. What things do you do to distract yourself or disassociate? How do you feel when you distract yourself? How do you feel afterward? What triggers you? How anxious do you feel around the people in your life? Who do you feel safe with? Who puts you on edge? What situations trigger impulsive or compulsive behaviors? Take notes. This activity is about becoming aware. You don't need to do anything; just peek inside yourself. Look under the hood. Get to know your anxiety.

2. Watch how you're healing; take note of that as well. It will happen incrementally, but it's important to note our improvements and changes. Give yourself regular reviews.

3. Seek help if or when you get stuck in any area or get in over your head. There are many no-charge support programs for mental health.

4. Here's a short list of my go-to recovery slogans I use when I'm in high anxiety. I didn't create them; they've been around recovery circles for many years. Feel free to borrow or create your own go-to list.

"What we resist, persists."

"Little by slowly."

"We don't have to like it; we just have to accept it."

"Easy does it."

"One day at a time."

"My soul can be at peace."

"God, grant me the serenity / To accept the things I cannot change, / Courage to change the things I can, / And wisdom to know the difference."

Learning to Live and Love Again

At least I don't run around actively seeking my own demise anymore.

—ANONYMOUS

O riginally I planned to separate the material in this chapter into two chapters: "Learning to Live Again" and
"Learning to Love Again." However, I decided sepa-
rately addressing living and loving wasn't the issue. The problem
many codependents encounter is learning to do both at the same
time. This chapter isn't just about romantic attachments; it's about
all our love relationships—friends, family, children, colleagues.

According to Earnie Larsen and others, the two deepest desires
most people have are (1) to love and be loved and (2) to believe
they are worthwhile and know someone else believes that too.[1]

Most of us have been trying, on some level of consciousness,
to meet these needs. To protect ourselves, some of us may have
blocked or shut off these needs. Whether we acknowledge or repress
them, they're still there. Understanding ourselves and our desires is

powerful information. What we need to learn to do is *fulfill* these desires, needs, and wants in ways that don't hurt ourselves or other people, in ways that allow maximum enjoyment of life.

For many of us, that means we need to do things differently because the ways we've gone about getting our needs met haven't worked. We've talked about some concepts that will help us do that: detachment, a non-rescuing approach to people, not controlling the objects of our attention, directness, paying attention to ourselves, and becoming undependent. I believe as we get healthier, love will be different. Love will be better, perhaps better than ever before, if we open up to and allow that.

Love doesn't have to hurt as much as it did before. We certainly don't have to let it destroy us. As one woman said, "I'm sick of being addicted to pain. I'm sick of being addicted to suffering. And I'm sick of letting people work out their unfinished business in my life!" We don't have to stay in relationships that make us miserable.

We can learn to recognize the difference between relationships that do and don't work. We can leave destructive relationships and enjoy the good ones. We can learn new behaviors that will help our good relationships work better.

I believe the universe allows certain people to come into our lives. But we're responsible for our choices and behaviors in initiating, maintaining, and/or discontinuing these relationships. We may want and need love, but we don't need destructive love. And we're not desperate anymore. When we know that, our message will come across clearly.

I believe our professional lives can be different and better. We can learn to take care of ourselves and our needs at work. And if we're not so absorbed in other people and their business, if we believe we're important, we're free to set our own goals and reach our dreams. We're able to capture a vision for our own lives—and speak up for ourselves. That's exciting because good things can, do, and will happen to us if we allow those things to happen and if we believe we deserve them. The good things probably won't happen without some struggle and pain, but at least we will be struggling and stretching for something worthwhile instead of simply suffering.

It's okay to have successful loving relationships and to enjoy all aspects of life. We may struggle and kick and want to hide our heads in the sand along the way. That's okay. That's how growth feels. If it feels too comfortable, too natural, or too easy, we're not growing, and we're not doing anything differently. We're doing the same things we always have, and that's why it feels so comfortable— it's familiar.

Learning to live and love again means finding a balance: learning to love and, at the same time, living our own lives; learning to love without getting so emotionally entangled with the objects of our affection; and learning to love others without forfeiting love for ourselves.

Much of recovery is finding and maintaining balance in all areas of our lives. We need to watch the scales so they don't tip too far to either side as we measure our responsibilities to ourselves and to others. We need to balance our emotional needs with our physical, mental, and spiritual needs. We need to balance giving and receiving; we need to find the dividing line between letting go and doing our part. We need to find a balance between solving problems and learning to live with unsolved problems. Much of our anguish comes from having to live with the grief of unsolved problems and having things not go the way we hoped and expected. We need to find a balance between letting go of our expectations and remembering we are important, valuable people who deserve to lead decent lives.

GETTING STARTED

Frequently I'm asked, where do I start? How do I get started? How do I even get my balance?

For some of us, getting our balance may seem overwhelming. We feel like we're lying flat on the floor of a dark cellar, and we cannot possibly crawl out. We can. Alcoholics Anonymous and Al-Anon offer a simple three-part formula for doing this. It follows the acronym "HOW": honesty, openness, and willingness to try. Change begins with awareness and acceptance, followed by assertive action.[2] That means doing things differently. Get honest, keep an open mind, and become willing to try to do things differently, and you will change.

Choose one behavior to work on, and when that becomes comfortable, move on to the next. I have heard we need to repeat an action twenty-one times to make it a habit. That's a rule of thumb to keep in mind. The checklist in chapter 4 may provide some clues about where to start. The activities at the end of the chapters may give us some ideas. Figure out where we want to start and begin there. Start where we're at. If we can't figure out where to start, start by going to Al-Anon meetings or another appropriate group. If we're in the basement, start crawling out. We'll learn to walk; we'll get our balance as we find and stay on our path to well-being.

At the beginning of my recovery from codependency, I felt hopelessly trapped in myself and my marriage. Gloom surrounded me, and depression seemed to have permanently confined me to my bed. One morning, I dragged myself into the bathroom to get dressed. My son burst in, insisting that I follow him. A raging fire was consuming my bedroom. It had spread to the curtains, the ceiling, and the carpet. My daughter was in school, my husband was at work. I grabbed a fire extinguisher and emptied it on the flames. Too little, too late. The fire raged on as Shane and I ran out of the house.

The house was gutted by the time the fire department arrived. It was two weeks before Christmas, and my children and I had to move into a small apartment with the most basic of comforts and minus most of our clothing. My husband decided it was all too much for him and decided he had to "go out of town for business." (Alcoholic talk for "I'm going to go on a binge.") I hit a low point of despondency and anxiety. I had already lost so much, including myself. My home had been my nest, my remaining source of emotional security, and now I'd lost that too. I'd lost everything.

As the weeks passed, life began to require a little more movement from me. Insurance inventories, negotiations, cleanup, and rebuilding plans demanded my attention. I felt anxious and insecure, but I had no choice. I had to think. I had to get busy. I had to do certain things. Once the actual reconstruction began, I had to do even more. I made choices about how to spend thousands of dollars. I worked hand in hand with the crews, doing everything I was able to do to help cut costs and expedite the project. That included physical activity, a part of my life that had become nonexistent. The busier I got, the better I felt. I began to trust my decisions.

I worked off lots of anger and fear. By the time my family and I moved back into our home, my balance had been restored. I had begun living my own life, and I wasn't going to stop. It felt good!

The important concept here is to get started. Light a fire under yourself.

GROWING FORWARD

Once we have gotten started, moving forward will become a natural process—if we continue to move. Sometimes, we'll take a few steps backward. That's okay too. Sometimes it's necessary; it's part of going forward.

Some of us may be facing tough decisions, decisions about ending relationships that are miserable and destructive. As Earnie Larsen used to say: If the relationship is dead, bury it. We can take our time, work on ourselves, and make the right decision when the time is right.

Some of us may be trying to repair damaged but still "alive" relationships. Be patient. Love and trust are fragile, living entities. They don't automatically regenerate on command if they've been bruised. Love and trust don't automatically reappear if the other person gets sober or solves whatever problem they had.[3] Love and trust must be allowed to heal in their own time. Sometimes they heal; sometimes they don't.

It's okay to be in a relationship, but it's also okay not to be in a romantic relationship. Find friends to love and be loved by; people who think you're worthwhile. Love yourself and know that you are worthwhile. Use your time alone as a breather. Let go. Learn the lessons you're meant to be learning. Grow. Develop. Work on yourself so when love comes along, it enhances a full and interesting life. Love shouldn't be the concern of our whole lives or an escape from an unpleasant life; we will only be as happy in a relationship as we were without one.

Whatever our situation, we can go slowly: Our hearts may lead us where our heads say we shouldn't go. Our heads may insist we go where our hearts don't want to follow. Sometimes our attraction to frogs may take us where neither our hearts nor heads choose to be. That's okay. There are no rules about whom we should or shouldn't love and relate to. We can love whomever we love, however we want to. But slow down and take the time to do it in a way that doesn't hurt you. Pay attention to what's happening. Love from your strengths, not from your weaknesses, and ask others to do the same. Make good decisions each day about what you need to do to take care of yourself. If you're in tune with your higher self, you'll figure out what to do and when to do that. I hope you will find people you enjoy loving—people who enjoy loving you and who challenge you to grow.

A word of caution. From time to time, you may lose your balance. You may start running, skipping, and jumping, then suddenly find yourself with your nose on the cement. All the old crazy feelings can come rushing in. Don't be frightened. This is normal. Codependent characteristics, ways of thinking, and feelings become habits. Those habitual feelings and thoughts may surface on occasion. Change (even good change), certain circumstances reminiscent of alcoholic insanity, and stress, may provoke codependency. Sometimes the craziness returns unprovoked. See it through. Don't be ashamed, and don't hide. You can pick yourself up again. You will get through it. Talk to trusted friends; be patient and generous with yourself. Just keep doing the things you know you need to do. It will get better. Don't stop taking care of yourself no matter what happens.

Getting our balance and keeping it once we've found it is what recovery is all about. If that sounds like a big order, don't worry. We can do it. We can learn to live again. We can learn to love again. We can even learn to have fun at the same time.

Acknowledgments

For helping make this book possible, I thank God, my mother, David, Shane, Nichole, Scott Egleston, and all those who generously shared their stories with me. I would also like to acknowledge Gary, who nudged me back to life.

Acknowledgment

Resources

BIPOC (BLACK, INDIGENOUS, PEOPLE OF COLOR) COMMUNITY

DEQH
DEQH is a culturally competent organization and hotline for South Asian/Desi LGBTQ+ individuals, family, and friends.
Website: deqh.org
Call: 908-367-3374

LATINX THERAPISTS ACTION NETWORK
The Latinx Therapists Action Network is a collection of Latinx mental health practitioners honoring and affirming the dignity and healing of migrant communities marginalized by criminalization, detention, and deportation.
Website: latinxtherapistsactionnetwork.org

THE LOVELAND FOUNDATION
The Loveland Foundation is a nonprofit committed to showing up for communities of color, with a particular focus on Black women

and girls. Through their Loveland Fund, they are able to pay for therapy sessions for Black women and girls who apply and meet financial criteria.

Website: thelovelandfoundation.org

STRONGHEARTS NATIVE HELPLINE

The StrongHearts Native Helpline provides a confidential and anonymous domestic violence and dating violence helpline for Native Americans.

Website: strongheartshelpline.org

Call: 844-762-8483

EATING DISORDERS

ANAD—NATIONAL ASSOCIATION OF ANOREXIA NERVOSA AND ASSOCIATED DISORDERS

ANAD is a peer-run and professionally supported organization catering to individuals struggling with eating disorders and body image issues.

Website: anad.org

Call: 888-375-7767

NEDA—NATIONAL EATING DISORDER ASSOCIATION

NEDA is a nonprofit dedicated to supporting individuals and families affected by eating disorders.

Website: nationaleatingdisorders.org

Online Chat link: https://chatserver.comm100.com/ChatWindow .aspx?siteId=144464&planId=467

Call: 800-931-2237. Translation services are available on the phone.
Text: 800-931-2237. Standard text messaging rates may apply.
*If you suspect you may have an eating disorder, NEDA has an online screening tool: https://www.nationaleatingdisorders.org /screening-tool.

GAMBLING ADDICTION

GAMBLERS ANONYMOUS

Gamblers Anonymous is a fellowship of individuals who share their experience, strength, and hope that they may solve their common problem and help others to recover from a gambling problem. The only requirement for membership is a desire to stop gambling. Website: gamblersanonymous.org

NCPG—NATIONAL COUNCIL ON PROBLEM GAMBLING

The mission of the National Council on Problem Gambling is to advocate for programs that assist people and families affected by problem gambling, facilitate community through conferences, and provide resources. They provide a twenty-four-hour confidential helpline.
Website: ncpgambling.org
Chat: ncpgammbling.org/chat
Call: 800-522-4700
Text: 800-522-4700

GAMING ADDICTION

COMPUTER GAMING ADDICTS ANONYMOUS

Computer Gaming Addicts Anonymous is a fellowship of individuals dedicated to supporting one another through the recovery from excessive gaming by offering information and meetings.
Website: cgaa.info

HOUSING AND FOOD

DIAL 211

Dial 211 is a comprehensive service organization run by the nonprofit United Way that assists people with finding food, paying housing bills, accessing free childcare, and other essential services.
Website: 211.org
Call: 211

USDA NATIONAL HUNGER HOTLINE

The USDA National Hunger Hotline provides information for families and individuals in need of food support.
Website: hungerfreeamerica.org
Call (to speak with someone in English) : 866-348-6479
Call (to speak with someone in Spanish): 877-842-6273
Text: 914-342-7744. Please note that these are automated texts.

LGBTQ+ COMMUNITY

TRANS LIFELINE

Trans Lifeline is a grassroots hotline and nonprofit offering direct emotional and financial support to trans people in crisis—for the trans community, by the trans community.

Website: translifeline.org

Call (US): 877-565-8860

Call (Canada): 877-330-6366

THE TREVOR PROJECT

The Trevor Project is dedicated to creating a safe and loving environment for LGBTQ+ and nonbinary youth. They provide a nationwide, twenty-four-hour, toll-free, and confidential suicide hotline and an online community for youth ages thirteen through twenty-four.

Website: thetrevorproject.org

Call: 866-488-7386

Text: START to 678678

MENTAL HEALTH

ADAA—ANXIETY AND DEPRESSION ASSOCIATION OF AMERICA

ADAA is a nonprofit dedicated to the prevention, treatment, and cure of anxiety, depression, OCD, PTSD, and co-occurring disorders through both science and education. This is not a direct service organization, but ADAA has a searchable database of therapists.

Website: adaa.org

IOCDF—International OCD Foundation

The International OCD Foundation is dedicated to helping those with OCD and other related disorders to live full and productive lives.

Website: iocdf.org

Mental Health America

Mental Health America is dedicated to promoting mental health as a critical part of overall wellness. They include prevention services, early identification, and intervention with an integrative and culturally competent lens.

Website: mhanational.org

Call: 800-273-TALK (8255)

Text: MHA to 741741

NAMI—National Alliance on Mental Illness

The National Alliance on Mental Illness is a nonprofit that provides mental health education and advocacy for individuals living with mental illness to gain understanding and build better lives.

Website: nami.org

Call: 800-950-NAMI (6264)

Text: NAMI to 741741

SAMHSA—Substance Abuse and Mental Health Services Administration

SAMHSA is a government-funded administration that provides information, directories, and twenty-four-hour hotlines for individuals and families facing mental health issues and/or substance use disorders.

Website: samhsa.gov
Call: 800-662-HELP (4357)
TTY: 800-487-4889

RECOVERY

AL-ANON
Al-Anon offers meetings for people worried about someone who struggles with substance abuse.
Website: al-anon.org

ALCOHOLICS ANONYMOUS
I've written a lot about AA in this book and over the years. It's informed my work and my life in profound ways.
Website: aa.org

RESPITE CARE

ARCH—ACCESS TO RESPITE CARE AND HELP
NATIONAL RESPITE NETWORK
The ARCH National Respite Network promotes the development and quality of respite and crisis care for individuals or adults with special needs. They also provide directories and resources to help families locate respite and crisis care in their communities.
Website: archrespite.org

SEX ADDICTION

SAA—SEX ADDICTS ANONYMOUS
Sex Addicts Anonymous offers online resources and a twelve-step meeting program to help those living with sex addiction.
Website: saa-recovery.org
Call: 713-869-4902

SEXUAL ASSAULT AND DOMESTIC VIOLENCE

NATIONAL DOMESTIC VIOLENCE HOTLINE
The National Domestic Violence Hotline is a twenty-four-hour hotline that provides essential tools and support to help survivors of domestic violence.
Website: thehotline.org
Call: 800-799-7233
TTY: 800-799-7233
*If you are unable to speak safely, text LOVIES to 22522 or log onto thehotline.org

RAINN—RAPE, ABUSE & INCEST NATIONAL NETWORK
RAINN is the nation's largest anti–sexual violence organization and provides a twenty-four-hour hotline and programs to support and advocate for sexual assault survivors.
Website: rainn.org
Call: 800-656-HOPE (4673)

SAFEHORIZON

Safehorizon offers support, anger management counseling, and resources to victims of anger and domestic violence and to those who
need assistance controlling their anger.

Call: 800-621-HOPE (4673)

SUICIDE PREVENTION

NATIONAL SUICIDE PREVENTION LIFELINE

The National Suicide Prevention Lifeline provides free and confidential emotional support to people in suicidal crisis or emotional
distress twenty-four hours a day.

Website: suicidepreventionlifeline.org

Call: 800-273-8255

TRAUMA AND DISASTERS

NATIONAL DISASTER DISTRESS HELPLINE

The National Disaster Distress Helpline is available for anyone
experiencing emotional distress related to natural or human-caused
disasters twenty-four hours a day.

Website: disasterdistress.samhsa.gov

Call: 800-985-5990

Text: TalkWithUs to 66746

Notes

INTRODUCTION

1. Janet Geringer Woititz, "Co-Dependency: The Insidious Invader of Intimacy," in *Co-Dependency, An Emerging Issue* (Hollywood, FL: Health Communications, 1984), 59.
2. Toby Rice Drews, *Getting Them Sober* vol. 1 (South Plainfield, NJ: Bridge Publishing, 1980), xv.

CHAPTER 1: MY STORY

1. Serge Daneault, "The Wounded Healer," *Canadian Family Physician* 54, no. 9 (September 2008): https://www.ncbi.nlm.nih.gov/pmc/articles/PMC2553448/.

CHAPTER 3: CODEPENDENCY

1. Paraphrase based on a quote by Joan Wexler and John Steidll (teachers of psychiatric social work at Yale University), in Colette Dowling, *The Cinderella Complex: Women's Hidden Fear of Independence* (New York: Pocket Books, 1981), 145.
2. Robert Subby, "Inside the Chemically Dependent Marriage: Denial and Manipulation," in *Co-Dependency, An Emerging Issue* (Hollywood, FL: Health Communications, 1984), 26.
3. All quotes and ideas attributed to Earnie Larsen throughout this manuscript come from one of the many handouts and lectures he shared as part of his work in the recovery field throughout the 1970s and '80s. While

Larsen is no longer with us, his ideas had a major impact on the field of recovery.

4. Robert Subby and John Friel, "Co-Dependency: A Paradoxical Dependency," in *Co-Dependency, An Emerging Issue*, 31.

5. Al-Anon Family Groups, *Al-Anon Faces Alcoholism* (New York: Al-Anon Family Group Headquarters, 1977).

6. Al-Anon protects the anonymity of its members and keeps no official record of membership data. However, the Minneapolis Intergroup office agreed this figure was probably accurate.

7. Terence T. Gorski and Merlene Miller, "Co-Alcoholic Relapse: Family Factors and Warning Signs," in *Co-Dependency, An Emerging Issue*, 78.

8. Subby, "Inside the Chemically Dependent Marriage," 26.

9. Subby and Friel, "Co-Dependency," 31.

10. Learn more about David Kessler and Elisabeth Kübler-Ross's Five Stages of Grief™ on the Grief.com website, accessed April 4, 2022, https://grief.com/the-five-stages-of-grief/.

11. Charles L. Whitfield, "Co-Dependency: An Emerging Problem Among Professionals," in *Co-Dependency, An Emerging Issue*, 53; Joseph L. Kellerman, *The Family and Alcoholism: A Move from Pathology to Process* (Center City, MN: Hazelden, 1984).

12. Wayne W. Dyer, *Your Erroneous Zones* (New York: Funk and Wagnalls, 1976); Theodore Rubin with Eleanor Rubin, *Compassion and Self-Hate: An Alternative to Despair* (New York: David McKay Company, 1975).

CHAPTER 4: CODEPENDENT CHARACTERISTICS

1. Scott Egleston and I facilitated many codependency groups together in the 1970s and '80s, before the world even knew the word *codependency*. We would consult each other before and after these sessions. The ideas attributed to him throughout this book come from these experiences. He is an excellent therapist and teacher.

2. Nathaniel Branden, *Honoring the Self: Personal Integrity and the Heroic Potentials of Human Nature* (Boston: Houghton Mifflin Company, 1983), 162.

3. Lydia Saad, "Substance Abuse Hits Home for Close to Half of Americans," GALLUP, October 14, 2019, https://news.gallup.com/poll/267416/substance-abuse-hits-home-close-half-americans.aspx.

4. Judi Hollis, *Fat Is a Family Affair* (San Francisco: Harper/Hazelden, 1986), 55. All subsequent citations refer to this edition unless otherwise noted.

5. Hollis, 53.

6. Subby and Friel, "Co-Dependency," 32.

CHAPTER 5: DETACHMENT

1. This quote is most often attributed to philosopher William James. I found it unattributed in Dyer, *Your Erroneous Zones*, 89.

2. Al-Anon Family Groups, *One Day at a Time in Al-Anon* (New York: Al-Anon Family Group Headquarters, 1976).

3. Hollis, *Fat Is a Family Affair*, 47.

4. Terence Williams, *Free to Care: Therapy for the Whole Family of Concerned Persons* (Center City, MN: Hazelden, 1975).

5. Hollis, *Fat Is a Family Affair*.

6. Carolyn W. *Detaching with Love* (Center City, MN: Hazelden, 1984), 5.

CHAPTER 6: DON'T BE BLOWN ABOUT BY EVERY WIND

1. William Backus and Marie Chapian, *Telling Yourself the Truth* (Minneapolis: Bethany Fellowship, 1980).

CHAPTER 7: SET YOURSELF FREE

1. Eda LeShan, "Beware the Helpless," *Woman's Day*, April 26, 1983, 50.

CHAPTER 8: REMOVE THE VICTIM

1. Stephen B. Karpman, "Fairy Tales and Script Drama Analysis," *Transactional Analysis Bulletin* 7, no. 26 (1968): https://karpmandramatriangle .com/pdf/DramaTriangle.pdf.

CHAPTER 9: UNDEPENDENCE

1. Rubin, *Compassion and Self-Hate*, 278.

2. Janet Geringer Woititz, *The Complete ACOA Sourcebook* (Deerfield Beach, FL: Health Communications, 2002), 163.

3. Rubin, *Compassion and Self-Hate*, 196.

4. Penelope Russianoff, *Why Do I Think I Am Nothing Without a Man?* (New York: Bantam Books, 1982).

5. Dowling, *The Cinderella Complex*.
6. Ibid., 152–53.
7. Ibid., 22.
8. Kathy Capell-Sowder, "On Being Addicted to the Addict: Co-Dependent Relationships," in *Co-Dependency, An Emerging Issue*, 23. Chart reprinted by permission. See also Stanton Peele and Archie Brodsky, *Love and Addiction* (New York: New American Library, 1975).

CHAPTER 10: LIVE YOUR OWN LIFE

1. Branden, *Honoring the Self*, 53.
2. Rubin, *Compassion and Self-Hate*, 65.
3. Ibid., 65.

CHAPTER 11: HAVE A LOVE AFFAIR WITH YOURSELF

1. Rubin, *Compassion and Self-Hate*; Branden, *Honoring the Self*.
2. Subby and Friel, "Co-Dependency," 40.
3. Rubin, *Compassion and Self-Hate*.
4. Branden, 76.
5. Toby Rice Drews, *Getting Them Sober*, vol. 1, 3rd ed. (Baltimore, MD: Recovery Communications, 1998), 4.
6. Branden, 1–4.

CHAPTER 12: LEARN THE ART OF ACCEPTANCE

1. Joseph L. Kellerman, *A Guide for the Family of the Alcoholic* (New York: Al-Anon Family Group Headquarters, 1984), 8–9.
2. Janet G. Woititz, *The Intimacy Struggle*, rev. ed. (Deerfield Beach, FL: Health Communications, 1993), vi.
3. Ibid., xiv.
4. Harold A. Swift and Terence Williams, *Free to Care: Recovery for the Whole Family* (Center City, MN: Hazelden, 1975).
5. Branden, *Honoring the Self*, 62–65.
6. Elisabeth Kübler-Ross, *On Death and Dying* (New York: Scribner, 2019).
7. The Five Stages of Grief™ are listed on David Kessler's Grief.com website.
8. Claudia L. Jewett, *Helping Children Cope with Separation and Loss* (Harvard, MA: The Harvard Common Press, 1982), 29.

NOTES 295

9. Claudia Jewett Jarratt, *Helping Children Cope with Separation and Loss*, rev. ed. (Boston: The Harvard Common Press, 1994), 66.
10. John Powell, *Why Am I Afraid to Tell You Who I Am?* (Grand Rapids, MI: Zondervan, 1999), 71.
11. Ibid., 71, 72.
12. Kübler-Ross, *On Death and Dying*, 110.
13. Donald L. Anderson, *Better Than Blessed* (Wheaton, IL: Tyndale House Publishers, 1981), 11.

CHAPTER 13: FEEL YOUR OWN FEELINGS

1. Jael Greenleaf, "Co-Alcoholic/Para-Alcoholic: Who's Who and What's the Difference?" *in Co-Dependency, An Emerging Issue*, 9.
2. Branden, *Honoring the Self*.
3. Powel, *Why Am I Afraid?*.

CHAPTER 14: ANGER

1. Janet Geringer Woititz, *Marriage on the Rocks: Learning to Live with Yourself and an Alcoholic* (Deerfield Beach, FL: Health Communications, 1979), 50.
2. Gayle Rosellini and Mark Worden, *Of Course You're Angry* (San Francisco: Harper/Hazelden, 1986).
3. Ephesians 4:26.
4. Drews, *Getting Them Sober*; Rosellini and Worden, *Of Course You're Angry*; and Scott Egleston.
5. Frederick S. Perls, *Gestalt Therapy Verbatim* (New York: Bantam Books, 1969).
6. Rosellini and Worden, *Of Course You're Angry*.
7. Woititz, *Marriage on the Rocks*, 29.

CHAPTER 15: YES, YOU CAN THINK

1. Drews, *Getting Them Sober*.

CHAPTER 16: SET YOUR INTENTION

1. David Schwartz, *The Magic of Thinking Big* (New York: Cornerstone Library, 1959), 162–63.

2. Ibid., 163–64.
3. Ibid., 164.
4. Dennis Wholey, *The Courage to Change* (Boston: Houghton Mifflin Company, 1984), 39.

CHAPTER 17: COMMUNICATION

1. Drews, Getting Them Sober, 76.
2. Powell, *Why Am I Afraid?*, 12.
3. Ibid.

CHAPTER 18: WORK A TWELVE STEP PROGRAM

1. Al-Anon Family Groups, *Al-Anon's Twelve Steps & Twelve Traditions* (New York: Al-Anon Family Group Headquarters, 1981), 131.
2. Greenleaf, "Co-Alcoholic/Para-Alcoholic," 15.
3. George E. Vaillant, *The Natural History of Alcoholism: Causes, Patterns, and Paths to Recovery* (Cambridge, MA: Harvard University Press, 1983).
4. Warren W. told this story in Minneapolis on August 23, 1985, borrowing it from circuit speaker Clancy Imislund, who used to operate LA's Midnight Mission.
5. Quiz taken from Al-Anon Family Groups, *Al-Anon: Is It for You?* (New York: Al-Anon Family Group Headquarters, 1983). Reprinted by permission of Al-Anon Family Group Headquarters.
6. Tony A., *25 Questions: Am I an Adult Child?* (Adult Children of Alcoholics® / Dysfunctional Families World Service Organization, Inc., 2015), https://adultchildren.org/wp-content/uploads/Literature/25_Questions_EN-US_LTR.pdf. Pamphlet adapted from *ACA Fellowship Text ("The Big Red Book")* (Lakewood, CA: ACA WSO, 2006), 18–22.
7. The Twelve Steps are taken from *Alcoholics Anonymous*, 59–60. Reprinted with permission.

CHAPTER 19: PIECES AND BITS

1. Toby Rice Drews, *Getting Them Sober*, vol. 2 (South Plainfield, NJ: Bridge Publishing, 1983), 52.
2. Russianoff, *Why Do I Think I Am Nothing Without a Man?*.
3. Capell-Sowder, "On Being Addicted to the Addict," 20–21.

4. Ideas discussed in this section are drawn from several articles in *Co-Dependency, An Emerging Issue*: Janet Geringer Woititz, "The Co-Dependent Spouse: What Happens to You When Your Husband Is an Alcoholic"; Gerald Shulman, "Sexuality and Recovery: Impact on the Recovering Couple"; Marilyn Mason, "Bodies and Beings: Sexuality Issues During Recovery for the Dependent and Co-Dependent"; and Janet Geringer Woititz, "Co-Dependency: The Insidious Invader of Intimacy."

CHAPTER 20: SOOTHE YOURSELF

1. *Lead Me Home*, directed by Pedro Kos and Jon Shenk, released September 3, 2021, on Netflix, 7:45, https://www.netflix.com/title/81240756.
2. Bessel van der Kolk, *The Body Keeps the Score: Brain, Mind, and Body in the Healing of Trauma* (New York: Penguin Books, 2015).
3. "Anxiety Disorders," National Alliance on Mental Health (NAMI), last updated December 2017, https://www.nami.org/About-Mental-Illness/Mental-Health-Conditions/Anxiety-Disorders.
4. Borwin Bandelow and Sophie Michaelis, "Epidemiology of Anxiety Disorders in the 21st Century," *Dialogues in Clinical Neuroscience* 17, no. 3 (2015): https://doi.org/10.31887/DCNS.2015.17.3/bbandelow.
5. Ry Gavin, "From 'American Idol' to Queen, Adam Lambert Is Going All the Way," *Hunger*, February 11, 2022, https://www.hungertv.com/editorial/from-american-idol-to-queen-adam-lambert-is-going-all-the-way/.

CHAPTER 21: LEARNING TO LIVE AND LOVE AGAIN

1. Abraham H. Maslow, ed., *Motivation and Personality*, 2nd ed. (New York: Harper & Row, 1970); Benjamin Wolman, ed., *International Encyclopedia of Psychiatry, Psychology, Psychoanalysis, & Neurology*, vol. 7 (New York: Aesculapius Publishers, 1977), 32–33.
2. Branden, *Honoring the Self*, 162.
3. Woititz, "Co-Dependency: The Insidious Invader of Intimacy," 59.

Bibliography

1. BOOKS

Al-Anon Family Groups. *Al-Anon Faces Alcoholism*. New York: Al-Anon Family Group Headquarters, 1977.

———. *Al-Anon: Is It for You?* New York: Al-Anon Family Group Headquarters, 1983.

———. *Al-Anon's Twelve Steps & Twelve Traditions*. New York: Al-Anon Family Group Headquarters, 1981.

———. *The Dilemma of the Alcoholic Marriage*. New York: Al-Anon Family Group Headquarters, 1971.

———. *One Day at a Time in Al-Anon*. New York: Al-Anon Family Group Headquarters, 1976.

Alcoholics Anonymous ("The Big Book"). 3rd ed. New York: Alcoholics Anonymous World Services, 1976.

Anderson, Donald L. *Better Than Blessed*. Wheaton, IL: Tyndale House Publishers, 1981.

Backus, William, and Marie Chapian. *Telling Yourself the Truth*. Minneapolis: Bethany Fellowship, 1980.

Baer, Jean. *How to Be an Assertive (Not Aggressive) Woman in Life, in Love, and on the Job*. New York: New American Library, 1976.

Branden, Nathaniel. *Honoring the Self: Personal Integrity and the Heroic Potentials of Human Nature*. Boston: Houghton Mifflin Company, 1983.

Co-Dependency, An Emerging Issue. Hollywood, FL: Health Communications, 1984.

Day by Day. San Francisco: Hazelden, 1986.

DeRosis, Helen A., and Victoria Y. Pellegrino. *The Book of Hope: How Women Can Overcome Depression.* New York: MacMillan Publishing, 1976.

Dowling, Colette. *The Cinderella Complex: Women's Hidden Fear of Independence.* New York: Pocket Books, 1981.

Drews, Toby Rice. *Getting Them Sober.* Vol. 1. 3rd ed. Baltimore, MD: Recovery Communications, 1998.

———. *Getting Them Sober.* Vol. 2. South Plainfield, NJ: Bridge Publishing, 1983.

Dyer, Wayne W. *Your Erroneous Zones.* New York: Funk and Wagnalls, 1976.

Ellis, Albert, and Robert A. Harper. *A New Guide to Rational Living.* Hollywood, CA: Wilshire Books, 1975.

Fort, Joel. *The Addicted Society: Pleasure-Seeking and Punishment Revisited.* New York: Grove Press, 1981.

Hafen, Brent Q., with Kathryn Frandsen. *The Crisis Intervention Handbook.* Englewood Cliffs, NJ: Prentice-Hall, 1982.

Hollis, Judi. *Fat Is a Family Affair.* San Francisco: Harper/Hazelden, 1986.

———. *Fat Is a Family Affair.* 2nd ed. Center City, MN: Hazelden, 2003.

Hornik-Beer, Edith Lynn. *A Teenager's Guide to Living with an Alcoholic Parent.* Center City, MN: Hazelden, 1984.

Jewett, Claudia L. *Helping Children Cope with Separation and Loss.* Harvard, MA: The Harvard Common Press, 1982.

Jewett Jarratt, Claudia. *Helping Children Cope with Separation and Loss,* rev. ed. Boston: The Harvard Common Press, 1994.

Johnson, Lois Walfrid. *Either Way, I Win: A Guide to Growth in the Power of Prayer.* Minneapolis: Augsburg, 1979.

Kimball, Bonnie-Jean. *The Alcoholic Woman's Mad, Mad World of Denial and Mind Games.* Center City, MN: Hazelden, 1978.

Kübler-Ross, Elisabeth. *On Death and Dying.* New York: Scribner, 2019.

Landorf Heatherley, Joyce. *Irregular People.* Georgetown, TX: Balcony, 2018.

Lee, Wayne. *Formulating and Reaching Goals.* Champaign, IL: Research Press Company, 1978.

Maslow, Abraham H., ed. *Motivation and Personality.* 2nd ed. New York: Harper & Row, 1970.

Maxwell, Ruth. *The Booze Battle.* New York: Ballantine Books, 1976.

McCabe, Thomas R. *Victims No More.* Center City, MN: Hazelden, 1978.

Peele, Stanton and Archie Brodsky. *Love and Addiction.* New York: New American Library, 1975.

Perls, Frederick S. *Gestalt Therapy Verbatim.* New York: Bantam Books, 1969.

Pickens, Roy W., and Dace S. Svikis. *Alcoholic Family Disorders: More Than Statistics.* Center City, MN: Hazelden, 1985.

Powell, John. *Why Am I Afraid to Tell You Who I Am?* Grand Rapids, MI: Zondervan, 1999.

Restak, Richard M. *The Self Seekers.* Garden City, NY: Doubleday and Company, 1982.

Rosellini, Gayle, and Mark Worden. *Of Course You're Angry.* San Francisco: Harper/Hazelden, 1986.

Rubin, Theodore. *Reconciliations: Inner Peace in an Age of Anxiety.* New York: The Viking Press, 1980.

Rubin, Theodore, with Eleanor Rubin. *Compassion and Self-Hate: An Alternative to Despair.* New York: David McKay Company, 1975.

Russianoff, Penelope. *Why Do I Think I Am Nothing Without a Man?* New York: Bantam Books, 1982.

Schwartz, David. *The Magic of Thinking Big.* New York: Cornerstone Library, 1959.

Steiner, Claude M. *Games Alcoholics Play.* New York: Ballantine Books, 1974.

———. *Healing Alcoholism.* New York: Grove Press, 1979.

———. *Scripts People Live.* 1974. Reprint, New York: Grove Press, 1990.

———. *What Do You Say After You Say Hello?* New York: Grove Press, 1972.

Twenty-Four Hours a Day. San Francisco: Hazelden, 1985.

Vaillant, George E. *The Natural History of Alcoholism: Causes, Patterns, and Paths to Recovery.* Cambridge, MA: Harvard University Press, 1983.

van der Kolk, Bessel. *The Body Keeps the Score: Brain, Mind, and Body in the Healing of Trauma.* New York: Penguin Books, 2015.

Vine, Phyllis. *Families in Pain: Children, Siblings, Spouses, and Parents of the Mentally Ill Speak Out.* New York: Pantheon Books, 1982.

Wallis, Charles L., ed. *The Treasure Chest.* New York: Harper & Row, 1965.

Wholey, Dennis. *The Courage to Change.* Boston: Houghton Mifflin Company, 1984.

Woititz, Janet Geringer. *Adult Children of Alcoholics.* Hollywood, FL: Health Communications, 1983.

———. *The Complete ACOA Sourcebook.* Deerfield Beach, FL: Health Communications, 2002.

———. *The Intimacy Struggle,* rev. ed. Deerfield Beach, FL: Health Communications, 1993.

———. *Marriage on the Rocks: Learning to Live with Yourself and an Alcoholic.* Deerfield Beach, FL: Health Communications, 1979.

Wolman, Benjamin, ed. *International Encyclopedia of Psychiatry, Psychology, Psychoanalysis, & Neurology.* Vol. 7. New York: Aesculapius Publishers, 1977.

York, Phyllis and David, and Ted Wachtel. *Toughlove.* Garden City, NY: Doubleday, 1982.

2. PAMPHLETS

Beattie, Melody. *Denial.* Center City, MN: Hazelden, 1986.

Burgin, James E. *Help for the Marriage Partner of an Alcoholic.* Center City, MN: Hazelden, 1976.

The Enormity of Emotional Illness: The Hope Emotions Anonymous Has to Offer. St. Paul, MN: Emotions Anonymous International Services, 1973.

H., Barbara. *Untying the Knots: One Parent's View.* Center City, MN: Hazelden, 1984.

Harrison, Earl. *Boozlebane on Alcoholism and the Family.* Center City, MN: Hazelden, 1984.

Hazelden Educational Materials. *Learn about Families and Chemical Dependency.* Center City, MN: Hazelden, 1985.

———. *No Substitute for Love: Ideas for Family Living.* Center City, MN: Hazelden. Reprinted with permission of Special Action Office for Drug Abuse Prevention, Executive Office of the President, Washington, DC, in conjunction with the Drug Abuse Prevention Week in 1973.

———. *Step Four: Guide to Fourth Step Inventory for the Spouse.* Center City, MN: Hazelden, 1976.

———. *Teen Drug Use: What Can Parents Do?* Center City, MN: Hazelden. Reprinted with permission of Department of Public Instruction, Bismarck, ND, Drug Abuse Education Act of 1970.

Kellerman, Joseph L. *The Family and Alcoholism: A Move from Pathology to Process.* Center City, MN: Hazelden, 1984.

———. *A Guide for the Family of the Alcoholic.* New York: Al-Anon Family Group Headquarters, 1984.

Nakken, Jane. *Enabling Change: When Your Child Returns Home from Treatment.* Center City, MN: Hazelden, 1985.

Schroeder, Melvin. *Hope for Relationships.* Center City, MN: Hazelden, 1980.

Scientific Affairs Committee of the Bay Area Physicians for Human Rights. *Guidelines for AIDS Risk Reduction.* San Francisco: The San Francisco AIDS Foundation, 1984.

Swift, Harold A., and Terence Williams. *Free to Care: Recovery for the Whole Family.* Center City, MN: Hazelden, 1975.

Timmerman, Nancy G. *Step One for Family and Friends.* Center City, MN: Hazelden, 1985.

————. *Step Two for Family and Friends.* Center City, MN: Hazelden, 1985.

W., Carolyn. *Detaching with Love.* Center City, MN: Hazelden, 1984.

Williams, Terence. *Free to Care: Therapy for the Whole Family of Concerned Persons.* Center City, MN: Hazelden, 1975.

3. ARTICLES

Anderson, Eileen. "When Therapists Are Hooked on Power." *The Phoenix* 5, no. 7 (July 1985).

"Author's Study Says CoAs Can't Identify Their Needs." *The Phoenix* 4, no. 11 (November 1984). From Family Focus, published by the *U.S. Journal of Drug and Alcohol Dependence.*

Bartell, Jim. "Family Illness Needs Family Treatment, Experts Say." *The Phoenix,* 4, no. 11 (November 1984).

Black, Claudia. "Parental Alcoholism Leaves Most Kids Without Information, Feelings, Hope." *The Phoenix* 4, no. 11 (November 1984).

Hamburg, Jay. "Student of Depression Sights a Silver Lining." *St. Paul Pioneer Press and Dispatch (Orlando Sentinel),* September 23, 1985.

Jeffris, Maxine. "About the Word Co-Dependency." *The Phoenix* 5, no. 7 (July 1985).

Kahn, Aron. "Indecision Decidedly in Vogue." *St. Paul Pioneer Press and Dispatch.* April 1, 1986.

Kalbrener, John. "We Better Believe That Our Children Are People, Says Children Are People." *The Phoenix* 4, no. 11 (November 1984).

LeShan, Eda. "Beware the Helpless." *Woman's Day.* April 26, 1983.

Ross, Walter S. "Stress: It's Not Worth Dying For." *Reader's Digest.* January 1985.

Schumacher, Michael. "Sharing the Laughter with Garrison Keillor." *Writer's Digest.* January 1986.

Strick, Lisa Wilson. "What's So Bad About Being So-So?" *Reader's Digest.* August 1984. Reprinted from *Woman's Day.*

4. MISCELLANEOUS

"Adult Children of Alcoholics." Handout. Author unknown.

"Detachment." Handout written by anonymous Al-Anon members.

Jourard, Sidney, with Ardis Whitman. "The Fear That Cheats Us of Love." Handout.

Larsen, Earnie. "Co-Dependency Seminar." Stillwater, MN, 1985.

Wright, Thomas. "Profile of a Professional Caretaker." Handout.

About the Author

A pioneering voice in self-help literature, Melody Beattie is the author of many bestselling books—including *The Language of Letting Go, Playing It by Heart, The Grief Club, Beyond Codependency,* and *The Codependent No More Workbook.* In 2009, *Codependent No More* was named one of the four essential self-help books of all time by *Newsweek.* She lives in California.